From Borderline Adolescent to
Functioning Adult: The Test of Time

From Borderline Functioning Adult:

A Follow-up Report of Psychoanalytic
Psychotherapy of the Borderline
Adolescent and Family

Adolescent to
The Test of Time

By

James F. Masterson, M.D.

*Clinical Professor of Psychiatry,
Cornell University Medical College—
New York Hospital (Payne Whitney Clinic)
Visiting Professor of Psychiatry, University of Toronto
Director, The Masterson Group for the
Study and Treatment of Character
Disorders (Adult and Adolescent)*

with

Jacinta Lu Costello, M.S.W., A.C.S.W.

Staff Social Worker, The Masterson Group

BRUNNER/MAZEL, *Publishers* • New York

This research was supported by The Masterson Group for the Study and Treatment of the Character Disorders, Adolescent and Adult.

Chapters 4 and 14 of this project have also been submitted in partial fulfillment of the requirements for the degree of Doctor of Social Work at Smith College, School for Social Work.

Library of Congress Cataloging in Publication Data

Masterson, James F.
   From Borderline Adolescent to Functioning Adult.

   Bibliography: p.
   Includes index.
   1. Adolescent psychopathology.   2. Personality, Disorders of.
3. Psychoanalysis.   4. Family psychotherapy.   I. Costello, Jacinta Lu,
joint author.   II. Title. [DNLM: 1. Psychoanalytic therapy—In
adolescence. WS463 M423t]
RJ503.M315   616.89'82   80-14270
ISBN 0-87630-234-7

To
WILLIAM V. LULOW, M.D.
(1913-1979)
Friend and Colleague

Preface

This book, reporting the range of effectiveness of psychotherapy of the borderline adolescent, takes this controversial and oft debated issue out of the realm of discussion and subjects it to the microscope of scientific investigation. It brings research evidence to bear on many vital questions. For example:

How effective is psychotherapy based on a developmental theory with the borderline adolescent?

Does psychotherapy produce changes only in symptoms and functioning or does it go beyond that to produce enduring change in ego structure and object relations?

Can borderline adolescents overcome their developmental arrest sufficiently to resume normal emotional growth?

Can the borderline adolescent internalize the effects of the psychotherapy so that the results endure after the treatment has stopped?

What are the clinical guidelines of progress in treatment?

How often does the patient have to be seen and over how long a period of time?

How do the results of outpatient treatment alone compare with inpatient treatment?

Is the borderline syndrome a stable diagnostic entity?

What were the clinical signs of a good prognosis or of a poor prognosis?

This book also presents evidence on questions about casework therapy of the parents. For example:

How did treatment affect the parents' attitudes toward themselves, toward the adolescent, toward the spouse, toward their role as a parent and toward the communication patterns in the family?

Did they learn to support their adolescent's separation-individuation?

How did the family adapt to the adolescent's emancipation?

Although the follow-up study involved only borderline adolescents treated with psychoanalytic psychotherapy, the book has reference to a much larger body of patients. The wide spectrum of borderline psychopathology includes many teenagers who comprise, both in terms of numbers and severity, some of society's biggest social problems: the juvenile delinquent, the school dropout, the alcoholic and drug addict, the sexual offender and many of those who cannot tolerate discipline or responsibility.

Another more subtle group consists of those adolescents who "drop out" of society to "find themselves" or establish their identity. While some are no doubt engaged in this task, many are borderline patients whose "search for identity" is really a smoke screen to conceal their need to avoid commitment and responsibility because of the abandonment depression they entail.

A third group consists of those adolescents who attempt to resolve the abandonment depression that impedes the development of a true self by giving up the struggle altogether and throwing in with an authority figure who will relieve them of the task of taking responsibility for themselves and provide them instead with an authority and a system of beliefs, including a set of rules or guidelines to direct their lives. Their loss of the self is hardly noticed in the relief at not having to continue the struggle on their own. These adolescents are a significant proportion of those who join the religious communities such as the Jesus Freaks or the Hare Krishna, as well as populate many of the communes. It is not America's social values they reject as much as the need to establish and take responsibility for a self.

A fourth group consists of those patients who function better but at terrible emotional cost: the phobic, the anorexic and the many, many individuals who never come to a psychiatrist but spend their entire lives in a regressed style of living, i.e., living at home with parents, holding jobs far beneath their abilities, avoiding the opposite sex, spending their lives tending to their headaches, constipation and other psychosomatic complaints.

A poignant vignette illustrates the human tragedy involved for both adolescent and parent when a borderline adolescent does not receive treatment and must fend for himself in his struggle between individuation or growing up and the depression it triggers.

I recently saw a mother and father in consultation regarding their only son. The father had come to this country as a refugee during World War II and, succeeding beyond his wildest dreams, had amassed great wealth. The mother had a successful career as an artist. The son had grown up a shy, inhibited boy, lonely and isolated, while his parents pursued their busy lives. He failed his senior year in high school, at which point the parents sent him to a boarding school. He left the school and joined a religious sect.

The consultation one year later was prompted by the father's sudden realization, upon receiving a letter from his son, that he had lost him forever. The son's letter glowed with satisfaction with his new life. His greatest joy came from being permitted to kiss the guru's toe.

The mother and father, overwhelmed with guilt and depression, emphasized the bleakness of their own future without their son and pleaded for ways to restore him to their home. I could only woefully confirm their worst fears, that indeed it was probably too late, that arguing would only alienate him further. "At least, I said, "he leads a healthy and relatively disciplined life."

The number of adolescents suffering from borderline problems, although difficult to estimate, is certainly great.

Acknowledgments

Dr. W. V. Lulow and Mrs. Jacinta Lu Costello shared equally with me the responsibility for the design of the study and all the interviewing. Their dedicated and tireless efforts made it possible to bring the study to fruition. Dr. Lulow's untimely death put an end to his further participation. The analysis of the clinical data and the writing were my responsibility except for the material in Chapters 4 and 14 on method and results relating to prognostic factors which was analyzed and written up by Mrs. Costello. Both Mrs. Costello and I would like to thank Dr. Roger Miller, Director of Program of Advanced Study, Smith College School of Social Work, for his unrelenting support and invaluable guidance in the study's formulation, design, development and realization.

I want to thank my longtime editor Miss Helen Goodell for smoothing out the rough spots of the prose. She is truly the reader's best friend. Finally, I would like to thank both my wife, Patricia, and my secretary, Mrs. Nancy Scanlan-Epting, for their help with the manuscript.

JAMES F. MASTERSON, M.D.

Contents

Introduction

This volume—a follow-up report of psychoanalytically oriented psychotherapy of hospitalized borderline adolescents and casework treatment of the parents—describes how well the treatment results obtained with 31 adolescents and their parents, between 1967-74, have stood the test of time. For comparison, it includes a follow-up report on two adolescents treated only as outpatients. It presents compelling evidence that supports the theory that the borderline syndrome is a stable diagnostic entity which is due to a failure of separation-individuation related to the mother's libidinal unavailability.

Our results demonstrate that a therapeutic approach based on this theoretical assumption has a wide range of effectiveness—depending on the patient—from relief of symptoms and improvement in functioning to profound and enduring change in intrapsychic structure, i.e., in ego development and object relations.

Beyond that, the study illustrates that the theory not only illuminates the daily clinical vicissitudes of psychotherapy but also serves as a powerful prognostic tool. It brings full cycle 25 years of research into and treatment of what was originally labeled in 1967 (85) the personality disorders in adolescents and has come to be labeled (1972) (84) the borderline syndrome.

THE PSYCHIATRIC DILEMMA OF ADOLESCENCE, 1967 (85)

The work began in 1954, in an effort to distinguish by means of follow-up between those adolescents whose psychiatric symptomatology was an expression of illness and therefore required treatment and those whose symptomatology was an expression of adolescent turmoil that would subside with further growth and therefore did not require treatment.

This latter notion, quite prevalent at the time, was reflected in the American Psychiatric Association's diagnostic category of adjustment reaction of adolescence, which had three criteria: 1. The symptoms could be of any form. 2. They must be related to the adolescent growth process. 3. They must be transient.

It was also reflected in the then prevalent psychoanalytic theory about adolescent turmoil, which can be summarized as follows: The ego structure in the adolescent is in a state of marked flux and weakness owing to the growth process. This condition of flux causes: 1. psychiatric syndromes, when present, to be vague and ill defined; 2. patients shifting from one category of disorder to another; and 3. often only later follow-up determining whether a given symptom picture represents psychopathology or merely an intensification of the difficulties of adolescence. A final facet of the theory suggested that psychiatric symptoms were common and transient in most adolescents.

A five-year follow-up study of 78 adolescent outpatients found that adolescent turmoil was at most an incidental factor subordinate to that of psychiatric illness in the onset, course and outcome of the various emotional disorders of our patients. Adolescence was but a way station in a long history of psychiatric illness which began in childhood and followed its own inexorable course, a course only temporarily colored by the developmental stage of adolescence. The decisive influence was psychiatric illness, not adolescent turmoil. The latter exerted its effect primarily by exacerbating and giving its own coloring to the preexisting psychopathology. The decisive influence of psychiatric illness was clearly seen in the outcome five years later when these patients had not grown out of their illnesses.

The difficulties in diagnosis in these patients lay not in the choice between an adjustment reaction of adolescence and psychiatric illness. When these patients were compared to a control group of relatively healthy adolescents, marked differences were found in symptomatology, functioning and family relationships.

A revision of the theory was suggested as follows: The psychiatric effects of adolescent turmoil may be viewed as a product of the interaction between the turmoil and the personality structure of the adolescent; in the healthy, whose personality structure was not only strong but flexible enough to withstand the onslaught, adolescent turmoil produced, at most, subclinical levels of anxiety and depression. In those with character neuroses, whose personality structures were rigidly organized with insufficient flexibility to withstand stress, it produced an acute clinical breakdown of psychoneurotic symptoms which subsided as the patient got older, leaving, however, a residue of pathologic character traits. In those with schizophrenia and personality disorders, whose personality structures were loosely and poorly organized with less ability to respond to stress, adolescent turmoil has its most chaotic effect by worsening the previous conditions, which then tended to persist into adult life.

This point of view was subsequently corroborated by research on normal adolescents (98-104), as well as by research on other adolescent patient populations (37, 41, 42, 43). Additionally, since 1967, there have been no research reports to contradict the findings.

Psychotherapy did not seem to significantly affect this course of events. Approximately one-third of the patients with a personality disorder received psychotherapy once a week for periods of time varying from six months to several years. Although the adolescents improved during their treatment, when seen five years later, they were found to be suffering from moderate to severe impairment.

The prominent theme reflected by the treatment was that of a patient with acting-out behavior who presented complaints of anxiety, depression and conflicts with parents and who ventilated his feelings about current conflicts. The behavior improved, the anxiety and depression subsided, as did the conflicts with the parents. The patient's functioning improved and the treatment was stopped.

However, what was giving the patient so much trouble five years later—his basic characterologic traits such as avoidance, passivity, dependency, negativism, etc.—had been dealt with hardly at all in the psychotherapy. Clearly, the psychotherapy had not been adequate.

These sober findings (published in 1967 (85)) caused our interest to shift from the adolescent turmoil versus psychiatric illness issue to an intensive study of the personality disorders in adolescents in an effort to better understand what was wrong, so that we might design a more appropriate and effective treatment.

TREATMENT OF THE BORDERLINE ADOLESCENT: A DEVELOPMENTAL APPROACH, 1972 (84)

In 1968, in order to study personality disorders in adolescents in microscopic detail, I took charge of an adolescent inpatient unit where the adolescents' 24-hour behavior could be monitored and correlated with interviews.

At about the same time, clinical research with adults in psychoanalysis clarified the clinical picture of one of the personality disorders in the adult—the borderline syndrome (25, 26, 27, 30-36, 47-58). This clarification was accompanied by a shift in emphasis in psychoanalytic theory from the oedipal and instinctual to developmental and object relations theory—a theoretical model dealing with how intrapsychic structures develop which was ideally suited for understanding the borderline (19, 39, 40, 44, 45, 53,

62-65). Developmental theories (44, 45, 117, 133, 138) were elaborated and put to the experimental test, first and foremost by Mahler (75-82), who studied the contributions of the stages of symbiosis and separation-individuation to normal ego development, and also by Bowlby (13-15), who studied the effects on ego development of separation from the mother between 18 and 36 months of age. At the same time, the clinical picture of the hospitalized adolescent was also being clarified (110).

Integration of all this work with our study of the adolescent inpatient and his family led to a concept of the borderline adolescent that resembled, in most respects, the concept of the borderline adult elaborated through psychoanalytic work with adults.

Beyond this, through a unique vantage point—observing patient and family interactions in joint interviews—a theory evolved that the cause of the developmental arrest of the borderline adolescent was the mother's libidinal unavailability at the child's efforts to separate and individuate. This key feature of the mother's libidinal unavailability, could arise from a number of causes. In most of our cases, it was due to the fact that the mother had a borderline syndrome or a more serious disorder herself which led her to reward regressive behavior in her child and withdraw from efforts at separation-individuation in order to maintain her own intrapsychic equilibrium. There are a number of other possibilities —for example, a long physical separation from the mother, a mother who is psychotic or depressed or is emotionally empty and unable to nurture, or one who spends too much time away from home, at work or, even worse, has a long illness or dies.

A specific therapeutic design—repair of the faulty separation-individuation through psychoanalytic psychotherapy—emerged and was found to be effective. These findings were published in 1972.

This book completes the cycle by reporting how well the treatment results obtained with 31 adolescents and their parents between 1967 and 1974 have stood the test of time. Detailed case reports illustrate four levels of follow-up impairment—minimal, mild, moderate, and severe—based on the clinical evaluation of symptoms and functioning. Beyond that, more enduring changes in intrapsychic structure, in ego development and in object relations are then brought into focus. The parents' response to casework treatment is described. The results of hospital treatment are then contrasted with two patients who received outpatient treatment alone. The perspective then shifts from the clinical method to the statistical in order to report prognostic factors. Finally, the implications of the findings for the developmental theory and for psychotherapy are discussed.

From Borderline Adolescent to Functioning Adult: The Test of Time

I. THEORY

1

A Development Theory of the Borderline Syndrome

Although the concept of the borderline syndrome has, since 1967, formed a general background and often a specific guide for our clinical decisions, from admission through treatment to discharge planning, it should be kept in mind that the theory itself evolved slowly over this period of time, becoming more comprehensive and more complex as our insight sharpened and we delved deeper. For example, the intrapsychic dimensions of the theory which could only be generally sketched out in 1972 were thoroughly explored by 1976 (91). This theory attempts to integrate four theoretical perspectives—the developmental, ego psychology, object relations, and classical instinctual theory—into an integrated developmental perspective on the borderline syndrome.

CONTRIBUTIONS OF STAGES OF SYMBIOSIS AND SEPARATION-INDIVIDUATION TO NORMAL EGO DEVELOPMENT AND THE DEVELOPMENT OF NORMAL OBJECT RELATIONS

The concept of separation-individuation as a normal phase of the mother-child relationship is relatively recent and has emerged as an outgrowth of the study of ego psychology and increased interest in mothering patterns. This theory was evolved through the work of many people, but most important are Benedek (5-8), Jacobson (44, 45), Spitz (116-123), and Mahler (75-82), who studied by direct observation the separation-individuation process of normal children. Bowlby contributed through his study of the pathologic effects on the child of physical separation from its mother during this vulnerable period (18-36 months). It is beyond the scope of this book to give a comprehensive discussion of this vast topic, and for further detail, the reader is referred to these publications. However, a brief discussion provides the background essential to understanding the role of separation-individuation in the borderline patient. A diagram is presented in Figure 1 to enable the reader to visualize the development of self and object representations. It can be of help as long as the reader keeps in mind the oversimplification inevitably involved.

Stage of Symbiosis

In normal development the separation-individuation stage is immediately preceded by the symbiotic stage. Symbiosis can be defined as an interdependent relationship in which the combined energies of both partners are necessary for the existence of each. Apart from each other, each member appears to "perish."

The child's image of himself and of his mother in this phase is of one symbiotic unit. The importance of the symbiotic phase, which usually spans three to 18 months, to the normal development of ego structure can hardly be overemphasized. For example, Spitz (117) suggests that it is the mother who mediates every perception, every action, every insight, and every bit of knowledge.

The emotional climate of the mother interacts with that of the infant in a stimulating mutual experience that propels the infant

Figure 1
NORMAL DEVELOPMENT OF SELF AND OBJECT REPRESENTATIONS

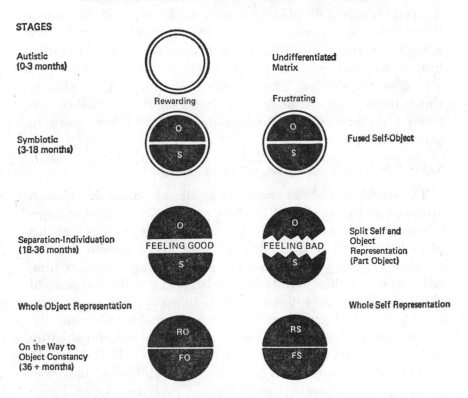

STAGES

Autistic
(0-3 months)

Undifferentiated
Matrix

Rewarding   Frustrating

Symbiotic
(3-18 months)

Fused Self-Object

Separation-Individuation
(18-36 months)

FEELING GOOD   FEELING BAD

Split Self and
Object
Representation
(Part Object)

Whole Object Representation   Whole Self Representation

On the Way to
Object Constancy
(36 + months)

into ever new and more involved experiences and responses. The quality of the mothering, the character, gifts, and talents of the mother, her ability to pick up cues and signals from her child, and her imagination in this complex interrelationship during the first year of the symbiosis seem to be the fertile soil in which ego development takes place (131). The mother functions as an auxiliary ego for the child, performing functions he or she is not yet able to perform—i.e., she controls frustration tolerance, sets ego boundaries, perceives reality and helps to control impulses.

Mahler (76) states that the child's dim awareness of the mother as a need-satisfying object marks the beginning of the symbiotic phase in which the infant behaves and functions as though he and his mother were a single omnipotent system, a dual unity within one common boundary. Mahler then emphasizes that the mother, because of the absence of an inner organizer in the human infant, must be able to serve as a buffer against inner and outer stimuli, gradually organizing them for the infant and orienting him to the inner versus the outer world in boundary formation and sensory perception. Thus, in the symbiotic stage, which continues through approximately the 18th month, the mother performs many of the ego functions the child will later learn to perform himself.

Separation-Individuation Stage—18 to 36 Months

The symbiotic stage so crucial to ego development should soon attenuate and be succeeded by the separation-individuation stage, which is equally crucial to development. Mahler suggests that this phase begins around 18 months and parallels the development of the child's capacity to walk and therefore physically separate himself from the mother. Mahler further suggests that the two-year-old child soon experiences his separateness in many other ways, enjoying his independence in exercising mastery with great tenacity. Accompanying these events, the infant's sense of individual entity and identity—the image of the self as an object—develops, mediated by bodily sensation and perception. The child now undergoes an intrapsychic separation and begins to perceive his own image as being entirely separate from the mother's.

Rinsley (109-113) has outlined some of the most important dividends of this achievement. There is an end to object splitting and the development of a capacity to relate to objects as wholes (see object constancy, page 10). Aggression becomes separated from positive or affectionate feelings, and energy is made available to the child's ego for further growth and development. The self and object representations have become more progressively differentiated as the child's perceptual apparatus matures, and these perceptions of the self and object then become associated with either positive or negative feelings. For example, the child's sense of a worthwhile or positive self-image springs in part from identifications during this phase with the mother's positive attitude toward him.

Three forces—1. the infant's unfolding individuality, 2. the mother's encouragement and support, that is, continuation of "supplies," and 3. pleasure in the mastery of new ego functions (see below)—press the child on his developmental pathway through the stages of separation-individuation toward autonomy.

Mahler (76) states that, from the end of the first year on, the average toddler seems to become so preoccupied with practicing his newly developed skills that he does not seem to mind his mother's short departures from the familiar playroom. He does not clamor for his mother's attention and bodily closeness during this practicing period. Some infants behave as though they were drunk with their newly discovered ability to walk in space and widen their acquaintance with large segments of reality. The infant does toddle up to the mother once in a while for "libidinal refueling," for facial expressions, utterances and gestures of approval and affectionate body contact, but his behavior seems to indicate that for the most part he takes his mother's emotional presence for granted.

Mahler further states that as soon as free locomotion is mastered, the toddler only returns to the mother to seek proximal communication with her. This behavior leaves no doubt that the representation of the self and that of the mother are now well on their way to differentiation. As the toddler masters the ability to move away from and to the mother, the balance dramatically shifts within the mother-toddler interaction from activity on the part of the mother to activity on the part of the child. Mahler concludes that the mother, as the catalyst of the individuation process, must be able to read the toddler's "primary-process" language. She emphasizes the resiliency with which the child's autonomy unfolds from within his own ego if he feels a fair degree of what she calls "communicative matching" on the mother's part. This term describes a process in which the mother perceives and responds with nonverbal approval and "supplies" to the toddler's nonverbal clues.

Ego Development

In the course of this separation, the normally developing child internalizes into his immature ego through the mechanisms of identification and introjection those ego functions that the mother had performed for him, and his ego structure becomes endowed with essential new functions: secure ego boundaries against which to differentiate inner from outer stimuli; strengthening of repression that makes more affect available for sublimation; improved reality perception; frustration tolerance; and impulse control. He develops the capacity to be alone (132), to tolerate anxiety and depression (139-142), to show concern and feel guilt (136).

Object Constancy

Object constancy, equally fateful for later interpersonal relations, also is a fundamental consequence of successful separation-individuation. This concept had origins in both general psychology (105-107) and psychoanalysis. Those interested in a complete discussion are referred to the excellent articles by Fraiberg (20) and McDevitt (97). The term as it is commonly used refers to the capacity to maintain object relatedness regardless of frustration or satisfaction. The relationship has relative autonomy from the fluctuations of need states. The emotional investment of the mother remains stable regardless of fluctuations in the infant's need states or externally imposed frustration. This quality is associated with, and some believe dependent on, the capacity to evoke a stable, consistent memory image or mental representation of the mother whether she is there or not. The achievement of this capacity has been variously placed, depending on the observer; for example, Spitz (117) places it at eight months; Mahler (76), however, places it around 25 months, specifically linking the attainment with the emergence of a stable mental representation that enables the child to tolerate separation from the mother.* These

---

* The further importance of object constancy is illustrated by the fact that it is a prerequisite for that process so vital to the repair of an object loss, that is, mourning. If one cannot evoke mental images of the lost object, how can one resolve all the painful feelings caused by this loss, to form new object relations? If one cannot mourn, he becomes fatally vulnerable to object loss.

new functions can be viewed as benefits of the achievement of separation and autonomy. Clearly, the mastering of this phase lays the foundation of ego structure.

Mahler (78) describes the separation-individuation process as being comprised of four identifiable subphases which blend into each other. It should be kept in mind that while the sequence of the four stages does not vary, the ages given are at best rough approximations and can vary widely.

1. Differentiation (three to eight months)—the child differentiates his body image from that of the mother's body image.
2. Practicing (eight to 15 months)—the child is actively exploring the new opportunities of the real world about him and seems oblivious of the mother.
3. Rapprochement* (15 to 22 months)—his practicing now completed, the child again turns to the mother with new demands for her responsiveness to his individuation.
4. On the Way to Object Constancy (22 to 36+ months?).

The Role of the Father in Normal Separation-Individuation

Contemporary psychoanalytic authors have viewed the father's first role as that of drawing and attracting the child out of the symbiotic orbit of the mother into the real world of things and people.

Mahler (78) confirmed Greenacre's formulations on this subject and integrated them with her own in the following words:

> The comparative immunity against contamination of the father image . . . can be understood fundamentally in the light thrown upon it by Dr. Greenacre—namely (through) the deep-going difference between the processes by which the two images take shape . . . the mother image evolves by being first differentiated within the symbiotic dual unity complex and then separated out from it: . . . the father image comes toward the child . . . "from outer space" as it were . . . as something gloriously new and exciting, at just the time when the toddler is experiencing a feverish quest for expansion.

---

* Rapprochement—a coming together; establishment of a state of good relations.

The father thus becomes "the knight in shining armor," and sometimes "the rescuer from the 'bad' mother."

Abelin (1) offered some tentative conclusions from his study of the role of the father in the separation-individuation process. His conclusions are summarized as follows:

1. The specific relationship with the father (e.g., the smiling response) begins in the symbiotic phase, somewhat later than it does with the mother and sibling. When the father is reasonably familiar to the infant, the latter shows no stranger anxiety toward him.

2. During the differentiation subphase, attachment to the father increases progressively, but the most conspicuous "turning toward the father" occurs at the beginning of the practicing subphase, when he becomes the "other," the "different" parent. He is a new, more interesting object for the child in the practicing subphase, whereas the mother is by now taken for granted as a "home base," for periodic refueling. The father comes to stand for distant, "non-mother" space—for the elated exploration of reality. A special quality of exuberance is linked with him.

3. Father and siblings are only the first landmarks in the expanding practicing space: "Out there" the male adults seem to represent the most different, the most fascinating group of objects. At first, stranger reactions to men are distinct, and often more violent than they are to women. This derives from the sequence and modes in which the specificity of father and mother have been established: The "stranger" is either too unlike or too similar to the parent(s). With the passing of the stranger conflict, a clear preference for men often emerges, patterned on the relationship with the father.

4. Girls tend to attach themselves to the father earlier than boys and, conversely, to be more wary of strange men and more discriminating with regard to unfamiliar persons in general. Boys approach male adults earlier and in a more

exploratory way. This is associated with their greater interest in distant space and in inanimate objects. Girls have been observed to be amazingly "feminine" and flirtatious as early as at the beginning of the second year, seeking passive physical affection with father substitutes.

5. The father is not consistently experienced as a rival for mother's loving attention; rather he remains an "uncontaminated" parental love object, while the relationship with the mother tends to become fraught with ambivalence during the rapprochement crisis. The role of the father as a rival may be foreshadowed more clearly and consistently in firstborn boys or in different cultural settings; in such cases, it may even bear some traits of the later oedipal conflict.

6. The symbolic representation of the father must be distinguished from the actual relationship with him. The rapprochement crisis is at first centered solely on the representation of the self and the mother. A few weeks later, the father begins to appear in the fantasy world of the toddler as the other, more powerful parent. *This father image may be necessary for the satisfactory resolution of the ambivalent rapprochement position.* The simultaneous representation of the three images of the self and both parents would constitute an even more elaborate step—perhaps representing the formal element of the oedipal complex. Thus, the development of these nuclear images after the rapprochement subphase would seem to recapitulate the earlier history of the actual specific relationship—in a distilled and schematized form. In cognitive development, Piaget (105) has called this recapitulation a "vertical lag."

The father becomes the first and most familiar of the "different" adults—the first step into the world of novelty, of external reality. As such, he comes to reflect the exuberant qualities of the practicing subphase, in which the push toward active exploration and autonomous functioning is dissociated in time and space from the "refueling," the periodic returning to the familiar and comforting mother. While this very source of comfort, if exclusive, threatens the infant's need for initiative, attachment to the father is apt to bind the new, wild centrifugal forces. The father responds exquisitely to the "need to function" of the child's newly maturing gross motor apparatuses.

There is implicit opposition between the centrifugal forces involved in practicing and the underlying need for the mother. Increasingly, as this need is brought to light and the two poles confront each other, the centripetal forces of rapprochement threaten to submerge the newly conquered reality in the whirlpool of the primary undifferentiated stage. But when this reality is genuinely anchored in a wide range of nonmaternal objects, when the father is firmly established as the "other, different" parent, then we need not be too concerned about the further development of the toddler toward final individuation and intrapsychic separation.

We might summarize the father's contribution to normal ego development in the separation-individuation phase of development as follows: 1. to serve as an object uncontaminated with symbiotic cathexis, to draw and attract a child into the real world of things and people; 2. in the rapprochement subphase to serve as a parental love object which aligns itself with reality and the forces of individuation as opposed to the regressive pull toward the mother and therefore to contribute to the successful resolution of the rapprochement phase; and 3. to participate in the construction of mental images of the self, the maternal object and the paternal object—the forerunner to the oedipal complex.

Having outlined the essential contributions of the mother and the father to ego development in the normal separation-individuation phase, let us now describe what goes wrong in the borderline patient's ego development.

The Mother's Role in the Genesis and Psychic Structure of the Borderline Patient—Interpersonal

The early mother-child interaction is so complex yet so fateful that it is both difficult and hazardous to try to tease out principal themes which can be generalized. Nevertheless, the stereotyped repetition of these maladaptive themes in our patients' lives and in the transference impel us to undertake this task in spite of its hazards, in hopes of unraveling some of its mysteries. While it is important to keep in mind the limitations, it is essential if we are to understand our patients' problems and their therapeutic needs.

Those mothers who were borderline, as has been the case with most of our patient population, furnish excellent illustrations of the phenomenon because, having been unable to separate from their own mother, they foster the symbiotic union with the child, thus encouraging the continuance of the dependency to maintain their own emotional equilibrium. They experience significant gratification during the child's symbiotic phase. They are threatened by and unable to deal with the infant's emerging individuality.

They depersonalize the child, cannot see him as he is but, rather, project upon him the image of one of their own parents or of a sibling. Or they perceive him as a perpetual infant or an object and use him to defend against their own feelings of abandonment. Consequently, even in the symbiotic stage they are unable to respond to the child's unfolding individuality, and he early learns to disregard certain of his own potentials to preserve his source of supplies (approval) from the mother.

The mother clings to the child to prevent separation, discouraging moves toward individuation by withdrawing her support. The crisis supervenes at the time of separation-individuation, specifically during the rapprochement subphase, when she finds herself unable to tolerate her toddler's ambivalence, curiosity and assertiveness; the mutual cueing and communicative matching to these essential characteristics of individuation fail to develop. The mother is available if the child clings and behaves regressively, but withdraws if the child attempts to separate and individuate. The child needs the mother's supplies in order to grow; if he grows, however, they are withdrawn.

The Abandonment Depression

Therefore, between the ages of 15 months and 22 months (rapprochement subphase) a conflict develops in the child between his own developmental push for individuation and autonomy and fear of the withdrawal of the mother's emotional supplies that this growth would entail. The normal developmental vicissitudes of the rapprochement subphase, the surge of individuation accompanying the acquisition of locomotion and speech, as well as the increased awareness of the separateness from the mother, which triggers the child's increased sensitivity and need for the mother, become unique vulnerabilities for the borderline child.

The very surge of individuation, which brings with it a greater need for the mother's support, actually induces withdrawal of that support, i.e., the vital process in which he is engaged produces the withdrawal that arrests the process and results in the abandonment depression. Such depression can, on occasion, be recognized at the age of three. Whether or not it is apparent at age three, it will later emerge and become manifest during adolescence.

This abandonment depression comprises not one feeling but a complex of six constituent feelings (the six psychiatric horsemen of the apocalypse): *depression, anger and rage, fear, guilt, passivity and helplessness, emptiness and void*. The intensity and degree of each of these component feelings will vary with the unique developmental traumas of each individual. However, each component will be present to some degree in every patient.

The Six Psychiatric Horsemen of the Apocalypse (84)

These feeling states (listed above) vie in their emotional sway and destructiveness with the social upheaval and destructiveness of the original four horsemen: famine, war, flood and pestilence. Technical words are too abstract to convey the intensity and immediacy of these feelings and, therefore, the primacy they hold over the patient's entire life. The adolescent patient's functioning in the world, his relationships with people, and even some of his physiologic functions are subordinated to the defense of these feelings.

Depression

The depression has qualities similar to that feeling state described by Spitz (116) as anaclitic depression: feelings that spring from the loss or the threat of loss either of part of the self or of supplies that the patient believes vital for survival. Patients often report this in physical terms comparable to losing an arm or both legs, or being deprived of vital substances such as oxygen, plasma or blood. This quality differs from the adult mid-life depression whose dynamics are predicated not upon the loss of vital supplies but upon the presence of a severe, punitive superego that punishes the ego until it breaks down.

The manner in which the depression emerges in therapy is itself a statement of its motivational power. In the first or testing phase of therapy, the patient may complain of boredom or a vague sense of numbness or depression, but his affect will appear quite bland and he will not seem to be suffering from a very intense feeling; this is a reflection of the fact that he is now well defended against the abandonment depression. As the defenses are successively interpreted in therapy sessions, his feelings become more intense, repressed memories emerge, and the patient quite obviously is suffering. The patient intensifies his struggle to maintain his defenses, but as the therapist continues to interpret them, the patient gradually slides into the bottom of his depression where lies, almost always, suicidal despair and belief that it will never be possible to receive the necessary supplies for living. At this point the patient is a genuine suicidal risk, and there is no longer any doubt in the observer's mind about the motivational power of the patient's depression.

Rage

The intensity of the patient's anger and rage and the rate of the emergence of these emotions in psychotherapy parallel that of the depression. The more depressed the patient becomes, the angrier he becomes. The content of the rage is first more general and very often projected upon contemporary situations. As memory of his feelings returns, the rage becomes more and more focused on the relationship with the mother. Thus the rage parallels and is companion to the depression throughout the stages of psychotherapy.

Fear

A third component is the fear of being abandoned, which may be expressed as fear of being helpless, of supplies being cut off, of facing death or of being killed. Two psychosomatic accompaniments of this fear that I have observed in patients in an abandonment panic are asthma and peptic ulcer. It is possible to theorize that these symptoms are an expression of the patient's separation fear. The former is a fear of suffocation and even death if supplies are cut off and the latter a hungering for but not daring to accept the lost supplies. The panic itself can dominate the clinical picture to the point where it conceals both the underlying depression and rage.

The degree to which fear participates in the clinical picture seems to be related to the degree to which the mother used the threat of abandonment as a disciplinary technique. The patients live with an almost constant fear of abandonment, waiting for the "Sword of Damocles" to fall. They recall childhood as: "It was like living in a permanent funeral, as if I might soon be buried."

The threat of abandonment apparently had been used as a disciplinary technique to inhibit the patient's self-assertion or expression of anger and to enforce compliance. Therefore, as the depression and rage emerge in psychotherapy, the fear of being abandoned for expressing these feelings rises in tandem, sometimes reaching panic proportions.

Guilt

Guilt, the fourth feeling component, is the "fifth column" behind the front line of the patient's defenses. This guilt, springing from the patient's introjection of the mother's attitude toward him, now becomes the patient's attitude toward himself. Since the mother greeted the expression of his self-assertion and his wish to separate and individuate with disapproval and withdrawal, the patient begins to feel guilty about that whole part of himself which seeks separation and individuation; that is, not only his actions but his thoughts, wishes and feelings. Consequently, to avoid guilt feelings, he suppresses moves in this direction (139) and sabotages, as by a "fifth column," his own autonomy. This aspect of the guilt is seen most clearly in treatment after the environmental conflict with the mother has been more or less resolved, when an intense intrapsychic battle comes to the fore between the patient's wish to individuate and the guilt that this entails.

Passivity and Helplessness

The mother withdraws her approval when the patient attempts to assert himself, since she views his self-assertion toward individuation as a threatened "loss" of her child. Therefore, the patient associates the fear of abandonment with his own capacity for assertion. When faced with a conflict, he becomes overwhelmed with feelings of passivity and helplessness, since the only tool that might give him mastery, self-assertion, brings with it the fear of loss of his mother's love, of abandonment.

Emptiness and Void

The sense of void is best described as one of terrifying inner emptiness or numbness; it springs partially from introjection of the mother's negative attitudes, leaving the patient devoid, or empty, of positive supportive introjects.

Defenses Against Abandonment Depression

Unable to tolerate the awareness of these feelings, the child handles them by denial (44) of the reality of separation, by projection and acting out of the wish for reunion by clinging, and by avoidance of individuation stimuli (139), all of which are fostered by the widespread employment of the splitting defense mechanism (21, 22, 23, 47, 86, 87).* Although separated, he continues to cling to the mother to defend himself against the return of abandonment depression into awareness. The clinging, splitting, denial and avoidance are secondarily reinforced by any number of the various defense mechanisms, which later determine the form of the clinical picture: for example, neurotic mechanisms such as those of the hypochondriac, the obsessive-compulsive, the phobic or the hysterical; schizoid mechanisms such as isolation, detachment, and withdrawal and suppression of affect.

The abandonment depression is then split off from awareness; its overwhelming but hidden force is observable through the tenacity and strength of the defense mechanisms used to keep it in check. These defenses, however, effectively block the patient's developmental movement through the stages of separation-individuation to autonomy. He suffers from a developmental arrest. Unlike the autistic or infantile psychotic child, the child with the borderline syndrome has separated from the symbiotic stage and has become fixated in one of the subphases of the separation-individuation stage—possibly the rapprochement stage (15-22 months), where the

---

* One crucial dividend of successful separation-individuation is the capacity to relate to others as individual whole objects—that is, both good and bad, gratifying and frustrating—and to have this relationship persist despite frustration at the hands of the object. This key characteristic, so essential for later satisfying interpersonal relationships, does not develop in the borderline; instead there is a persistence of the primitive defense of object splitting (paranoid position of Klein, 62-65). In other words, the borderline relates to objects as parts, either totally gratifying or totally frustrating, rather than as wholes.

The child's intense oral dependency and need for affection and approval from his mother to build ego structure and grow are so absolute and his rage and frustration at the deprivation of these very supplies on the part of the mother so great that he fears these feelings may destroy her and himself. To deal with his fear and to preserve the feeling of receiving supplies, the infant splits the whole object of the mother into two parts, that is, a good rewarding mother and a bad frustrating mother. Both feelings remain conscious but are kept apart by this splitting defense.

The images of the good and bad mother are never integrated as one object, a manner of relating that persists throughout his later life. He does not relate to people as one whole object but as if they were either good, that is, gratifying, or bad, that is, frustrating. Both sides of this split are equally unrealistic. In other words, he does not achieve the depressive position described by Klein (62-65).

mother's sharing of approval and encouragement is such a vital catalyst to the achievement of full separation for the child and to the establishment of a trusting relationship with the mother.

DEVELOPMENT ARREST OR NARCISSISTIC-ORAL EGO FIXATION

To understand the disastrous consequences of these events for the development of the child's ego structure, we must shift to another framework, that is, Freud's psychosexual continuum, which has common meeting points with the one we have been discussing and which, although not specifically emphasized here, is implied as an integral part of the developmental process. Freud spoke of two phases, the autoerotic and the narcissistic (23) phases, that precede the oral phase of development. Symbiosis is a narcissistic phase and separation-individuation is ushered in by orality. It is likely that the developmental arrest of the borderline occurs either in the narcissistic or early oral phase. The earlier the arrest occurs, the more likely the patient's clinical picture will resemble the psychotic; the later this occurs, the more likely the clinical picture will resemble the neurotic. In either case, the developmental arrest produces severe defects in ego functioning.

Those functions that the mother had performed for the child, which the normal child internalizes through identification, are not internalized because of the arrest. Consequently, the ego defects consist of poor reality perception, poor frustration tolerance and impulse control, and fluid ego boundaries, that is, difficulty in distinguishing between inner and outside stimuli. These are the ego defects referred to by Kernberg (49) as nonspecific ego weakness.

The ego structure is further characterized by the persistence of the primitive defense mechanisms of splitting and the specific defenses against separation: projection, projective identification, acting out the wish for reunion by clinging, denial of the reality of separation, denial and avoidance (63-65) of individuation.

The arrest results in a failure to achieve object constancy. This has far-reaching clinical significance: 1. The patient does not relate to objects, that is, persons, as wholes but as part-objects (62-65). 2.

The object relationship does not persist through frustration but tends to fluctuate widely with need states. 3. The patient is unable to evoke the image of the person when he is not present. When the person is not physically present, the borderline patient feels he has literally disappeared and is not going to return. 4. He cannot mourn. Any object loss or separation becomes a disastrous calamity. This can be seen clearly in the transference relationship during the therapist's vacation period; because the patient does not feel that the doctor will return, he sets his defensive operations in motion well in advance to protect himself. Some styles of defenses that patients exhibit during therapy are: emotionally withdrawing from the interviews in advance, actually physically leaving the doctor before he can leave the patient; complete emotional detachment; acting out by starting an affair; carrying through a previously tentative marriage possibility; and trying to provoke the therapist by, for example, coming late for appointments.

Role of the Father in the Borderline Patient's Life

Life never seems to be so difficult that it can't get worse. Does the borderline child, whose growth is already heavily burdened by the mother's regressive pull, get the "average expectable" help from a father who influences him toward growth and reality, who forms a "bridge" out of the symbiotic whirlpool? For the most part, the answer is no.

The father of the borderline child may have any one of the severe forms of character pathology, or even schizophrenia. The key feature is that he is not available to the child as an uncontaminated object to support the forces of individuation and mastery of reality (91).

Although the specifics vary with each case, the father's influence almost always is towards a reinforcement of the mother-child exclusive or clinging relationship, rather than either opposing the relationship or making efforts to lead the child away from it. The marital contact often seems to consist of the mother's permitting or even encouraging the father to distance himself from the home, as long as the father allows the mother to have exclusive control of the child. It is instructive to note in these cases the amount of absence the father is permitted without any complaint from the mother. Beyond the fact of his frequent absence, the specific dynamics of his relationship with the mother and child when he is present again reinforce the mother-child exclusive relationship.

The Mother's Role in the Genesis and Psychic Structure of the Borderline Patient: Intrapsychic (91)

It is now necessary to take the issue a step further by presenting a microscopic, detailed view of just how this interaction with the mother and father relates to the developing intrapsychic structure of the borderline child—i.e., the split ego and the split object relations unit.

The developmental cause of the fixation of the borderline ego is to be found in the mother's withdrawal of her libidinal availability (that is, of her libidinal supplies of approval, affection and love) as the child makes efforts to separate-individuate during the rapprochement subphase (15-22 months). Further, the fixation comes into existence at exactly that phase of development because the child's individuation constitutes a major threat to the mother's defensive need to cling to her infant and, as a consequence, drives her toward removal of her libidinal availability.

Split Object Relations Part-Unit

The images of the two mothers, the one rewarding and the other withdrawing, are powerfully introjected by the child to form a split object relations unit which consists of two separate part-units, each of which comprises a part-self representation, and part-object representation with an affective component linking the two together. These may be termed the withdrawing part-unit and the rewarding part-unit. The withdrawing part-unit is cathected predominantly with aggressive energy, the rewarding part-unit with libidinal energy, and both remain separated from each other through the mechanism of the splitting defense (see Table 1).

TABLE 1

Summary of the Borderline's Split Object Relations Unit

WITHDRAWING OR AGGRESSIVE PART-UNIT**

Part-Object Representation	Affect	Part-Self Representation
A maternal part-object which is attacking, critical hostile, angry, withdrawing supplies and approval in the face of assertiveness or other efforts toward separation-individuation.	Abandonment depression, anger, rage, fear, guilt, hopelessness, helplessness, emptiness, void.	A part-self representation of being inadequate, bad, helpless, guilty, ugly, empty, a flawed trophy, a paraplegic, an indentured slave.

REWARDING OR LIBIDINAL PART-UNIT*

Part-Object Representation	Affect	Part-Self Representation
A maternal part-object which offers approval support and supplies for regressive and clinging behavior.	Feeling good, being loved, gratification of the wish for reunion.	A part-self representation of being the good, passive, compliant child.

* Referfed to hereafter in the text as RORU
** Referred to hereafter in the text as WORU

Split Ego

It is necessary now to inquire into the basis for the persistence of the split ego in these cases. As the child's self representation begins to differentiate from the object representations of the mother, i.e., as the child begins to separate, he now experiences the abandonment depression in the wake of the threat of loss or withdrawal of supplies; at the same time, the mother continues to encourage and to reward those aspects of her child's behavior—passivity and regressiveness—which enable her to continue to cling.

Thus the mother encourages and rewards in the child the key defense mechanisms of denial of the reality of separation, which in turn allows the persistence of the wish for reunion (clinging), which later emerges as a defense against the abandonment depression. Thus, part of the ego fails to undergo the necessary transformation from reliance upon the pleasure principle to reliance upon the reality principle, for to do so would mean acceptance of the reality of separation, which would bring on the abandonment depression. The ego structure is split into a pathological (pleasure) ego and a reality ego, the former pursuing relief from the feeling of abandonment and the latter following the reality principle. The pathological ego denies the reality of the separation, which permits the persistence of fantasies of reunion with the mother, which are then acted out through clinging and regressive behavior, thus defending against the abandonment depression and causing the patient to "feel good." Extensive fantasies of reunion are elaborated, projected onto the environment and acted out, accompanied by increasing denial of reality. The two, operating in concert, create an ever-widening chasm between the patient's feelings and the reality of his functioning as he gradually emerges from the developmental years of childhood into adolescence.

The Relationship Between the Split Object
Relations Unit and the Split Ego

The splitting defense keeps separate the rewarding and the withdrawing object relations part-units, including their associated affects. Both remain conscious but do not influence each other. Although both the rewarding and the withdrawing part-units are pathological, the borderline experiences the rewarding part-unit as increasingly ego-syntonic, as it relieves the feelings of abandonment associated with the withdrawing part-unit, with the result that the individual "feels good." The affective state associated with the rewarding part-unit is that of gratification at being fed, hence, "loved." The ensuing denial of reality—i.e., the lack of confidence in a self—seems but a small price to pay for this affective state.

An alliance is now seen to develop between the child's pathological ego and either his rewarding object relations part-unit or his withdrawing part-unit, the primary purpose of which is to promote the "good" feeling and to defend against the feeling of abandonment.

Rewarding Part-Unit (RORU)—Pathologic Ego Alliance

The withdrawing part-unit remains internalized and is experienced as abandonment depression, which is defended against by projection and acting-out (or externalization) of the RORU onto the environment. This is seen clinically by dramatic or subtle clinging, compliant behavior. The patient projects the part-object representation of the RORU onto a person in the environment, behaves in a compliant manner, and expects that person to resonate with the projection and provide approval and support. This promotes the denial of separateness and potentiates the acting-out of reunion fantasies, thus relieving the abandonment depression.

Withdrawing Part-Unit (WORU)—Pathologic Ego Alliance

The withdrawing part-unit is externalized by projection and acting out and therefore is not experienced as internal. This would be observed clinically not by compliant behavior but by the projection of the part-object representation of the withdrawing unit, with its critical, hostile attitudes, onto a person in the environment, resulting in various behaviors to defend against the projected hostility. The RORU remains internalized and is expressed with hidden fantasies.

The withdrawing part-unit (part-self representation, part-object representation and feelings of abandonment) is activated by actual experiences of separation (or of loss) or as a result of the individual's efforts toward separation-individuation within the therapeutic process, which symbolize earlier life experiences which provoked the mother's withdrawal of supplies. If the pathological ego's alliance is with the withdrawing part-unit, this activation of the WORU would activate the defense mechanism of projection of hostile attitudes on the environment. If the defensive alliance is between the rewarding part-unit and the pathological ego, the rewarding unit would in turn be activated by the resurgence of the withdrawing part-unit. The purpose of this operation would be defensive, i.e., to restore the wish for reunion, thereby to relieve the feeling of abandonment. These two alliances thus become the borderline's principal defenses against the painful affective state associated with the withdrawing part-unit, i.e., either externalize it or defend against it with the rewarding unit. In terms of reality, however, both part-units are pathological; it is as if the patient has but two alternatives—to feel bad and abandoned (withdrawing part-unit) or to feel good (rewarding part-unit), at the cost of denial of reality and self-destructive behavior.

The Therapeutic Alliance (92)

The patient begins therapy feeling that the behavior motivated by the alliance between the rewarding part-unit and the pathological (pleasure) ego or by the externalization of the WORU is ego-syntonic, since it makes him feel good. The self-destructiveness of either behavior is denied.

The first objective of the therapist is to render the functioning of this alliance ego-alien by means of confrontive clarification of its destructiveness. Insofar as this therapeutic maneuver promotes control of the behavior, the withdrawing part-unit becomes activated, which in turn reactivates the rewarding part-unit with the appearance of further resistance. There results a circular process, sequentially including resistance, reality clarification, working-through of the feelings of abandonment (withdrawing part-unit), further resistance (rewarding part-unit), and further reality clarification, which leads in turn to further working-through. This process of the alternate activation of the two part-units and the defenses of the pathological ego in the transference demonstrates the patient's intrapsychic structure.

In those cases in which the circular working-through process proves successful, an alliance is next seen to develop between the therapist's healthy ego and the patient's embattled, traumatized reality ego. This therapeutic alliance (92), formed through the patient's having internalized the therapist as a positive external object who approves of separation-individuation, proceeds to function counter to the alliance between the patient's rewarding part-unit and his pathological (pleasure) ego, battling with the latter, as it were, for ultimate control of the patient's motivations and actions. The structural realignments which can then ensue in the wake of this working-through process have been described elsewhere. In summary, the patient works through the pathological mourning (rage and depression) associated with separation from the mother and, through the mechanisms of internalization and identification, forms a new intrapsychic structure based on whole object relations. This process, which begins in therapy with the therapist gradually extends to others in the patient's environment as it becomes firmly internalized.

The next chapter presents a recent addition to the theory and explores the details of the psychopathology of the self in the borderline patient.

2

Psychopathology of the Self in the Borderline

INTRODUCTION

The adolescents in this study who improved demonstrated again and again that their clinical improvement was related to the emergence and consolidation of the self. This observation impelled me to reevaluate the psychopathology of the self in the borderline, which hitherto had been generally included within the concept of "failure to individuate"—a notion too general to do adequate justice to these findings. This chapter specifies the psychopathology of the self in the borderline and contrasts my own views with those of Winnicott (137) on the same psychopathology which he called the false self. The differentiation of the psychopathology of the self in the borderline from that found in the narcissistic disorder, as described by Kohut (66-72), is too complex and theoretical to be appropriate to this volume, and can be found elsewhere (96a).

There is a consensus among clinicians as to the observed phenomena referred to as difficulties with the self—poor self-regulation, low self-esteem and inhibition of self-expression. Patients report these difficulties quite clearly, and they are not difficult to observe and identify. This consensus at the clinical level gives way to confusion and conflict when it comes to theories about these difficulties: What is the self? What are its functions? What is the difference between the experiential and the theoretical self? What are the constituents of the self? How does the self develop? The fact that it is a holistic, overriding concept that goes well beyond such discrete notions as the self-representation or the intrapsychic structure contributes further to the confusion.

We frequently made the clinical observation in our borderline patients of a false self similar to that described by Winnicott (137). However, we viewed it as only one of a broader spectrum of clinical difficulties with individuation or self-expression, difficulties which have also been observed and described by Kohut as defects in the structure of the self.

Many borderline patients—adult and adolescent—clearly and concretely express a collection of complaints that are more or less loosely related to self-expression. Some who have these problems cannot complain, as the awareness of the problem is submerged in their pathological behavior. Others express a wide range of complaints, from an inability to identify what they want—their own individuative thoughts, wishes and feelings—to all degrees of inhibitions of and difficulties in initiating, activating and implementing in reality those thoughts and wishes reflective of individuation that they can identify. There is always an associated lack or inhibition of self-assertion—an inability to support and sustain individual interests if, when activated, they come under environmental pressure. There is also always an associated distortion of self-image related to an inability to autonomously regulate self-esteem. It is, then, a syndrome of the following roughly related complaints:

1. self-image disturbance;
2. difficulty identifying and expressing in reality one's own

individuated thoughts, wishes and feelings and in autonomously regulating self-esteem; and
3. difficulty with self-assertion.

These complaints do not exist in a vacuum. Although they may
sometimes predominate, more often they are presented tangentially
by the patient alongside his or her other complaints of depression,
difficulty in relationships and functioning, and other symptoms.

The degree of self-image distortion can be used to devise a
clinical spectrum, from no self-image at the one end to the false
self-image in the middle and the poor self-image at the other end.

No self-image refers to those patients whose motivations and
behavior are so completely dominated by the need to cling to the
object and to suppress individuation that few individuative stimuli
can break through. Those that do occasion great anxiety. The
patients are quite unaware of this state of affairs until the need for
the clinging defense has been sufficiently lessened so that individuation can begin. At this point they describe themselves as having
been "caretakers of the mother," or as "not being a person," or as
having "no self." For example, a 32-year-old married woman complained of depression, frigidity and anger at her husband. After a
year of psychotherapy, as she became aware that she projected the
intrapsychic negative image of the maternal part-object on the
husband, she also became aware that she had spent her developmental years as mother's caretaker. "It was my job to keep mother
feeling good. She used me as an object for her pleasure. It was as if
she or her presence filled the whole house. I had no self; I was not
a person in my own right."

The *false self*—less serious in degree than no self-image—also
represents a collection of behaviors, thoughts and feelings that are
motivated by the need to cling to the object with avoidance and
suppression of individuative stimuli. This pattern the patient
comes to identify as his or her self. Like the patients with no self-
image, these patients may not recognize until well into treatment
that it is a false self or collection of defensive behaviors rather than
an expression of the true individuated self. As a matter of fact,

some patients in treatment, as they improve, go through an identity crisis as they begin to lose their false façade, reacting as if they were losing their true individuated self.

> An 18-year-old girl with marked obsessive-compulsive defenses was seen in her senior year of high school for a depression. Her defensive behavior was so well integrated that it took a series of interviews to determine that, despite the fact that she was suicidally depressed each night, she managed to carry on during the day at school and at home without anyone noticing. Both parents, who described her as having been the perfect compliant child throughout childhood, were completely unaware of her distress and stunned to discover how sick she was. The patient described herself as "split in two"— identifying her daytime compliance as her real self and the nighttime anger and depression as a loathsome stranger she must fight.

> A 21-year-old girl whose long-term depression surfaced on college graduation presented a façade of the cute, bright, intellectual and intellectualizing little girl who entertained older men with her chatter, while her own feelings were handled by detachment. This role was blatantly acted out with her depressed father—her life task being to maintain his emotional equilibrium through this role. Not until she became aware that she had sacrificed her own individuative wishes— particularly her desire for a real relationship with a man— did she also become aware that what she had thought was herself was a false self.

The *poor self-image* is the least severe of the three. The patient is aware of and reports his poor self-image, his difficulty in articulating his wishes and feelings in reality, and his difficulty with self-assertion. For example, a 21-year-old male who chose economics as a major in college out of desperation at not being able to decide what he wanted to do recently graduated and found himself in the same quandary when it came to getting a job. He articulated clearly his desperation, his avoidance of this difficulty throughout high school and college by drifting and drugs, and his passivity and reticence about self-assertion. Thus, he didn't know what he wanted and was unable to express it if he did.

We can now add this additional vector to the psychopathology of the borderline patient. There is a distortion of self-image and difficulty in identifying and activating individuative thoughts, wishes and feelings into reality, as well as difficulty with self-assertion. This aspect of the borderline psychopathology has been implied in my use of the phrase "a failure to individuate," but its importance was overshadowed by the abandonment depression and the ego and superego fixation. To these must now be added and equally emphasized the parallel failures of self-expression.

A DEVELOPMENTAL OBJECT RELATIONS THEORY

Developmental object relations theory provides a framework to understand one aspect of the normal development of self-expression and some of the difficulties caused by arrests of that development. The base would be the self representation which emerges from the fused symbiotic self-object representation of the dual mother/child unit as the child passes through the symbiotic phase (3-18 months), through the stages of separation-individuation (18-36 months), to the stage of being on the way to object constancy (36 months plus). This emergence of the self probably occurs under the influence of: 1. genetic drives, 2. pleasure in the mastery of new functions, and 3. the mother's appropriate cueing and matching to the child's individuation. As the child becomes a toddler and develops the capacity to separate from the mother, the task of separation-individuation ensues, during which time the child develops an image of himself as separate from the mother. This emerges first as two part-images—a good self representation and a bad self representation—which then coalesce into a whole self representation, both good and bad. During the rapprochement stage of this process, through phase-appropriate frustration and disappointment, the child loses the grandiose image of self and the omnipotent image of the object, preparatory to moving towards whole-self and whole-object representations. In the course of this evolution towards an autonomous self, the child develops a whole self-image (both good and bad) about which he feels adequate esteem, which is based for the most part on the achievement of the capacity to utilize self-assertion to identify and activate in reality his own individuative thoughts, wishes and feelings.

The difficulties with self-expression in the borderline patient are revealed in psychotherapy as being due to the need to avoid identifying and activating those very individuated thoughts and wishes, in order to defend against the abandonment depression that such activation would trigger. This sacrifice of self-expression to defense adds an additional negative increment to the already negative self part-image of the borderline patient as a result of the operation of the withdrawing object relations part-unit, i.e., loss of approval from the mother for signs of self-expression.

To compensate for the fact that self-expression is not available for motivation, the patient turns instead to the alliance of the RORU (or WORU) and the pathological ego, which, while providing him with a defense against the abandonment depression, at the same time provides him with responses to deal with the environment—a form of adaptation. As these patterns become familiar, stereotyped and repetitive, the patient identifies them as his self. This is, however, a false self based on a need for a form of adaptation that provides a defense against individuation, rather than one which is an expression of the solutions arrived at by the dynamic experiment and interplay between the evolving individuating self and the environment.

The follow-up reports presented here of the successfully treated patients demonstrate that, as the rage and depression are worked through, the patient begins to separate and individuate, and the self gradually emerges and assumes its functions. The patient develops new thoughts, wishes and feelings (individuation or self-expression), identifies them and assertively activates them in reality, thereby turning away from his old rewarding part-unit— pathological ego alliance to this new motivation for his behavior. Over the course of time there is eventual consolidation of the self.

We were able to observe and describe the gradual emergence and various degrees of consolidation of the self which paralleled the patients' clinical improvement.

TRUE AND FALSE SELF: WINNICOTT (137)

Winnicott (137) described a clinical state of the false self as follows: A patient, although quite successful in external adaptations, had the feeling that she had not started to exist, that she had always been looking for a means of getting to what she called her true self. He emphasized that the link between intellectualizing and the false self created a special danger—a deceptive clinical picture in which there is seemingly extreme external success so that it is difficult or impossible to believe the real distress of the person concerned who feels "phony, the more phony the more successful they are." He dramatized the point by reporting a patient who had much futile analysis on the basis of the false self, cooperating vigorously with the analyst who thought this was the whole self. The patient said, "The only time I felt hope was when you told me that you could see no hope, and you continued with the analysis." He emphasized that in psychoanalysis it is possible to see analyses going on indefinitely because they are done on the basis of work with a false self.

Winnicott's theory of true and false self relied on Freud's division of the self into a part that is central and powered by the instincts, the true self, and a part that is turned outward and related to the world presumably the false self. This definition springs from structural theory and poses a false dichotomy. The true self emerges as an entity reflecting the individuation process and probably involves parts of the outside world that are internalized as well as the instincts.

In his development of the concept of the true self, however, Winnicott seems closer to the point. For example, he states that, "the true self is the theoretical position from which comes the spontaneous gesture and personal idea. The spontaneous gesture is the true self in action. Only the true self can be creative and feel real" (137).

This concept of the true self goes awry, however, in his description of what he calls the normal equivalent of the false self: "There is a compliant aspect to the true self and healthy living, an ability of the infant to comply and not to be exposed, an ability to compromise. . . . The equivalent of the false self in normal development is that which can develop in the child into a social manner, something that is adaptive" (137). This analogy is in error because in normal development the true self, the separated individuated self, has a sense of being alert, alive, creative, spontaneous and real and through its ego functions interacts with the environment and does form adaptations and compliances. The true self can comply or adapt without necessarily compromising its essence or integrity.

Winnicott felt that the defensive function of the false self was to hide and protect the true self. I do not feel that this is so because there is not at this point any true self. The true self is in a state of limbo or atrophy—it is only a potential. The defensive function of the false self is to rationalize and provide a false sense of identity for those regressive, compulsive behaviors that reflect the adaptive side of the RORU or WORU—pathological ego alliance necessary to defend against the abandonment depression.

In his discussion of etiology, Winnicott described the crucial variable: "The good enough mother meets the omnipotence of the infant and responds to it. A true self begins to have life through the strength given to the infant's ego by the mother's implementation of the infant's omnipotent expression" (137). In more current idiom, the true self begins to have life through the mother's providing reward and approval for steps toward separation-individuation. This spurs individuation and gives a sense of a true self as the child begins to separate from the mother.

Winnicott states: "The mother who is not good enough is not able to implement the infant's omnipotence and so she repeatedly fails to meet the infant gesture, substituting her own which is to be given sense by the compliance of the infant. This compliance on the part of the infant is the earliest stage of the false self and belongs to the mother's inability to sense her infant's needs" (137). Again, in more current idiom, the mother's withdrawal of approval for separation-individuation produces an abandonment depression. However, since the mother rewards regressive clinging, the child defends himself against the depression by regressive compliance with the mother's projections, thus setting up a system of regressive, pathologic defense mechanisms—avoidance, denial, clinging, acting-out, splitting, projection, etc.

The image of the rewarding mother is internalized as one part of a split object relations unit—the rewarding unit—which allies with the regressive defense mechanisms to form a defense against the other part of the split object relations unit—the withdrawing unit. This alliance, which defends against depression, becomes the basis for the false self. Neither of the part-self-images of the two units is the true self, since the latter, a developmental achievement, only comes about through separation of the self-image from the maternal image based on growth and development through the mode of self-assertion, facilitated by the mother's mirroring and matching responses. The child develops a false self not to hide the true self, since the true self has not emerged, but to rationalize the adaptive function of his regressive defenses against the abandonment depression—a depression created by his efforts to develop a true self in the first place. This false self reacts to the mother's projections with compliance, developing a parallel and complementary set of pathologic defense mechanisms. This intrapsychic system is then internalized and projected on the environment and constantly reactivated, so that the infant may develop a false self which does relate to external reality on the same basis as the infant's false self related to the mother.

Winnicott pointed out that in extreme examples there is no spontaneity but mainly compliance and imitation; there is more concreteness than use of imagination and symbol formation. As he illustrated, there can be varying degrees of the false self and sometimes, as in the "as-if" personality, the false self can be mistaken for the whole personality. In other cases, for example with actors, there may be a kind of sublimation. He stressed that the true self had the capacities of spontaneity, creativity and the use of symbols,

Certainly creativity and spontaneity spring from full individuation where the self-assertion is unfettered and free to apply itself.

Let us now answer the six questions that Winnicott raised about the true and false self.

1. *How does the false self arise?* The mother's libidinal unavailability for the child's efforts toward separation-individuation during that crucial phase of development produces the abandonment depression, against which the child defends by conforming to the mother's projections, which enable her to continue to cling—through projecting, splitting, acting-out, denial and avoidance. These regressive pathologic mechanisms enabling the mother to continue to cling produce a developmental arrest, but they also relieve abandonment depression and separation anxiety and enable the child to "feel good" as if he were receiving supplies. These defense mechanisms—the alliance between the rewarding unit and the pathologic ego—become rationalized as the child's self, but it is a false self.

2. *What is the function of the false self?* As described above, its function is to defend against separation anxiety and abandonment depression.

3. *Why is the false self exaggerated or emphasized in some cases?* It will be exaggerated depending upon the exaggerated projections of the mother or perhaps some combination of constitutional inadequacies of the child and exaggerated projections of the mother.

4. *Why do some people not develop a false self system?* If there are no constitutional inadequacies and the mother provides adequate mirroring and approval for separation-individuation, there will be no need for a false self system.

5. *What are the equivalents of the false self in normal people?* There are none.

6. *What is there that could be named a true self?* A true self is a self representation that is whole, both good and bad, and based on reality; it is creative, spontaneous and functioning

through the mode of self-assertion to regulate self-system in an autonomous fashion.

SUMMARY

To summarize briefly, the psychopathology of the self in the borderline comprises the following:

1. self-image disturbance;
2. difficulty identifying and expressing in reality one's own individuated thoughts, wishes and feelings and in autonomously regulating self-esteem; and
3. difficulty with self-assertion.

The degree of self-image distortion can be used to devise a clinical spectrum from no self-image through false self-image to poor self-image.

The difficulty with self-assertion is due to the need to avoid individuation in order to defend against the abandonment depression. The distorted self-image springs from the patient's identifying as his self the actions motivated by his need to defend against the abandonment depression, i.e., the RORU (or WORU)—pathologic ego alliance.

As the patient improves in treatment and begins to individuate, the true self emerges with newfound thoughts, wishes and feelings, to assume its functions and become the new basis for the formation of a realistic self-image, which is founded not on defensive behavior but on experimentation with new ways of coping.

II. METHOD

3

Clinical Diagnosis and Model of Treatment

A Psychodynamic Approach to Clinical Diagnosis of the Borderline Adolescent

Understanding the role of separation-individuation enables us to predict the components of the clinical picture: The overt manifestations will consist of the patient's particular style of defenses against his feelings of abandonment which are handled by splitting, avoidance, denial, etc. These defenses not only determine the form of the present illness, but also reflect the style of the patient's character. They occur in many different combinations and are as varied as the number of patients one sees, but there is usually a predominance of one or two defenses which assists in further categorizing the clinical picture.

The clinical picture I have seen most commonly is also the one

43

that causes the most diagnostic confusion—the adolescent whose defense is aggressive acting-out.

Five factors in the clinical picture aid in making the diagnosis:

1. the present illness—the patient's defenses against the abandonment depression;
2. the precipitating stress—the environmental separation experience;
3. the past history—evidence of narcissistic oral fixation;
4. type of parents—parents with a borderline syndrome or more serious illness, their character structure and capacity to parent;
5. type of family communication—deeds or acts, not words.

Diagnosis

The diagnosis should be made at two levels—the presenting symptomatic episode (even though the history may be four or five years in duration), and the underlying character structure within which this symptomatic episode is taking place. Some of the difficulties encountered both in obtaining the clinical facts necessary for the diagnosis and in conceptually ordering these facts into a comprehensive whole are discussed below.

Present Illness

The key to the diagnosis is not the subjective symptoms which the patient will report but his acting-out behavior, which is obvious to all but which he is very reluctant to report. The adolescent will not tell you he is depressed; he wishes to avoid the whole affair. Not only will he deny, avoid, and evade it, but also he probably will "holler bloody murder" if you confront him with it too soon.

Much of the evidence, therefore, must be obtained from the reports of the parents, who, suffering from a borderline or more serious syndrome themselves, are not good observers. They may be unaware of their adolescent's behavior because of guilt or denial on their part, or they may have been unconsciously provoking this behavior to obtain vicarious satisfaction. Therefore, very often the diagnosis must be made on the basis of evidence supplied by unqualified observers. In the face of this situation, the examiner must realize that the story he has obtained from patient and parents is probably at best only the tip of the iceberg of the patient's total behavior. The therapist must press for facts from the patient in as much detail as possible, since most of the history and details of behavior are submerged in the dark sea of resistance and denial. It may not be until many months later that the true story will be uncovered, when control of the adolescent's acting-out brings his depression to the surface, and when the parents, having worked through their guilt, are able to reveal the true facts.

The Patient's Defense Against the Abandonment Depression

Having pressed the issue, what kinds of acting-out are found? It may begin with mild boredom, restlessness, difficulty in concentrating in school, hypochondriasis, or even excessive activity (physical and sexual). Finally, more flagrant forms of acting-out appear—antisocial behavior, stealing, drinking, use of drugs such as marijuana, LSD, methedrine, and heroin, glue-sniffing, promiscuity, running away, having car accidents and behaving like a hippie, that is, having long hair, wearing sloppy dress and keeping hippie companions. These companions form an excellent target upon which the parents can project their guilt about their own role in their adolescent's difficulties. They will say that their adolescent has been enticed away by bad companions, not driven by conflicts at home.

Another common form of acting-out (based on object-splitting as described in Chapter 1) is the use of a sexual relationship to substitute for reunion with the maternal figure, that is, clinging, dependent relationships with older males or females.

Having now obtained the clinical history of acting-out, the examiner should keep in mind a number of issues in making the diagnosis. Acting-out may serve many functions; for example, it may be a defense against psychosis in those who are schizophrenic or against anxiety in those who are neurotic. In these borderline syndrome patients, it is neither of these but specifically a defense against feeling depressed and remembering the desperation, abandonment and helplessness associated with the pain of separation from the parent.

Precipitating Stress—The Environmental Separation Experience

The separation experience itself, although sometimes blatant and obvious, is more often hidden and must be winnowed out of a great deal of chaff by selective questions. Actual separations such as in death or divorce are obvious, but often the separation experience involves subtle occurrences such as an older sibling's going away to college, the illness of a grandparent, a governess or maid, or merely some change in the focus of the symbiotic partner's behavior; for example, the mother may become involved in an affair or become depressed or be forced to attend a sick sibling. It is important to keep in mind that neither the patient nor the parent has any awareness of the profound significance of the separation experience, the examiner must ferret this out by himself.

The Past History of Underlying Character Structure: Narcissistic-Oral Fixation

The difficulties in obtaining the clinical facts necessary for the diagnosis of the oral fixation in the underlying character structure are similar to those encountered for the presenting symptomatic episode. The parents, almost universally suffering from borderline or more serious syndromes themselves, are most often quite unaware of the fact that the patient has failed to achieve the usual developmental milestones. The mother has unconsciously received gratification from the fact that the child remains "tied to her apron strings," even though she fails to give the kind of mothering he needs to achieve autonomy. Therefore, again, the therapist must pursue the developmental history on his own, looking for signs of prolonged dependency and passivity, as well as of developmental defects in ego structure, such as poor frustration tolerance, poor impulse control, and faulty reality perception, which give rise to a host of symptomatic expressions from very early in life. These include such varied problems as disciplinary problems at home and in school, difficulties in developing social skills with peers, and somatic symptoms such as enuresis, headaches and gastric upsets.

Particular attention should be paid to the possibility of traumatic experiences during the separation-individuation stage, that is, 18 months to three years. For example, the birth of another sibling who falls ill and requires the mother's attention, or the death of the maternal grandmother and a subsequent depression in the mother may be important. In addition, an early history of clinging, following the mother after learning to walk, separation anxiety at first going to school, or childhood phobias should be looked for. Attention should also be paid to the prepubertal period, ages 10 to 12, for symptomatic evidence of increased anxiety or for separation experiences. The mother's and patient's collaboration in regressive, dependent modes of relating is one of the most difficult clues to unearth because of their mutual defensiveness. Once an accurate developmental history has been obtained, the clinician must look for a difference between developmental level and chronological age.

Parents' Character Structure and Capacity to Parent

The parents suffer as much from a lack of parenting as do their adolescents. Consequently, having been inadequately mothered and fathered, they have great difficulty performing the tasks of a mother and a father.

The fathers are, for the most part, passive men who are dominated by, but maintain great distance from, their wives. They relinquish their paternal prerogatives in exchange for complete freedom to immerse themselves in their work.

The mothers are demanding and controlling women who need and vigorously maintain the symbiotic tie with their child. They do not object to the father's distancing as long as he permits them complete control over the child. This unconscious bargain often surfaces for the first time when the decision must be made as to whether to undertake treatment, the father leaving the decision to the mother.

The parents' affect hunger drives them to perceive the child not as he is but rather as a parent, peer or object. The child's emotional needs for supplies to effect separation and individuation go unmet. The child does receive supplies and nurture for those needs that are not related to separation and also receives them when his behavior meets the parents' narcissistic needs, that is, when his achievements gratify a wish of the parent that life had frustrated, such as the mother who had wanted to be a pianist rather than a housewife. It is the crucial area of separation-individuation that spotlights the parents' inadequate parenting.

When the abandonment finally occurs and the acting-out begins, the parents' permissive-punitive response only furthers the adolescent's sense of abandonment and throws him back on the anarachy of his own impulses.

Type of Family Communication

Behavior as a Plea for Help

Adolescents had an undeserved reputation of not being unmotivated toward treatment. Some of these youngsters do need to reject treatment in order to be able to accept it eventually. The initial refusal, springing as it does from conflicts over passivity versus activity, is only a first and needed step toward eventual acceptance of treatment. It is impressive how deeply interested they are subsequently in treatment.

Curiously, our borderline patients, rather than even appearing unmotivated, are actually desperate for help, although they are not able to verbalize this desperation. They express it by an act— a plea for help—which expresses exactly and poignantly the trapped crying out for succor and aid. The act that brings the patient to treatment usually occurs at the end of a long series of gradually escalated acts whose goal is somehow to break through the seeming vacuum of unawareness, even of indifference, created by the parents' inability to see the adolescent as the child he is. The adolescent is drowning in his struggle; he is floundering in this stormy sea, unable to swim; he cries out for help as he is about to go down for the third and perhaps last time.

The long history of pleas for help in the form of acts by these adolescents is dramatic testimony to the strength of the parents' resistance. To each, the parents respond with apparent unawareness which then leads to an even more flagrant and dramatic act on the part of the patient, until intervention finally occurs—and even then the intervention often is still not at the behest of the parents, but rather from some outside figure such as a friend, a school teacher or even the police or a wise judge.

The parents' resistance influences the initial contact with the doctor. They often "doctor shop," not in the ordinary sense of the term—to find the "best" doctor—but to find one who will give some "treatment" without really getting into the issue of separation from the adolescent. Consequently, it behooves the doctor to be very cautious in his initial comments to the parents, lest he raise their anxiety so much that they sense his therapeutic intent to foster separation-individuation and then go elsewhere.

However, the doctor's behavior toward the adolescent must be quite different. It is clearly of the utmost importance that the clinician sense and respond to the underlying distress and alarm that the adolescent is not able to verbalize. This response is as much a true rescue operation as the action of the lifeguard who dashes into the water with a life preserver. The doctor's response becomes the life preserver that assists the adolescent in keeping afloat long enough for more definitive measures to be taken— in other words, until the therapy begins to help him in his struggles.

A question arises here: Why a soundless act rather than a simple verbal request for help? The individuals in these families, both parents and adolescents, have borderline syndromes, and significant, if not all meaningful, communications between them occur in the form of acts and not words. Feelings are communicated by doing and not by saying. It is small wonder that when the adolescent is in danger, he turns to this most familiar vehicle to express his distress—an act of violence.

THE THERAPEUTIC MODEL

Why an Inpatient Service?

The usual indications for hospitalization are protective in nature: A person who is severely disorganized, homicidal or suicidal should be hospitalized. There is another, more positive indication for hospitalization of the borderline adolescent—when ambulatory therapy cannot bring enough influence to bear on his defenses to enable him to work through the abandonment depression. The structured environment of the inpatient service has the unique advantage of monitoring the patient's entire 24-hour behavior and of funneling all of the patient's thoughts, feelings and actions toward the psychotherapeutic interview. This makes it extremely difficult for the patient to maintain his characteristic defenses of splitting, clinging, denial, avoidance, projection, protective identification and acting-out.

Our treatment program (at the Payne Whitney Clinic of the Cornell University Medical College-New York Hospital) was designed to meet the borderline adolescent's therapeutic needs based on the presenting psychopathology, that is, abandonment depression, orally fixated ego structure, distorted object relations and the implications of these for pyschotherapy.

The salient characteristics of the borderline adolescent are the following:

1. A history of severe oral deprivation and frustration.
2. An orally fixated character structure with ego defects manifested by the following: motivation by the pleasure principle, seeking immediate satisfaction and immediate relief of tension; low frustration tolerance, poor reality testing, poor ego boundaries, and inability to tolerate the frustration of containing feelings, hence the tendency to act them out; resort to fantasy rather than reality

for gratification and emphasizing passivity and irrational acting-out rather than rational activity in dealing with emotions and life situation.

3. The prominent use of maladaptive defense mechanisms such as splitting, denial, projection, avoidance and acting-out. The management of acting-out is particularly crucial for therapy. Acting-out discharges feeling, thereby preventing it from arising to consciousness and being available for therapeutic use in the interview.

4. Maladaptive object relations. The borderline adolescent has no basic trust and tends to be at times withdrawn, isolated, provocative, manipulative and hostile. Because of the introjection of his parents' attitudes, the patient has very poor object relations. His relationships with others are based on projection of these inner attitudes derived from his parents and, therefore, represent fantasy rather than reality. He deals with people as reproductions of his parents who are going to abandon him, rather than as real individuals who may be potential friends.

5. Maturational lag as seen in inadequate development of social and achievement skills. One of the principal developmental tasks of ages six to 12 is the acquiring of social and achievement skills—the tools for mastery of the environment. Most of our patients have been either on drugs during some of this time or so unable to be assertive that they have not learned these skills.

Design of Milieu

The milieu was designed to deal with these characteristics as follows:

1. The oral deprivation and frustration. An inpatient facility with a high staff-patient ratio and a carefully designed structure of discipline gratified to some extent the patient's oral, dependent wish to be cared for and, on this basis alone, decreased frustration and aggression and began the process of enabling the patient to feel that we were interested in him and his problem. For some of these patients, it was the first time in their lives that they had received

any effective assistance in dealing with the anarchy of their impulses. For others, it was the first time they had experienced satisfaction from achievement and social relationships rather than from fantasy.

2, 3 and 4. Ego defects, maladaptive defenses and object relations. The staff set up a standard of consistent expectations of realistic, healthy behavior, and when the patient deviated from this standard in one way or another, it was brought to his attention. The manner in which this was done varied from a simple remark all the way to a graduated series of room restrictions from 15 minutes to 24 hours long. While restricted to his room, the patient was asked to think about his behavior, which was then discussed in the next interview. The confrontation focused the patient's attention on the meaning of his behavior, as the therapist attempted to relate the behavior to his feelings. This attention to behavior reinforced the patient's feeling that we were interested and could help. By helping him control his impulses, we were doing for him what his parents were unable to do for him and what he was unable to do for himself.

At the same time as the defense is interrupted, the patient's depression came to the fore. Control of the acting-out shut off this escape valve for feelings and caused them to rise to consciousness, where they became available for discharge in the interview. Thus the stage was set for interview psychotherapy and the development of insight. A constructive discharge of feelings in the interview was substituted for destructive discharge by acting-out.

The patient's distortions in his attitude towards the staff could be brought to his attention thereby, becoming grist for the psychotherapeutic mill. At the same time, as the patient was externalizing the old, negative introjections he began to make new, more positive introjections from the attitudes of the staff and their expectations. In this way, he replaced his maladaptive defenses with more constructive ones and began to learn new ego techniques of self-mastery and adaptation to the environment.

5. Maturational lag. Meanwhile, in school, in occupational therapy and recreational therapy, he began for the first time to

learn new social and achievement skills which were left by the wayside in earlier developmental periods.

Whether in school, on the floor, in occupational therapy or recreational therapy, the staff confronted the patient with his deficiencies in dealing with reality and emphasized the necessity of dealing with reality constructively. For example, a patient might prepare for a test inadequately, but, not perceiving either his inadequate preparation or his poor performance, might think he did quite well. The teacher would point out his poor performance and then question his preparation, stressing that one must make realistic preparations to meet a real challenge and implying that this required effort and delay of immediate satisfaction. Emphasis was also placed on realistic achievement, as opposed to fantasy, for gratification. This could also be done in occupational therapy; a patient building a cabinet might plan it poorly and execute it impulsively and then try to assert that it looked better than it actually did.

The goal of these policies was to provide an environment that through consistent expectations and appropriate limits: 1. demonstrated our competence to treat the adolescent and relieved his need to test our intentions; 2. helped to undo the pathology of his earlier developmental years; 3. prepared him for interview therapy; and 4. provided him with constructive learning experiences. We anticipated that he would learn to develop self-control, the only basis for self-respect and true autonomy. We expected that instead of being a slave to his impulses he would gain an ego structure strong enough to enable him to decide which impulse he would express where and in what manner he would express it.

The Setting of Limits

There are two horns to the dilemma of setting limits: arbitrary rules without logic or reason to back them up will repeat the parents' rigidity, and inadequate rules will be interpreted as weakness and disinterest. We tried to steer a middle course: a reasoned, individuated and gradually escalated response to the patient's behavior with the goal of teaching control. We preferred to accept mistakes in judgment rather than the hazards inherent in the alternatives of rigidity or permissiveness. Since we were attempting to develop ego control, the limits that were set were, as much as is humanly possible, based on reason and on an individual response to each situation. This had the additional goal of helping the patient to broaden his perception of reality and to learn to use this broadened perception of the reasons why things occur to better understand his own inner life and the world around him.

Restrictions

Room restrictions were a necessary part of the limit-setting. The duration of the restriction was directly related to the degree of lack of control that the patient demonstrated. The less control, the longer the restriction. When a patient was out of control, the nurse would ask him to go to his room. His doctor would come to see him as soon as possible to examine briefly—while the issue was still "hot"—what the patient was feeling before he lost control. The doctor would then restrict the patient for a period of time ranging from 15 minutes to 24 hours. The incident would then be examined in full in the next regularly scheduled session.

We called this "the velvet glove within the velvet glove" technique. The inexperienced often think of restrictions as being punitive. They are just the opposite, since they meet the patient's emotional needs. The only factor that supports the restriction is the patient's willingness to substitute our authority as a means of control for his lack of control. We did not permit use of force.

In some patients, it was not until we instituted 24-hour room restrictions—which indicated to the patient how seriously we viewed his behavior and how firmly we intended to deal with it—that the therapy got "off the ground." The restrictions were not an end in themselves but a means to an end. They had to be combined with efforts to focus on a therapeutic understanding of the feelings underlying the act. Otherwise, they would become simply another arbitrary use of punishment to maintain control. Restrictions were usually necessary only in the first phase of therapy before the working-through had begun. Thereafter, behavioral episodes could usually be handled by interpretation rather than by restriction, since we assumed that the patient now had the capacity to control his behavior. It was fascinating to observe the effort and will a patient would employ to control his behavior once he had become aware of its destructive import.

Drug Therapy

Drugs were used rarely for a panic attack or a psychosis that did not yield to other measures. We hesitated to use drugs for a number of reasons:

1. Most of our adolescent patients had made destructive use of drugs to manage their feelings for years.
2. We were attempting to strengthen frustration tolerance, impulse control and ego functions in general.
3. Administering drugs placed us in the position of reinforcing the RORU—pathological ego alliance and contributed to further regressive resistance.
4. We had a very high staff-patient ratio and were usually able to have staff available for a patient having difficulty.

Psychotherapy

The milieu therapy described in the preceding section provided the essential framework for the psychotherapy. The psychotherapy had many of the qualities of a scientific experiment, since its design was guided by the developmental theory.

For example, two steps were designed to deal with the theory that the patient's clinical picture reflected his use of acting-out as a defense against the feelings involved (mourning and depression) in separating from a symbiotic relationship: 1. physical separation in a hospital, and 2. control of acting-out by setting limits. The effectiveness of these two steps could then be verified by whether or not the patient began to experience the mourning and depression when he was deprived of these defenses. This was exactly what happened.

The goal of treatment was as specific as the developmental theory and the therapeutic design: the resolution of the acute symptomatic crisis (the abandonment depression) and the correction and repair of the ego defects that accompanied the narcissistic-oral fixation by encouraging growth through the stages of separation-individuation to autonomy.

The treatment model was a process, a continuous series of changes, one laying the groundwork for and flowing into the other in a natural and logical manner. Smooth transition from one phase to the next depended on the application of the appropriate therapeutic procedure. As the therapist dealt on a day-to-day basis with each clinical issue, the patient presented a sequence of clinical changes occurring with such regularity as to form a treatment model. Although for purposes of exposition I have divided the model into the three phases of 1. testing (resistance), 2. working-through (introject work or definitive), and 3. separation (resolution), the reader should keep in mind that these are major trends and there is much overlapping and back and forth movement. However, each phase has its own characteristics, which are briefly outlined below.

Phase I: Testing

This phase extends from the onset of treatment to the control of acting-out, the beginning of the depression, and the establishment of a therapeutic alliance.

1. The goal: the control of acting-out and the establishment in the eyes of the patient of the therapist's competence and trustworthiness.
2. The patient's clinical condition: The patient, motivated by the protest and wish for reunion instigated by parental abandonment, has been acting out to defend himself against feeling the depression and remembering the abandonment. Thus, underneath the acting-out he is depressed and feels hopeless. He resists the therapist's efforts in order to prevent final separation with its associated depression. The control

of acting-out which brings affect to awareness and memory into consciousness enables the patient to begin the painful work of mourning involved in separation.

3. Therapeutic relationship: The patient is resistant, and significant communication occurs in actions, not words. He is constantly testing the therapist's competence ad trustworthiness, challenging him with a variety of defiant acts. There is no therapeutic alliance in Phase I.

4. Therapeutic activities: The therapist sets limits to control the acting-out, defining it as self-destructive. Repeatedly, he points out the relationship of affect to behavior.

Phase II: Working-Through

This phase extends from the control of acting-out through the period of depression until separation is achieved and the depression subsides.

1. The goal: to achieve separation by working through the rage and depression associated with mourning.

2. The patient's clinical condition: The patient is very depressed, his acting-out is progressively reduced, he has a greater awareness of the relationship of feeling to behavior, and he is better able to control behavior and to express feelings in words.

3. Therapeutic relationships: The testing phase having been successfully passed, a rather shaky but definitely working therapeutic alliance develops between therapist and patient —the patient begins to trust his therapist. Problems and conflicts now tend to be verbalized in the interview rather than expressed through acting-out and efforts to manipulate people, and it is possible now to use words more effectively than actions.

4. Therapeutic activities: When the patient gives up the acting-out, a second line of defenses ensues against the depression such as withdrawal, evasion, denial, and blocking. The therapist removes these defenses by interpretation and guides

the patient back to the depression. He encourages verbalization as an alternative to acting-out for relief of the depression and begins to investigate the origins of the depression in the conflict with the parents. At this point he deals with any regressive acting-out by interpretation rather than setting physical restrictions as he did in Phase I.

5. In the later part of this phase joint interviews with the parents are begun.

Phase III: Separation

This phase extends from the resolution of the depression until the termination of hospitalization. Its duration varies a great deal.

1. The goal: repair of ego defects and pathological character traits, and the reworking through of anxiety over separation from the therapist and over becoming independent and autonomous.

2. The patient's clinical condition: Depression has abated. The patient now functions better but he experiences great anxiety over separation from the therapist and over becoming autonomous. He defends himself against this by clinging to the therapist and also by transient episodes of regressive acting-out.

3. Therapeutic relationship: The patient, now reexperiencing with the therapist a repetition of the original anxiety over separation from the mother, clings to the therapist in order to avoid the anxiety.

4. Therapeutic activities: The doctor supports the patient's autonomy and interprets his regressive defenses.

In Phase III, after the family has begun to work out new patterns of relating, the patient, in line with the need for autonomy and independence, is encouraged to visit out of the hospital with the family. He is also encouraged to deal with his conflicts with the parents by himself on these visits. After each visit, conflicts that arose with the parents are analyzed in interviews with the doctor and the social worker. It must be kept in mind that there is not sufficient time to completely work through the patient's separation anxiety, and this then becomes the focus of his later outpatient psychotherapy.

Treatment of the Parents

The parents were not permitted to see the patient during Phase I in order to minimize the resistance of both. Separation was as painful for the mother as for the patient, and she resisted it accordingly, as did the father.

However, the parents were seen weekly by the social worker, whose treatment goals were as follows: 1. to enable the parents to verbalize their rage at the separation and thereby to relieve their guilt and attenuate their resistance; 2. to investigate the nature of their conflicts as parents, as well as the source of these conflicts in their own development; 3. to discuss the open conflicts between the parents that impair their parental role with the patient; 4. to interpret the unconscious conflicts interfering with the parental role; 5. to give support, advice, and guidance as to what the appropriate parental role should be; 6. to investigate destructive patterns of family communication and to suggest more appropriate ones; and 7. to prepare the parents to deal with the confrontation with the patient.

Joint Interviews

In the latter part of Phase II, when the patient had verbalized his homicidal rage and suicidal depression and when the parents had become aware of their conflicts in the parental role and had, to some extent, learned a more appropriate parental role, it was necessary for parents and patient to be brought together.

These joint interviews had a specific and limited purpose: not to do family therapy as such but 1. to expose the family myth, the collection of family rationalizations designed to obscure psychopathology; 2. to restore more appropriate patterns of emotional communication in the family, the patient doing now what he was unable to do originally, that is, express his rage and verbally work it through with the parents; and 3. to find more constructive ways of dealing with family conflicts. This initial confrontation always aroused great anxiety, which immediately led to regression on the part of both parents and patient. However, after successful confrontation and catharsis of the underlying emotions, the family was freed to seek better patterns of adjustment. This crucial operation finally brought a strong shaft of hope to the patient.

The therapeutic model included having a halfway house where the patient could stay after discharge from the hopsital, until he felt ready to live on his own. This would have been ideal in that it would have provided a continuous source of support when needed, and yet, would have left to the patient the initiative for the final move to live on his or her own. Despite intense efforts (for example, soliciting 65 foundations), we were not able to get financial support for this endeavor and had to do without the halfway house. As I shall discuss later (see Chapter 15), this lack produced obstacles to all our discharge planning and saddled the patient with an additional burden at a very crucial time in his treatment.

It is the purpose of this volume to demonstrate how well the results achieved by this treatment model have stood the test of time. However, before turning to the results, it is necessary in the next chapter to review the method of follow-up.

4

Method of Follow-Up Study

INTRODUCTION

Since we were evaluating the follow-up results of a treatment based on a theory, ideally we would have liked to have had a hypothesis-testing type of research to test the effectiveness of the theory and the therapy outlined in the first three chapters. However, both practical and theoretical considerations made this impossible so that the research method was exploratory and descriptive in character.

METHOD

The accumulated data were approached from both a clinical and systematic point of view. One of the researchers (J.L.C.), interested in studying prognostic factors, used the systematic method described in pages 82-93, with definition of the variables to be studied, specific efforts to control bias, employment of coding schemes, data analysis and statistical calculations.

The majority of this report is based on the clinical approach which consisted of a case-by-case clinical review integrating all the data into a comprehensive clinical picture of the onset, course and outcome of these illnesses. Nevertheless, as will be described below, efforts were made by all three researchers (Masterson, Lulow and Costello) to control for individual bias and to define to some extent the variables studied.

Selection of Cases

Fifty-nine patients were admitted to the unit between 1967 and 1974. These patients were admitted neither consecutively nor at random, but only after a thorough evaluation suggested that the diagnosis was borderline and that they had a good potential for response to psychotherapy. The evaluation procedure was extensive: The chief resident of the unit spent four to five hours interviewing patients and parents and presented a report to the author who then also interviewed patient and parents. The author had to approve all admissions. Frankly schizophrenic and psychopathic patients, those with organic disease and those without at least one parent were excluded. A few patients admitted for continued diagnostic six-week evaluation were also excluded from the study sample.

In order to obtain a sample of patients who had stayed long enough to have received an adequate exposure to the treatment, we eliminated 22 of 24 patients who were hospitalized for less than 12 months. We included two, one who stayed nine months and one who stayed 10 months, in order to get an adequate size for the sample. The sample then consisted of 37 patients, 35 of whom stayed for 12 months or longer.

At the beginning of our follow-up study, case-finding was quite successful but took a long time and required multiple resources. We located 31 of our patients and 33 sets of parents out of the 37 patients who qualified for inclusion in the study.

The social worker obtained a master list of all patients which had been compiled when the unit closed in August, 1975. The list included the patient's name, age at admission, dates of admission and discharge and parents' last known addresses. Telephone directories and telephone operator assistance confirmed addresses and produced phone numbers of all parents. Former staff members helped to locate some parents. Most of the parents gave us their adolescent's address spontaneously. Some parents were initially fearful that our contact would harm their adolescent, but in all but one case, this fear was dissipated as the parents became more comfortable with the social worker and more familiar with the aim and scope of the study. The one mother who would not provide her adolescent's address was quite eager to be involved for herself, even asking for an additional interview, but she refused to allow us to get in touch with her daughter.

Patients who had maintained contact with each other over the years also helped us to locate nine subjects.

Case Recruiting

Three informed independent judges reviewed the entire sample before any actual contact with parents was made in order to exclude any former patients for whom a follow-up contact might be therapeutically contraindicated. No one was excluded.

A letter signed by the author, outlining the researcher's interest in knowing how the patients were doing now and requesting their participation in a follow-up study, was drafted. The letter also noted that their views of their own therapeutic experience would be helpful in assisting us develop future adolescent treatment programs. The confidentiality of the information was stressed and a brief description of the study design was described. Patients were thus given an idea of what their involvement would entail and informed of parental involvement. It was also noted that the social worker would telephone or write them within two weeks for an appointment. Duplicate letters were sent to the patients and their parents at the parental address.

Most parents, when approached, spontaneously gave their adolescent's whereabouts, explained that they had forwarded the letter or offered to give us the adolescent's address. Eighty-five percent of the parents located also agreed to be interviewed.

The parents' receptiveness and desire for involvement varied tremendously. Many felt indebted to the program for the help it provided them and their adolescents. These parents offered their time as a token of their gratitude. Some had continuing concerns about their adolescents and were indirectly looking for additional help. Others had mixed feelings about the program and seemed to want to use this opportunity to vent them.

Some difficulty was encountered recruiting those parents who continued to have angry feelings about the program and/or its staff. When parents were reluctant to participate in the study, the social worker went out of her way to facilitate their involvement by suggesting another contact later, arranging a home visit or, when all else failed, suggesting a telephone interview. Only three sets of parents overtly refused to be involved on any level but an additional three sets of parents covertly refused. The latter initially agreed to be involved but then failed to respond to our subsequent requests.

Recruitment of the adolescents was more complicated. Many were enrolled in distant schools, employed in other parts of the country or unreceptive to our initial contact. Parents or other patients frequently provided the endorsement we needed to engage reluctant patients. Time was also a factor. Adolescents who were initially quite resistant when they received our letter later agreed to be interviewed. They often explained having experinced strong emotional reactions to the introductory letter, which later subsided. Others reported that they were feeling particularly vulnerable when the letter arrived and unable to respond at that time. For a number of these more reluctant adolescents, our patience, repeated contacts and ancillary support from parents and other patients were effective.

The adolescent's motivations for involvement were similar to parental motivations. Many were proud of their accomplishments and wanted to share them. Others were curious about their fellow patient's whereabouts and outcome. Still others used the follow-up as a way of reworking, integrating and understanding their hospital experience as it related to their present functioning.

Six of the 37 qualified patients were either not located (two) or refused to participate in the study (four). Two of these were reached by phone but angrily objected to talking about themselves. While one of these same adolescents later agreed to speak to his former therapist by telephone, the data obtained were not complete enough to be included in the analysis. A third former participant failed to appear at several scheduled appointments and did not respond to subsequent phone calls and letters. A fourth adolescent lived on the West Coast, had no phone and did not respond to several letters. The fifth and sixth patients were not located. Both adolescents and their families had moved from the New York area, left no forwarding address and apparently had no contact with former staff or other patients following discharge from the program.

No ancillary source of follow-up data was available for any of the six lost patients. Parents of these adolescents were either not located or refused to participate in the study.

Study Sample

The obtained sample consisted of 31 of a potential 37 subjects (83.8 percent). There were 20 females (64 percent) and 11 males (35 percent) in the group. The two to one female-male ratio was the same for the 31 as for the original group of 37. It is also significant that 73 percent of all admissions ($N = 59$), regardless of duration of their hospitalization were females (see Table 2). There are several possible explanations for the high female population: Our culture has traditionally tolerated more symptomatic acting-out in boys. Parents and other authorities have rationalized acting-out behavior in adolescent boys with clichés like "boys will be boys." The same behavior in girls would cause serious alarm. It is possible, therefore, that girls were more frequently referred for admissions, whereas boys with similar symptomatic pictures were maintained in the community. It is also a fact that recent statistics

TABLE 2

Number and Sex Distribution by Year of Adolescents
Who Qualified and Who Participated in Program

Admission Years	Total		Sample		Lost Sample	
	Female	Male	Female	Male	Female	Male
1968	2	3	1	2	1	1
1969	4	2	3	2	1	0
1970	1	3	1	3	0	0
1971	8	1	6	0	2	1
1972	1	2	1	2	0	0
1973	3	1	3	1	0	0
1974	4	0	4	0	0	0
1975	1	1	1	1	0	0
Totals	24	13	20	11	4	2

show an increase in serious acting-out behavior in adolescent girls.
However, this increased rate of female acting-out in the general
population cannot account entirely for the higher proportion of
girls admitted to this specific unit.

A third possible contributive factor to the high female population may relate to the structure and function of this specific unit.
The program was highly organized and had as its initial focus the
control of acting-out behavior. Female adolescents may have been
better able to make the necessary adjustments needed for continuance in the highly structured program, whereas the male
adolescents, in the face of constraints, either refused admission or
left the unit prematurely. This is supported by the fact that 55
percent of all boys admitted to the unit left prematurely. Only 26
percent of all the females left before they were considered ready for
discharge.

The high female population did affect that character of the unit.
There were times when only one male adolescent was on the unit.
This phenomenon raises definite developmental issues and issues
regarding the representativeness of this sample to populations of
hospitalized adolescents in general.

The two-factor index of social position was used to determine the
social status of both the obtained and lost samples (43A). The

parental, educational and occupational levels were used, since the majority of subjects had yet to complete their educations or settle into a definite occupation. Twenty-three (74 percent) came from Classes I and II. The remaining eight (26 percent) came from Classes III and IV. There were no significant differences found with the lost sample. The hospital records were used to determine educational and occupational levels for the lost sample. The majority of patients came from upper-middle and upper socio-economic strata.

All of the adolescents were of at least average intellectual ability. Psychological testing was routinely done when subjects had not had evaluations prior to admissions. Complete batteries were also given during the treatment stay when they promised to provide information which would facilitate the therapeutic process. There was a considerable number of adolescents who were underachievers prior to admission, but this was, for the majority, felt to be functionally caused. Several did manifest soft signs of minimal brain dysfunction, which had necessitated tutorial and specialized academic services in the past, but in no case was the impairment severe enough to have warranted special class placement.

The ages at the time of admission of the obtained sample ranged from 13.0 to 18.1 years, with a mean of 15.7 years. The age at admission tended to diminish over the life of the program (see Table 3).

TABLE 3

Mean Ages of Subjects at Admission

Admission Year	Age Means for Total (37)	No.	Age Means for Sample (31)	No.	Age Means for Lost Subjects	No.
1968	16.7	(5)	15.5	(3)	16.3	2
1969	15.9	(6)	16.4	(5)	13.1	1
1970	16.9	(4)	17.6	(4)	—	
1971	15.8	(9)	15.9	(6)	15.9	3
1972	15.5	(3)	15.5	(3)	—	
1973	15.0	(4)	15.0	(4)	—	
1974	14.5	(4)	14.5	(4)	—	
1975	15.8	(2)	15.8	(2)	—	
Overall Means	15.7	(37)	15.7	(31)	15.1	6

Hospitalization was typically precipitated by a serious suicidal or homicidal gesture, which generally occurred following a gradual escalation of acting-out and increasing severity of symptomatology, associated with the onset of puberty at around 13 years of age. It is, therefore, not surprising that most of adolescents were between 14 and 16 years of age at admission. Admissions of older patients occurred more often during the earlier years, probably because it was only with increased experience with the model and increased numbers of referrals that the trend toward younger admissions occurred.

Hospital stays ranged from nine to 24 months, with a mean stay of 14.48 months (see Table 4). During the early and later years,

TABLE 4

Means of Duration of Hospital Stays in Months

Admission Year	Means for Total (37)	No.	Means for Sample (31)	No.	Means for Lost Subjects	No.
1968	11.4	5	12.6	3	12.0	2
1969	16.2	6	16.8	5	13.0	1
1970	14.6	4	14.8	4	—	
1971	14.8	9	14.8	6	13.1	3
1972	16.6	3	16.6	3	—	
1973	14.2	4	14.2	4	—	
1974	13.5	4	13.5	4	—	
1975	9.0	2	9.0	2	—	
Totals	13.9	37	14.5	31	12.7	6

stays were shorter. Initial experience with the model suggested that longer stays were therapeutically necessary. In later years, however, the anticipated closing of the unit necessitated abbreviating the duration of the hospital stays for many adolescents. No one who was still considered a suicidal risk was discharged to home, but there were a good number who were released when it was felt they could have benefited from a longer hospital stay. Mean age at discharge was 16.7 years (see Table 5).

TABLE 5

Mean Ages at Discharge from Program

Admission Year	Mean Ages for Total (37)	No.	Means Ages for Sample	No.	Means for Lost Subjects	No.
1968	17.7	5	16.6	3	17.3	2
1969	17.3	6	17.8	5	14.2	1
1970	18.2	4	17.4	4	—	
1971	17.1	9	16.9	6	17.0	3
1972	16.9	3	16.9	3	—	
1973	16.2	4	16.2	4	—	
1974	15.6	4	15.6	4	—	
1975	16.4	2	16.4	2	—	
Totals	16.9	37	16.7	31	16.2	6

Follow-up contacts were made between October 1976 and August 1977. The mean length of time between discharge and follow-up was 3.9 years with a range of 1 to 7.4 years (see Table 6). The

TABLE 6

Means of Time Between Discharge and Follow-up by Year

Admission Year	Mean of Total 37	Mean Sample	Mean of Lost Sample
1968	7.3 years	7.2 years	7.5 years
1969	6.0	6.0	6.1
1970	5.4	5.6	—
1971	4.4	4.6	4.3
1972	3.0	3.0	—
1973	2.5	2.5	—
1974	1.3	1.3	—
1975	1.0	1.0	—
Totals	4.3	3.9	5.7

greatest period of time elapsed at follow-up for those adolescents treated in the earliest years of the program.

Timing of follow-up contacts has been discussed in the literature. Gossett et al. (37) noted that follow-ups with adolescents are best conducted a year or more following discharge. Their review of follow-up studies showed that it generally takes about a year for the adolescent's functioning to stabilize. Although we would have preferred to have seen all subjects at a fixed interval from the time of discharge, the circumstances of the study precluded that possibility. We were confident that all had had sufficient time to have stabilized because all patients had been discharged for at least a year, and that our evaluations of post-treatment adaptation would not be colored by the transitional turmoil cited in previous studies.

There was, however, some concern about the adolescents who had been discharged more than three years prior to the follow-up contact. The literature (37) noted that beyond three years one is hard put to associate post-treatment adaptation to any specific treatment intervention.

Since the major project aim was to understand this patient population better and not to prove the universal efficacy of this therapeutic model, the length of time since discharge was not felt to be crucial. The design did address, however, the influence intervening life stress would have on post-treatment adaptation. It was hypothesized that adolescents with benign life experiences following discharge would fare better than those adolescents who had experienced intervening life stress, particularly separation stress. This hypothesis, however, was not limited to any specific time period. It was felt that it would be valid regardless of the amount of time that elapsed following discharge.

The average age of patients at follow-up was 20.6 years with a range of 16.8 to 25.1 years (see Table 7). The wide range had to be taken into account when functional assessments were made. The expectations for older patients were naturally different than the expectations for the younger ones.

Differences between the quality of the retrospective views of patients' treatment experience were also anticipated, but not encountered. It was expected that older patients, being the most removed from the hospital experience, may have repressed a great deal or so integrated their experiences that they might offer more generalized reflections about their individual hospital experiences.

TABLE 7

Mean Ages at Follow-up

Admission Year	Means of Ages of Total 37	No.	Mean Age of Sample	No.	Means Ages of Lost Subjects	No.
1968	25.0	5	23.8	3	24.8	2
1969	23.3	6	23.8	5	20.3	1
1970	23.6	4	23.0	4	—	
1971	21.5	9	21.4	6	21.3	3
1972	19.9	3	19.9	3	—	
1973	18.7	4	18.7	4	—	
1974	16.9	4	16.9	4	—	
1975	17.4	2	17.4	2	—	
Overall Means	21.2	37	20.6	31	22.2	6

This did not occur. Older patients were just as much in touch with their feelings about their hospital experiences as were more recent discharges. Their distance from the program and maturity enabled them to offer more balanced and less emotionally charged assessments of the model. In general, all patients, regardless of age, were quite articulate and eager to share their views.

Twenty-four or 77.7 percent continued in treatment after discharge. The duration of that treatment had a range of one month to 6.9 years, and a mean of 29.4 months.

The almost universal eagerness of the former patients to participate in the research, regardless of the period of time which had elapsed since discharge, seemed easily explained. All patients had spent a considerable period of their adolescence in a highly structured, intense and confined setting. Whether they felt they benefited or not, these patients had invested enough of themselves to want to participate.

In summary, the obtained sample consisted of 31 patients from upper-middle-income families who were of at least average intellectual ability. Admission to the program occurred at a mean age of 15.7 years, with mean hospital stays of 14.5 months. Follow-up contacts occurred between 1 and 7.4 years following discharge with a mean of 3.9 years. The ages at follow-up ranged from 16.8 to 25.1 years, with a mean age of 20.6 years.

Lost Sample of Six Patients

No dramatic differences emerged between the lost sample (six patients) and the obtained sample (31 patients). There were several nonsignificant characteristics, however, which are noteworthy. All six subjects from the lost sample participated in the program during its first four years, and the two unlocated subjects were hospitalized in 1968 and 1969. It was expected that it would be most difficult to find those subjects who were out the longest and surprising that the majority of early admissions were found. The mean age of the entire lost group at admission (15.4) was lower than for the obtained sample (15.7). The difference between these groups is diminished when one of the lost subjects, who was the youngest (13.1) ever admitted to the unit, is not included in the averaging.

The average length of stay for the lost patients was 12.7 months, while the mean for the obtained sample was 14.5 months. In addition, three of the six patients left the hospital against medical advice and refused to return. Five of the same six patients were also discharged with fair and/or guarded prognosis. The prognoses for the obtained sample were more varied and seemed more reflective of what one would anticipate.

In summary, the lost patients had shorter hospital stays, left the program prematurely, and had poorer prognoses at discharge than the obtained sample. The obtained sample would, therefore, best represent those borderline adolescents who had an optimal chance of having achieved the goals of this therapeutic model.

FATE OF THE 22 HOSPITALIZED PATIENTS EXCLUDED FROM THE STUDY

These patients were excluded from the study sample because of their shorter length of stay. Nevertheless, efforts were made by an independent investigator to follow up these 22 patients. These efforts were disappointing.

Nine of these 22 patients (40 percent) were found. Personal interviews were had with three and interviews with at least one parent for the remaining six. The functional outcome of the group was poor. Two of these patients received 18 months or more of treatment at another hospital, and their impairment rating was mild. One, a woman, age 24, was working and living independently the life of a homosexual; the other, a boy, 16, was a senior in high school. Two of the remaining seven were rated as having mild impairment, but there was strong clinical evidence that the underlying basis for this adjustment was psychopathic and, therefore, extremely tenuous. All five remaining patients were moderate to severely impaired, their conditions unchanged from that seen during hospitalization, despite the passage of time. They were unable to continue in school or to hold jobs, suffered from a plethora of symptoms, had poor relations with both family and peers and seemed to drift from crisis to crisis, unable to impose any direction on their lives.

Any conclusions from these findings must remain tentative, since only 40 percent of the group were found.

Data Collection

Interview Procedure

Where possible, two interviews were held with each patient and one interview with each set of parents. Efforts were made to conduct all interviews at the author's offices in Manhattan. The author and William V. Lulow, M.D. served as the informed interviewers. Both had supervised the primary therapists of most of the adolescents, participated in weekly case conferences on all patients and were involved in the daily routine of the program. Each interviewed approximately one-half of the sample. Their assignments were made according to time availability, relative familiarity with the patient and the specific requests of the patients themselves. The social worker (Mrs. Costello) also interviewed each subject, with no prior information beyond that provided by the master sheet or by the parents in the first interview. The social worker, however, did have clinical experience with this age group and was well versed in the theories relating to normal development, border-line pathology and the treatment model under study.

We were initially concerned about the sequence of the interviews. We thought that the patients might be more guarded in their responses to the informed interviewers because of their previous interactions with them at the hospital and that this guardedness might be carried over into the second interview with the social worker. In view of this, we decided that the social worker interviews would be conducted first.

We were unable to maintain this procedure because of scheduling difficulties and experience revealed that the ordering of interviews was unimportant. Patients did not seem to be any more guarded when seen first by the informed interviewers than when first seen by the social worker. There were differences in the kinds of information shared with the interviewers, but this seemed to be a function of other factors. Patients tended to be more critical of the program and more open about their sexual behavior and drug use with the social worker, perhaps because she had not been connected with the program.

The interviews with parents were also conducted by the social worker. The former caseworker of the unit (Mrs. Grace Christ) had planned to share the task of interviewing parents but had to withdraw from the project because of other commitments. Two sets of parents were interviewed by her. In one case, the social worker also saw the same parents.

When it was impossible to schedule parental interviews at the senior author's office, other arrangements were made. In eight cases, the interviewer held sessions at parents' homes. Parents were seen conjointly.

It was possible to conduct two individual interviews with the patient and one interview with the parents for 23 of the patients. In addition, three adolescents were seen for single interviews and five adolescents had no interviews.

In two cases, it was only possible to arrange for one clinical interview with the adolescent, and one with their respective parents. Both adolescents were residing in the western part of the country. Dr. Masterson interviewed one while on a speaking tour in that area. The other adolescent spoke with the social worker by phone on several occasions. In both cases, the resultant data appeared reliable, were supported by parental interviews and were included in the analysis.

In four other cases, parents were not interviewed, but each adolescent did have two clinical interviews. One parent absolutely refused to to be involved and expressed extreme hostility toward the program because of the cost. This same parent felt the program had turned her child into a "selfish, egocentric" individual with whom she wanted no contact. Two parents of this same group agreed to participate but then passively resisted by failing to keep appointments and not returning phone calls. The last parent in this group lived a great distance away, had recently suffered from a serious illness and failed to respond to repeated phone calls. These losses were not believed to seriously affect our data, since parental interviews served primarily as a means of collaborating the self-reports of the patients. In none of the four cases where parents were not seen was either interviewer concerned about the reliability of the adolescent's report.

There was one alternation of the design that did give cause for concern. In five cases, the parental interview was our only source of data for post-treatment adaptation of the adolescent. Two adolescents were hospitalized and could not be interviewed. One parent sabotaged the involvement of her adolescent by telling her that she had already seen us and that we wanted to see the adolescent to tell her she needed to be hospitalized. One adolescent was reportedly functioning well, but was extremely antagonistic toward the program and one had committed suicide.

The failure to interview the adolescents in these five cases caused us great concern. The purpose of the clinical interviews was to make a functional, dynamic and structural assessment at follow-up. This kind of assessment is often problematic even with multiple diagnostic sessions with a patient, let alone attempting the same using one ancillary source of information. Though the dilemma could not be completely resolved, several measures were adopted to compensate. The caseworker (Mrs. Grace Christ) who had worked with these parents was consulted first. The social worker (Mrs. Costello) asked for her clinical assessment of the parents' ability to give accurate reports of their respective adolescents. The caseworker was confident that reliable reports would be given in four cases. The fifth parent would have obvious difficulty. The social worker incorporated this knowledge into her approach to offset the possibility of obtaining distorted data. Extra interviews were arranged with all five sets of parents. This gave the social worker additional time to gain the parent's confidence, elicit more supportive evidence to make more refined judgments, and review or pursue areas which remained vague or were not covered in previous sessions.

In addition, when it became clear that there would be some adolescents for whom only ancillary sources of data would be available, a small experiment was attempted with a subgroup of parents. After interviews with four sets of parents were completed, the investigator wrote up post-treatment adaptation evaluations on each of the respective adolescents. These evaluations were put aside and the same adolescents were then interviewed in the usual manner by both the social worker and the informed interviewers. Post-treatment adaptation evaluations were then completed independently by each interviewer. These evaluations were then compared to the ones based on parental interviews alone. In three of the four cases, the conclusions were essentially the same. In the fourth case, the investigator suspected the parents of minimizing the adolescent's difficulties, but she did not suspect the degree of distortion that existed. This small experiment, though less than conclusive, did give us increased confidence in utilizing the parental interviews alone to make inferential assessments of post-treatment adaptation, when the adolescent was not available. This was particularly true when the parents were historically known to be accurate reporters.

In summary, 93 interviews were conducted (see Table 8). Eight telephone interviews were conducted when all efforts to schedule in-person appointments failed. It has generally been shown that

TABLE 8

Sources of Data for Obtained Sample (N = 31)

Source	Type of Contact	Number of Cases	Number of Interviews
Adolescent	Duplicate Interviews	23	47
	Single Interviews	3	3
	No Interviews	5	
	Totals:	31	50
Parents	Parent and Child Interviews	23	76
	Child—No Parent Interviews	3	6
	Parent—No Child Interviews	5	11
	Totals:	31	93
Hospital Records	Reviews	31	

telephone interviews do not elicit the same depth of material one can get with a personal interview. The use of multiple telephone contacts served as a means of establishing rapport with the subject, reviewing the goals of the research and preparing the way for a more in-depth interview later. Subjects who were quite guarded initially gradually became quite spontaneous and open with repeated contact. The social worker's experience with the multiple contacts suggests that the approach offers a viable way of overcoming the inherent problems of telephone interviews for other investigators.

Adolescent Interviews

The major aim of the adolescent interviews was to assess each patient's functional adjustment at the time of follow-up in terms of normal developmental expectations, the characteristics and dynamics of borderline pathology and the realization of this model's treatment aims. The social worker was also interested in identifying and assessing the effects of intervening life stress and compensatory experiences on each patient's follow-up status.

Duplicate interviews of patients with Mrs. Costello and with Drs. Masterson or Lulow were arranged to broaden and deepen the data base and contribute to the accuracy of final functional assessments.

A semi-structured clinical interview format was adopted. Patients were given another explanation of the study aims and an overview of the areas to be covered. Areas of inquiry included a chronology of life experience since discharge and a description of the present life situation. The social worker also asked patients to share their retrospective views of their hospital experience, their perceptions of the program's effect on themselves and their families and their specific recommendations for future adolescent treatment programs. Beyond this general overview, no fixed ordering of topics or questions was imposed, and the remainder of the interview resembled a clinical consultation. Patients discussed areas in the order they were most comfortable with and interviewers pursued clinical leads as they arose. Illustrative information was encouraged when needed for clarification or to support final conclusions. At the end of the interview, subjects were given an opportunity to ask questions and were asked to sign releases giving us permission to review their hospital records and to publish the results.

The time length of interviews varied among patients and interviewers. Interviews ranged from 45 minutes to two hours. The informed interviewers generally had briefer sessions because they were familiar with the patients, had narrower aims, had more experience in doing follow-up interviews and had time restraints.

Evaluation forms were devised for independent completion after each interview (see Appendix I). This protocol served to organize the data in a comprehensive, consistent and relevant manner. It provided space for evaluative and descriptive data in the following areas: an overall functional assessment rating, symptomatology, psychodynamics, ego structure, object relations, and developmental achievements in areas of independence, intimacy, and creativity. Later an additional category was added to provide descriptive material on overall functioning. Data relating to subjects' impressions of the program and its effects, as well as their recommendations were also written up. The duplicate evaluation forms, interview notes, descriptive material and releases were filed for later analysis.

Parental Interviews

The primary aim of parental interviews was to provide an additional reliability check on the former patients' self-reports. Parents were asked to share their views of the adolescent's functioning since discharge in the areas previously outlined. A second line of inquiry focused on the parents themselves. Since the theory holds that parents significantly contribute to their children's inability to separate, it was hypothesized that specific parental change would be essential if these patients were to overcome their difficulties around separation.

Parents were seen conjointly by the social worker. The format resembled the adolescent interviews. The study aims were reiterated and areas of inquiry outlined. Parents were asked to describe the adolescent's life experience since discharge and assess his or her present adjustment. They were then asked to share their views of their own involvement in the program, program effects on the patients, themselves and other family members and their recommendations for future programs. Releases to review hospital records and report our findings were requested at the end of the interview.

Parental interviews averaged one and one-half hours in length. The social worker took notes throughout. Processing this data was less rigorous, since the major aim of parental sessions was to support, refute or substantiate data relating to the patient's post-discharge and follow-up adjustment. A descriptive report on each parental couple relating to their views of their own involvement and its effects on them as parents, spouses and individuals was composed and filed in the adolescent's files with the interview notes and releases.

Hospital Records

After adolescent and parental interviews were completed and releases obtained, the hospital records were examined. Information about the patient's pre-hospital adjustment and development, admission status, hospital course and discharge status were explored. Former prognostic studies, the literature on borderline pathology and specifically on this treatment model provided direction in the selection of those variables which gave promise of predicting outcome status. The experimental nature of the unit, training requirements of psychiatric residents and proclivity for this patient population to fragment staff insured the maintenance of comprehensive records. All potential patients were thoroughly evaluated prior to acceptance to insure a borderline diagnosis and suitability for the unit, as stated earlier.

All histories became part of the official record. These same records became the central vehicle for teaching, communication among staff and monitoring of patient's daily progress. All of these factors contributed to the compilation of comprehensive records which would provide information relevant to the project aims.

A protocol* was developed to facilitate the extraction of information in an economical, consistent and comprehensive fashion. It consisted of four major sections: demographic information and early history, admission status, hospital course, and discharge status and planning.

Demographic Information

This section provided demographic data about the subjects and their families. This would later be used to describe the characteristics of the sample. Also included here was a section on significant early parental histories. The interest in parental histories was stimulated by the literature, which cites a generational pattern in the development of borderline pathology. Masterson (91) states that parents of borderline adolescents are "at best" borderline

---

* See Appendix II.

themselves and had similar separation-individuation problems in their own development. It was hoped that data would be available to support or refute this belief. This section was later omitted from the analysis because the records did not provide uniform and comprehensive data about parental histories.

Early History of the Patient

It was assumed that all subjects' histories would show pathological deviations during the separation-individuation and subsequent phases of development. In spite of this, differences in the degree of subsequent functional impairment and severity of symptomatology were anticipated. It was hypothesized that intervening life stress and/or compensatory life-experience would compound or minimize the severity of the pathological sequelae of separation-individuation and partially explain the functional, structural and symptomatic variations among patients at admission. Material regarding all areas of functioning, symptomatology, developmental achievements, intervening life stress and object relations from birth to the onset of adolescence or the illness leading to hospitalization was abstracted.

Status at Admission

All facets of functioning from the onset of adolescence or the illness to actual admission to the hospital were then reviewed. A comprehensive picture of each adolescent at admission promised to serve later as a means of comparison with the follow-up status of each patient and comparison among patients at admission. It was therefore necessary to tap the same areas which were covered on follow-up. In addition, factors which gave promise of having significant prognostic value were also tapped. These factors included: age at admission, duration of the illness, severity of symptomatology, degree of functional impairment, quality of object relations, precipitant to admission, patient awareness of problems, and patient amenability to treatment.

Hospital Course

Here we were interested in capturing the character of each patient's therapeutic experience, assessing how closely the treatment model was realized for each patient, and identifying those variables which either contributed to or interefered with the realization of the model. A determination of each patient's success in achieving the treatment goals was also made. These aims seemed feasible because of the clarity and specificity of the model and extensive treatment notes kept on each patient. All staff members made notations in each patient's chart after every contact, and therapists were expected to make detailed entries after all therapy sessions. In addition, three-month and final-treatment summaries were included in all charts. The concern about therapist bias in recording was dissipated, because most residents did not initially know the therapeutic model but learned it as they practiced. Their primary interest in recording was to report individual patient's daily behavior and their verbal content in sessions, not to prove that their patient was realizing a specific model.

Psychological testing results were also abstracted when available. Review of these tests would later provide substantiation that all patients were of at least average intellectual ability.

Discharge Status

Each patient's discharge status was assessed in terms of treatment-goals realization and those discharge variables which gave promise of having prognostic significance. The following were also examined: discharge prognosis, rationale for discharge and disposition plans.

ORGANIZATION AND ANALYSIS OF DATA

The data were organized and analyzed from the two points of view—in the service of clarity we have identified them as the *clinical* and *systematic* approaches. The aim of the clinical approach was to provide comprehensive descriptive analysis of the follow-up functional status and changes in intrapsychic structure in patients. The aim of the systematic approach was to identify the salient pre-admission, admission, hospital and post-discharge prognostic factors. These somewhat differing goals necessitated two methods of data organization. In this section a description of both the clinical and systematic methods is presented.

Clinical Method

At the time of the interview, each of the two interviewers rated the patient's impairment at follow-up using his or her clinical judgment and the American Psychiatric Association's impairment rating as follows: minimal 0-10 percent, mild, 20-30 percent, moderate up to 50 percent, severe over 50 percent. Functional impairment was defined as "the degree to which the patient's total capacity to function is impaired by his psychiatric illness.

Following that, all the material on each patient was reviewed by the two psychiatrists to make a final impairment rating for each patient. Differences between the two were discussed and resolved. Each patient's follow-up record was then thoroughly reviewed to study specifically each of the categories listed below:

1. Functional impairment
2. Symptoms
3. Capacity to deal with separation stress
4. Persistence of pathological defenses
5. Change in self representation
6. Change in object representation
7. Degree of autonomy
8. Degree of intimacy and
9. Degree of creativity.

After the follow-up status was rated, the patient's entire hospital treatment record was reviewed to get a clinical impression of the important contributing factors. All of the residents who conducted this treatment were supervised by Drs. Masterson or Lulow or a third colleague. Therefore, it was possible to make judgments as to the adequacy of the therapist's contribution to the treatment process.

Systematic Data Processing

The parents' interviews were then studied to answer the following questions: Did the parents benefit from the treatment? How much did the parents support or resist the patient's separation-individuation? How did the parents compensate in the family for the adolescent's separation-individuation? What psychopathology remained in the family?

Clinical Outcome of Parents

The aim of the systematic analysis was to determine what pre-admission, admission, hospital and post-discharge factors had prognostic value.

In order to achieve this end, an index of follow-up outcome status was calculated. Patients were first ranked using a seven-point scale on each of the ten follow-up or outcome functional variables (see p. 87). Score values ranging from 7 to 1 were assigned to each of the points on the scale, the higher scores reflecting the least impairment. These scores were then added up to obtain a *final follow-up index* for each patient. This index reflected the relative within-group standing of each patient with regard to follow-up functioning.

Patients were then ranked using a seven-point scale on a series of 12 pre-admission, admission, and hospital variables (see pp. 88-89). Score values ranging from 7 to 1 were then assigned to each of the points on the scale. The higher scores reflected the least impairment on that variable. A *final admission index* was calculated by summing the scores on admission variables. This final admission index represented the relative within-group functional standing of each adolescent at admission.

Correlation coefficients were then calculated between the follow-up indices and score values on the pre-admission, admission and hospital variables to determine which factors were significantly related to outcome.

Rationale and Procedures

The raw data base included process notes and reports of the adolescent interviews, process notes of parental interviews and abstracted data from the hospital records.

The plan for organizing data was adopted after an inspection of the raw data suggested that patient distribution on most variables resembled a normal curve and that a seven-step discrimination among patients could be achieved reliably. That is, only a few patients showed extreme manifestations of the variables, while the majority seemed to reflect intermediate manifestations. Thus, on each variable, each patient would be placed on a seven-point scale with a frequency distribution predetermined to conform to a normal curve. A score value ranging from 7 to 1 was then assigned to each of the seven points along the scale—the higher score indicating more adequate standing on the particular dimension. This schema utilized on all variables is shown below.

Points on the Scale	I	II	III	IV	V	VI	VII
Frequency Distribution	2	3	6	9	6	3	2
Score	7	6	5	4	3	2	1

The adoption of this plan served to facilitate reliable discriminations among patients and had the advantage of providing a common standard deviation across all variables. The latter then justified the use of interval statistics in the analysis.

There were, however, a few variables where the data did not allow for a seven-point discrimination. In these cases, a five-point scale was adopted. Since the symmetrical shape of the distribution was maintained, no change in the choice of statistics was necessary.

The rating procedure, conducted by Mrs. Costello and resembling a Q Sort Technique, was used on all variables. Initially, all 31 subjects were rated on a continuum assuming no predetermined number of points on the scale or predetermined frequency distribution. This provided a natural grouping of patients and manageable data base from which more refined inter-patient discriminations could be made. At this point, the seven-point scale and predetermined frequency distribution were employed. Since reliable discriminations are most easily achieved at the tails of a distribution (where differences are most obvious), Mrs. Costello began here and then worked gradually toward the center, where inter-patient differences became less discernible or tended to cancel each other out. Thus the two most and the two least impaired subjects on a specific variable were placed at the ends of the continuum. This procedure continued until all 31 subjects were placed on the continuum. A score value ranging from 7 to 1 was then assigned to each of the seven points on the scale. On any one variable it was, therefore, only possible for two subjects to receive a score of 7, three subjects to receive a score of 6, six subjects to receive a score of 5, nine subjects a score of 4, six subjects a score of 3, three subjects a score of 2, and two subjects a score of 1.

The scores on relevant variables were later summed to calculate final follow-up and final admission indices on each patient.

Outcome Variables

The data sources utilized in the ratings of subjects on outcome variables were the process notes and written reports of adolescent interviews and the process notes from parental interviews. Mrs. Costello did the ratings on all follow-up variables. Each subject's outcome was evaluated along four dimensions: Independence and Autonomy, Ego Functioning, Object Relations and Symptomatology. Subscales were devised on the last three dimensions because they promised to contribute a more comprehensive understanding of each adolescent. For example, it was anticipated that a subject might have a better within-group standing in terms of Symptom-Recognition than he might on Symptom-Type and Severity. In order to tap various aspects of all three dimensions, two scales were adopted for Ego Functioning, three subscales for Object Relations and four subscales for Symptomatology.

Outcome Variables*

Subjects were rated on the following ten outcome variables:

1. Independence and Autonomy
2. Ego Functioning—Self-Regulatory Functioning
3. Ego Functioning—Defensive Structure
4. Object Relations—Parental
5. Object Relations—Peer/Sexual
6. Object Relations—Peer/Nonsexual
7. Symptomatology—Recognition
8. Symptomatology—Type and Severity
9. Symptomatology—Source of Conflict
10. Symptomatology—Social and Psychic Cost to Functioning.

A final follow-up index was calculated by summing the actual score for the Independence and Autonomy scale with the mean scores from the three Object Relations, four Symptomatology and two Ego Functioning scales. A composite score was used because each of the four dimensions, though interrelated, contributed something unique to the outcome profile which no one dimension could. It was also justified by the fact that all 10 scales were positively correlated with each other. These correlation coefficients ranged from .65-.96, with a median of .85. The means of the Object Relations, Ego Functioning and Symptomatology scales were used (rather than the raw score) in the final index to insure that each of the four dimensions carried equal weight.

In summary, the final follow-up index was comprised of the actual score on the Independence and Autonomy variable and the mean scores on the Object Relations, Ego Functioning and Symptomatology variables. The theoretical range of this index was 4.0-28.0. Higher indices reflected less overall impairment. The outcome index, therefore, represented each patient's outcome standing in relation to all other patients.

---

* Operational definitions are included in Appendix III.

Prognostic Variables

The prognostic variables were limited to those where the data were consistently available on all subjects. They consisted of three types: *qualitative,* where relative within group clinical judgments were made regarding patients pre-admission, admission and hospital experiences; *objective,* where data were quantifiable; and *subjective,* where patients' perceptions of the effectiveness of their parents' concomitant counseling was scaled.

The data source for the qualitative prognostic variables was the abstracted information from the hospital records. Mrs. Costello made within group ratings on all but the Patient-Therapist-Supervisor Match variable. Dr. Masterson, director of the unit, was involved directly or indirectly in the treatment of all patients. His personal knowledge of all patients, therapists and supervisors made his rating subjects on this variable logical.

These data were processed in the same manner as for the follow-up variables with clinical within-group judgments made on the following variables:

*Qualitative Prognostic Variables**

1. Pre-admission—Life Stress
2. Pre-admission—Early Academic Functioning
3. Pre-admission—Early Social Functioning (Object Relations)
4. Admission—Ego Self-Regulatory Functioning
5. Admission—Independence and Autonomy
6. Admission—Object Relations
7. Admission—Symptomatology—Chronicity
8. Admission—Symptomatology—Recognition
9. Admission—Symptomatology—Social and Psychic Cost to Functioning
10. Final Admission Index

---

* Operational definitions included in Appendix III.

11. Hospital—Model Realization
12. Hospital—Patient-Therapist-Supervisor Match
13. Hospital—Prognosis at Discharge

The final admission index variable was calculated by summing the actual score on the Ego Self-Regulatory Functioning, Independence and Autonomy and Object Relations scales with the mean score of the Symptomatology scales. The use of a mean for three Symptomatology scales insured that equal weight of all dimensions would be reflected in the admission index. This index represented the within-group health standing of each adolescent at admission. The theoretical range of admission indices was 6.6-41.2.

The objective prognostic variables included those data which were quantifiable from hospital records and, therefore, did not necessitate judgments.

Objective Prognostic Variables

14. Age at Admission
15. Duration of Hospital Stay
16. Continuation of Post-Discharge Treatment
17. Duration of Post-Discharge Treatment

The subjective prognostic variable was derived from the subjects' retrospective views and personal perceptions about the effectiveness of the parental counseling. Patients' comments were then reviewed by Mrs. Costello and rated on a three-point scale. The three points were: parents made definite gains, there was no change, or parents worsened. A score ranging from 3 to 1 respectively was then assigned.

Subjective Prognostic Variable

18. Patient Perception of the Effectiveness of Parents' Concomitant Counseling

In summary, there were 18 prognostic variables. These consisted of 13 qualitative variables, including the final admission index, four objective variables and one subjective variable.

Check for Investigator Bias

The study design involved the making of comparative within-group clinical judgments on 22 variables: ten relating to outcome status; three relating to pre-admission experiences; six relating to admission status and three relating to hospital experiences (qualitative prognostic variables).

Efforts were made to check the reliability of these judgments because of the small sample size, interrelationships among variables and the sheer volume of judgments. This check for systematic bias consisted of a review of the distribution of a subsample of subjects on each variable by a judge familiar with the data. The judge was asked to review the relative placement of subjects on each variable and note any disagreements that emerged. Where differences arose, they were discussed and resolved. Although this method did not constitute a strict reliability check, it did provide a way of insuring that no gross misappraisal of subjects had been made.

Dr. Masterson served as the judge for the ten outcome scales which were originally rated by Mrs. Costello. There was complete agreement on six scales. Differences emerged on the remaining four scales: Object Relations—Peer/Sexual; Object Relations—Peer/Nonsexual; Symptomatology—Type and Severity; and Symptomatology—Source of Conflict. Five changes were necessary. In four cases, the change involved one step and in the fifth case, two steps. Thus, though there were alterations of the original distributions, the original judgments were not grossly questioned, and subjects' scores were only changed by at most two points.

The discussion of differences also served to determine the basis for the emergent disagreements. Though the basis did vary, one trend did emerge. Both Mrs. Costello and Dr. Masterson had a tendency to more heavily weigh the data they had collected personally. The discussion, therefore, allowed for a better integration of all data sources in those cases where bias was most apt to have existed.

The original distribution on the Patient-Therapist-Supervisor Matching was done by Dr. Masterson. Dr. Lulow served as the judge for this variable. He reviewed the original distribution and made note of any differences. Where disagreements arose, they were discussed and resolved. Two changes were decided upon as a result of the conference. The disagreements were clearly a function of the raters' deriving their distribution from a slightly different data base. Though both were involved in all subjects, Dr. Ludlow had personally supervised the individual treatment of subjects where changes were indicated. His personal knowledge provided additional information which supported a change in the original distribution. In both cases, the changes involved only a one-step difference. The review, therefore, supported our belief that no gross misappraisals had occurred; initial rankings of subjects were realistic.

Since the review of the outcome and the Patient-Therapist-Supervisor matching variables did result in some minor changes, a similar check for bias was done on the remaining 12 qualitative prognostic variables. Ms. Joan Stearns, an experienced social worker who was well versed in the relevant theory and this specific treatment model, served as the judge for all 12 scales. A subsample, randomly chosen, of the original distribution on each of the scales and the raw data were presented. A review of the total distributions on all variables was not feasible because it would have necessitated a total familiarity with the data on all subjects. Ms. Stearns was asked to familiarize herself with the raw data on a subsample of subjects and then review Mrs. Costello's distribution. There was complete agreement on seven scales. On the remaining four scales, four one-step changes were required. The 89 percent agreement supported the contention that no major systematic bias existed.

In conclusion, the review of the distributions on all scales where within-group comparative clinical judgments had been made revealed substantial between-judge agreement and provided an avenue for understanding and resolving differences in judgment when they did arise. As a result, there was no reason to believe that the scores assigned reflected a systematic bias or gross errors in appraisal.

Analysis

The aim of the analysis was to determine whether the differences in outcome status were related to differences in pre-admission, admission, hospital, and post-discharge factors. The organization of the data justified the use of internal statistics in most cases. When internal statistics were not appropriate, other non-parametric statistics were used. Since the latter was more the exception than the rule, they will be reported as used in the systematic findings chapter. The Pearson Product-Moment Correlation Technique was utilized to calculate whether relationships did exist between the outcome indices and the other variables. Values were also calculated to determine the level of significance. The other statistics included chi-squares and the Point Biserial Correlation Technique.

The list below comprises all the variables which were correlated with the final follow-up indices.

Pre-Admission

1. Life stress
2. Social functioning prior to onset of illness leading to hospitalization
3. Academic functioning prior to onset of illness leading to hospitalization

Admission

4. Age at admission
5. Ego self-regulatory functions
6. Degree of independence and autonomy
7. Quality of object relationships
8. Symptomatology—chronicity

9. Symptomatology—recognition, how ego alien, awareness of need for treatment
10. Symptomatology—social and psychic cost to functioning
11. Symptomatology mean of 8, 9, 10
12. Final admission index sum of 5, 6, 7. 11

Hospital

13. Duration of hospital stay
14. Realization of therapeutic model
15. Quality of patient-therapist-supervisor match
16. Prognosis at discharge

Post-Discharge

17. Effect of counseling on parents (chi-square)
18. Continuation of treatment (Point Biserial Correlation)
19. Duration of post-discharge treatment

III. RESULTS

5

Clinical Outcome: From Borderline Adolescent to Functioning Adult

How well did the treatment results stand the test of time? Did the patients relapse, stay the same or continue to develop and grow?

Fifty-eight percent of the 31 patients had maintained their improvement four years later. In evaluating these results, it must be kept in mind that these disorders began early in childhood (18 to 36 months), were consistently reinforced throughout childhood and adolescence, and were therefore tenacious and difficult to modify.

The results are presented first in terms of functional impairment as defined by the *American Psychiatric Association* manual: "the degree to which the patient's total capacity to function is impaired by his psychiatric illness."

Table 9 presents follow-up functional psychiatric impairment:

TABLE 9

Follow-up Functional Impairment

Level of Impairment	Number of Patients	Percent
Minimal (0-10%)	5	16.1
Mild (20-30%)	13	41.9
Moderate (30-50%)	7	22.6
Severe (more than 50%)	6	19.4
Total	31	100.0

Sixteen percent of the patients had minimal impairment, 41.9 percent mild, 22.6 percent moderate and 19.4 percent severe impairment. To summarize, 58 percent were adapting well, whereas 42 percent (moderate and severe) continued to have serious trouble.

To shed more light on these results, we compared them with the results of the follow-up study done ten years previously on adolescent outpatients. It was these dismal results which prompted this work. Although the group cannot serve as a control (since they were not controlled for age, race, socioeconomic status, etc., and they were outpatients as opposed to inpatients), the results can form a useful backdrop against which to contrast the present findings.

Table 10 presents the follow-up functional impairment of those patients diagnosed personality disorder in our 1968 study (89).

TABLE 10

Follow-up Functional Impairment (1968)

Level of Impairment	Number of Patients	Percent
Minimal (0-10%)	6	14.0
Mild (20-30%)	5	11.6
Moderate (30-50%)	16	37.2
Severe (more than 50%)	16	37.2
Total	43	100.0

If we compare the two tables, we note that there is a relatively dramatic shift of patients from the moderate and severe impairment categories to the minimal and mild. The 75 percent of the patients who were moderate to severely impaired at follow-up in 1968 decreased in the present study to only 42 percent. The mildly impaired improved almost four-fold from 11.6 percent in 1968 to 41.9 percent in the present study. The described treatment has more than doubled the number of patients who are doing well.

From another perspective, the number who maintained their improvement on follow-up four years later was almost the same as the number improved on discharge—i.e., 18 versus 20. Examining further, we found that they were the exact same patients—90 percent of those who improved maintained their improvement.

An additional, more refined evaluation of the therapeutic process itself was made from those cases where the therapeutic input was optimal. The second-year residents who conducted the psychotherapy lacked knowledge and were prone to massive countertransference reactions. This single factor caused much prolonging and stretching out of the therapy. However, our mission included teaching as well as research. The principal task of the supervision was to help the resident to resolve his countertransference. We found that if the supervisor could help the resident with his countertransference, the adolescent would teach him what he needed to know about treatment.

To better evaluate the treatment approach, we selected out a subsample of 12 patients whose treatment was relatively free of contamination by countertransference. Nine (75 percent) of these patients did well (minimally or mildly impaired)—perhaps the truest measure of the effectiveness of the treatment.

The statistical correlations reported in detail in Chapter 14 show a highly statistically significant correlation between the degree to which the patient's clinical course followed the optimum therapeutic design and follow-up status, i.e., the closer the patient's course came to the design, the better the outcome; the more the patient's course deviated, the worse the outcome. A statistical correlation of prognosis on discharge with later outcome showed the same statistically significant relationship.

SUMMARY

All of these patients were ill enough to have to be hospitalized for suicide attempts or other expressions of desperate pleas for help. They had exhausted their adaptive capacities and had hit the rock bottom of emotional despair. Without treatment many of them would, no doubt, be dead, in hospitals or in prisons.

The fact that 58 percent of the 31 patients were doing well four years later suggests that this work done in psychotherapy was not superficial or temporary but had been internalized by the patients, producing new, more effective and enduring capacities for adaptation. Further, the fact that 90 percent of those discharged as improved maintained that improvement suggests that the treatment had a profound influence on the course of the lives of a substantial number of these adolescents. For many, it represented a true triumph over tragedy.

Beyond that, this outcome was highly correlated with the degree to which the patient's clinical course followed the therapeutic model and could be predicted with great accuracy by prognosis at discharge. These are two powerful arguments for the accuracy and the effectiveness of this treatment model.

6

Minimal Impairment

Chapter 5 reported a macroscopic level of observation. The next five chapters (6-10), in an effort to get closer to the extraordinary variations in detail, summarize each of the four impairment categories and illustrate each with four cases.

This report gives special attention to the degree to which the previous pathologic defense mechanisms had subsided and been replaced by more adaptive mechanisms, changes in the capacity to manage separation stress, the degree to which the patient had individuated and developed whole self and object representations and object constancy, and the development of the capacities for autonomy, intimacy and creativity.

MINIMAL IMPAIRMENT

These were five patients who, at follow-up, exhibited minimal impairment (Table 9, p. 98) and showed the most dramatic improvement. They had worked through the rage, depression and despair of their abandonment depression, separated from the symbiotic relationship with mother, and received the resultant benefits for ego development and the development of object relations. Four of these patients are described in this chapter.

Their object relations developed approximately to the stage of object constancy, with whole self and object representations that were realistically based. There was strengthening of the ego as splitting and the other pathologic defense mechanisms (projection, acting-out, passivity, avoidance and denial) were replaced by higher level mechanisms. Regressive behavior gave way to self-assertive attempts to cope and adapt to reality. The vulnerability to separation stress was drastically reduced, the capacities for creativity and autonomy developed and, as individuation took place, the self emerged to be consolidated and expressed in a flowering of newly found wishes and interests. Intimacy still posed some problems which were being dealt with by experimentation rather than avoidance and denial.

BETTY

Follow-Up 18 Months After Discharge

History of Illness at Admission

Betty, 14, gave a history of at least a year of increasing isolation and depression in the setting of the escalation of the marital conflict between her alcoholic and dependent mother, who expected Betty to take care of her, and her intellectual, remote and detached father, who denied emotion and spent most of his time working away from home. Betty felt a responsibility to settle this battle, but became increasingly depressed and isolated and withdrew more and more into a fantasy life, daydreaming of events that would bring the conflict to a successful resolution.

One day Betty truanted from school and went to a local guidance center for help, but her parents refused to cooperate, saying that she went to the center just to excuse her not attending school. At one point she became ill with an infection and had to stay in bed for a month, felt "bored" and depressed and noted that her mother spent most of the time on the phone and ignored her.

Several months before admission, Betty began to act out sexually, had intercourse for the first time with her off and on boyfriend of two years, became pregnant and made arrangements to have an abortion without telling her parents. However, she inadvertently left the report of the pregnancy test on her father's desk. When the parents found it, they supported the idea of an abortion, denying its implications. The father said: "It's just a normal adolescent happening." After the abortion, Betty's parents continued to deny that anything of special significance had happened.

Betty's depression deepened. She took a razor and slashed her wrists. She felt that she was not trying to kill herself but had to do something "drastic" to make her parents aware of her desperate emotional condition.

Past History

Her past history was not particularly remarkable except for some increased stranger anxiety around the age of two and repetitive episodes of underachievement at school, which the father thought were due to her lack of intelligence. "We adjusted our standards downward for Betty."

Hospital Psychotherapy

Betty's initial behavior—her defenses against her abandonment depression—consisted of acting out her dependency on the staff in a helpless, compliant manner, retreating into fantasy while expressing herself in vague and ambiguous ways with her therapist. Meanwhile, she denied that these activities might be harmful.

Betty was defending herself against her abandonment depression through clinging, splitting, projection, acting-out, avoidance and denial. Confrontation of these defenses, when integrated, led to the working-through of her abandonment depression. The anger with which she struggled for several months was reflected in fantasies of murdering her mother or killing herself.

She recalled vivid memories of her mother's flagrant behavior when drinking, of the mother's use of her as an object for the mother's security, and of the father's depersonifying her as a "beautiful, stupid ornament." When she had worked through much of her abandonment depression, she then worked through the communication problems and the depersonification of her mother and father in family interviews. She entered the last phase of treatment, and, after some efforts to provoke the therapist into taking over for her, she was able to deal with her separation anxiety and leave the hospital.

What stands out in this report of the hospital treatment is Betty's use of the pathological defense mechanisms to deal with her abandonment depression at cost to herself. She described on follow-up her feeling about herself before treatment—a view expressed by many of the patients—"I was not a person, I had no self, I had to take care of my mother." (See the description of the false self in Chapter 2.)

Follow-up at 18 Months after Discharge

Betty, seen at 17 years of age, was a different girl. She was discharged to attend a local Catholic boarding school, where she had difficulties with the authorities whom she felt suppressed her self-expression. Nevertheless, she finished her sophomore year. She then lived at home for the summer, worked off and on, and continued in treatment as an outpatient with the same doctor as she had in the hospital.

She had more and more open conflict with her parents, particularly with her mother who attacked her for her independence and attempted to get her to resume her old role as caretaker. Betty, however, battled her mother: "I demanded what I wanted. I expressed my anger. I tried to protect myself against my mother. I told her I couldn't listen to her problems, as this had screwed me up, and I had my own. I felt confident of myself, but lonely and totally on my own."

By the end of that summer, Betty decided that she had to get away from her parents and managed to get herself accepted at a good private girls' boarding school, where she began the eleventh grade. The academic standards were too high for her background, and the school wanted her to drop back a year. Betty fought with the school authorities to allow her to continue in the eleventh grade. They reluctantly agreed, and she did manage to finish the year successfully although with a great struggle. "I made a lot of new friends and got into new things with people on an equal basis without being stepped on." However, she decided that the school was in reality too difficult for her and returned home for her senior year at her local high school. Fearful of living at home, she was able to arrange to live with one of the teachers in the school. She was still living there at the time of the follow-up.

She reported having felt some depression over the conflict with her parents, but she made a point of mentioning that she never felt hopeless or helpless. "I know I can get myself out of this; I know I can manage myself on my own." She did not report separation anxiety or any other symptoms. There seemed to be no resorting to excessive fantasy or to role-playing in the old sense with the parents. The pathologic defense mechanisms had given way to more constructive coping efforts. She was getting a B average in school and felt quite content there.

There had been an explosion of new interests, in particular a great interest in Outward Bound, "a symbol of everything I felt." She was able to be responsible for herself. She was a proctor for her hall and a member of the Student Council. She had joined a trail club and a dramatic club, gone skiing and camping, and attended first aid classes at the YWCA.

She was dating a number of boys without any serious involvement. She felt that the sexual episode that preceded her admission and the long relationship with her father had left her guarded with boys, and she wanted to take some time before again getting involved with a boy. "I don't want to play a role and to be a possession of a boy. I want to be a girlfriend, I don't want to submit. I am more aware when that is being pushed on me, and I am able to stop it now. For a while I had to be opposite and rebel against it, so I went from one extreme to the other; now I seem to be coming to a mid-point." She had ended treatment with her doctor nine months after discharge on her own initiative, feeling that she wanted to manage on her own, and although she experienced anixety and depression, she managed to work through the separation.

Parents of Betty

Betty's parents were dramatically affected by the hospital treatment program. The mother reported that she had become aware of how her own difficulties interfered with her daughter's development. She viewed her casework therapy as follows: "They said we needed to clean up our own house and that we didn't have to worry about Betty." She felt grateful to Betty for forcing her to look at her own problems.

She noted that prior to treatment she had denied her conflict with her detached and unavailable husband, drank heavily and leaned on her daughter.

The mother has returned to work as a geriatric nurse. Initially, she had difficulty separating from her other children because she felt guilty, but she now believes it has been better for her and the other children. She still has a tendency to become depressed and wants to lean on Betty, but so far she has restrained herself.

The father had great praise for the treatment program and talked on and on about his gains. He believed that he had never been a consistent, stable, secure model for the children but with the help of the therapy had become one. However, he saw Betty as a phony, selfish adolescent who was trying to squeeze him for everything. His feeling was: "You wanted to leave, so why depend on me?" It was striking that he was the one who encouraged her to leave boarding school to live at home, promising to buy her a car. He does wonder in retrospect whether it was the best thing for Betty.

Betty described her mother as more self-reliant, and although she still tended to get depressed, she coped, was "predictable, natural and nonintrusive." She "wanted something out of life for herself."

Betty viewed her father, on the other hand, as quite disturbed.

Prior to treatment, he was completely "a loner, aloof from the family," but ever since he had been "unpredictable, intrusive and twisted." "One minute he says you're on your own, and the next minute he's making ridiculous demands, interfering and treating me like a baby." For example, after he agreed to pay for her food and rent in a boarding house, he insisted that Betty give him a list of all the food she bought each week so he could check to see if she were eating well. Betty avoided him as much as possible. The mother showed obvious discomfort with the father's anger and seemed unable to cope beyond offering weak disagreement with his perceptions.

There were three siblings still at home—a girl a year younger than Betty and a preadolescent boy and girl. An older sister attended college. Everyone denied that any adjustment problems existed except for Betty and her year-younger sister, who apparently calmed down when Betty did. The interviewer, however, sensed that somehow the father and the siblings felt Betty to be an egocentric traitor for leaving home. It seems quite possible that they viewed her and/or her individuation as "bad" and were excluding her for her independence.

Clinical Impression

Betty illustrated how the self emerged under the influence of treatment. Her passive-regressive defense of submitting to the projected roles of caretaker of the mother and of brainless object for the father, with denial of the self, was dramatically evident.

She began treatment with no image of herself. She was unable to motivate herself, but instead played a role in relationship with both mother and father and life in general. The mode for this was passivity rather than self-assertion. She could not identify her own wishes, activate them, or protect her self-esteem.

On follow-up, Betty was clearly aware of her own positive self-image: "I feel good about myself. I think I can manage myself, cope with my problems." She was coping through the use of self-assertion, identifying her own goals and pursuing them if necessary against the regressive influence of her parents' rules and differences with school authorities. She was able, to a considerable extent, to regulate her self-esteem in this fashion. This represents a profound recapture and flowering of the real self.

There are similar changes in object relations. She sees both of her parents as whole objects, is quite aware of her mother's regressive projections and is able to challenge them. The idealization and dependence are gone. She relates to her peers through liking and common interests rather than through clinging and compliance.

She certainly has handled severe post-hospital separation trauma without an abandonment depression, despite the intensity of the separation stress. Her pathological defense mechanisms—avoidance of individuation, clinging, denial, resort to fantasy and regressive behavior—are, for the most part, gone. She deals with her life through efforts to cope with and master reality.

There has been a flowering of new thoughts and interests as further evidence that she has reached the stage of ego autonomy. Her being used as an object by her father and by the boy who impregnated her has left her with a fear of being used so that she still has not achieved a level where she can experiment with intimacy. However, she is changing from rebelling against or complying with the object to a need for a real relationship on an equal level. This remains to be worked out, but since she is only 17, one can anticipate that, with other functions intact, she should be successful in this area also. If not, she may need more treatment to expand her capacity for intimacy.

MARIE
Follow-Up 18 Months After Discharge

History of Illness at Admission

Marie, age 14, was admitted to the hospital after a suicide attempt. She gave a five-year history of anorexia, vomiting, weight loss, hyperactivity and depression.

The illness began at age nine, during the summer of her first major trip away from home for a skating competition. She became depressed and escalated her already heavy skating practice schedule. The depression and overactivity continued episodically for the next two years until her eleventh summer, when Marie, at camp for the first time, became depressed and began at eat poorly, with selective rejection of protein food. During her twelfth year, she felt "pressured" at school and was angry with herself when she did not get "the top grades." That year, she became terrified at a party when the other adolescents began to play a kissing game. She began to cling to her best friend and said she was "turned off" by boys. In her thirteenth year, her brother began to withdraw from the family in preparation for his leaving for boarding school the next year, and Marie took over many of his household tasks. During her thirteenth summer, she again went away to camp and reexperienced depression and anorexia, which cleared upon her return.

At 14, her breasts began to develop, and she became interested in boys, but at the same time, she lost ten pounds. Her mother than developed a severe depression in response to the death of the governess who had raised her, and the patient's older brother left for boarding school in September. Marie became depressed, and in a few months (November) her selective eating pattern became more noticeable. She was "moody and irritable." By March, she vomited regularly, and by April, she was limiting her diet exclusively to vegetables. Attempts of the pediatrician to help were of no avail, and in early September her parents found a suicide note saying she was sorry she was such a burden and describing suicidal attempts made by scratching her lower abdomen and attempting to gag herself to death.

Past History

Marie, the second of three children, had a normal birth and early development. She was breast-fed until three or four months of age, at which time her mother, on stopping, felt: "a separation, a loss of a feeling of closeness like when she was in the womb; this seemed like a second separation."

Marie had a succession of nine maids who took care of her. At bedtime she often stood in her crib and screamed. Her brother comforted her. Mother said, "There was no point in going in, that would prolong the agony. I was quite upset with guilt feelings." The mother revealed her projections by describing the patient's first year as: "helpful, never a complainer, never a discipline problem, a clown, mimic and independent, adventuresome, daring, obstinate."

Marie was increasingly unhappy during her second year of life, as her governess was dismissed, her mother gave birth to her sister, became depressed and sent Marie for several months to live with her paternal grandparents. The parents recall little of Marie between two and five years. Marie was anxious on starting nursery school to the point that her mother went to school with her each morning for a month.

At age four, in nursery school, Marie was settling down after some minor reports of attention-getting behavior, when the parents went away for a long weekend and returned to find Marie "dissolved, depressed" and again anxious about school. The mother had to return accompanying her to school again in the mornings for a few weeks. After a tonsillectomy at seven, she became "hysterical" and would not let the nurses near her so that the mother had to take care of her. She did well at school, both academically and socially, until the last two years. On her mother's prompting, the patient took up ice skating at age six and age nine was deeply involved in practice and competition.

Parents' History

The parents each received individual psychotherapy once a week and group therapy once a week for 16 months. Space limitations require the briefest of summaries.

Marie's mother was an only child whose mother had died at her birth. She was raised by a governess with whom a strong mutual symbiotic relationship developed. The governess forced food on her charge and tried to influence her to become a champion ice skater. When Marie's mother was 16, her governess was dismissed by her father who had remarried, and she reacted with severe depression.

When Marie was born, the mother felt consciously that her dream had come true, that her mother had returned in the person of her daughter. The symbiotic themes of reunion, dissolution, fusion and death that sprang from the mother's relationship with the governess were repeated with Marie, including the problem with food and the ice skating ambition.

These themes were evidenced in the family sessions when Marie said she no longer wanted to skate. Mother later reported Marie "freezing her out." She said, "I feel so hurt; it's like death. I withdraw." While working through her intense rage and depression at Marie's efforts to separate, she dreamed of Marie's death, of endless empty rooms. She gradually came to see Marie and herself as separate and to support Marie's individuation while looking more realistically at her own life and desires.

Marie's father, a lawyer, was the eldest son of a wealthy, socially powerful family dominated by his mother. He was the "good" son fulfilling all the family expectations of him, and he and his wife continued to live close to and be dominated by his mother up to the time of admission. He had a sister, two years younger, who had died at the age of 23 of anorexia nervosa. There was evidence of unconscious collusion on the part of Marie's father and the rest of the family in this death. The father named Marie after his sister because, "I guess I wanted to resurrect her, to have another chance." It became clear that Marie and this dead sister were fused in the father's mind. In treatment the father began for the first time to mourn the loss of the sister and to explore the formerly repressed feelings of envy, rage, guilt and sexual desire that he had towards her. He began to see parallels between his interaction with Marie and her symptoms and his past interactions with his sister. He reported dreams of trying unsuccessfully to merge two faces (daughter and sister) on one body. Gradually he was able to separate the two, which enabled him to become a father to his daughter.

Marie—Intrapsychic Structure

Marie's intrapsychic structure, as derived from the history and from the recapitulation of the part-units in the transference, could be outlined as follows:

The rewarding object relations unit consisted of a part-object representation of an omnipotent mother who was perpetually caring and gave her special attention, a part-self representation of a good child who was loved for behaving as if she were sick and helpless and could not manage for herself and an affect of feeling good, a cosmic feeling of safety and protection.

The withdrawing object relations part-unit consisted of a part-object representation of a mother who varied from indifferent to one who was "not there" and "hated her," a part-self representation as "a nobody, evil, fat pig, like I committed ten terrible sins, am ruining the whole family" and an affect of abandonment depression.

An explanation of the defense mechanisms of the pathological ego were as follows: denial of separation, splitting and acting-out through clinging of the rewarding object relations part-unit with a projection on the mother and on others of the wish for reunion. Behavior was helpless, childish, compliant, with avoidance, inhibition and denial of individuative thoughts and feelings—to the point of "not thinking." This partly accounted for the anorexia symptom, the distortions of body image and the helpless self-image. The anger of the withdrawing object relations part-unit was expressed partly in the anorexia symptom, and was partly reflected back on the self as well as projected on any and all who confronted her acting-out of the rewarding object relations part-unit fantasy.

Hospital Psychotherapy

During the course of her 15 months in the hospital, Marie presented an intense, clinging, helpless, dependent behavioral façade with anorexia, overcompliance and hyperactivity. Confrontation of the destructiveness of these behaviors which forced Marie to face the anger in her feelings resulted in long periods of resistance manifested by silence or in anger projected on her therapist. Her difficulty in individuation was closely linked to the anger at her mother which she couldn't express because of her fear of being abandoned. In addition, Marie had such severe separation experiences throughout infancy and childhood that she reacted strongly to every one of her therapist's vacations. She finally worked through her abandonment depression with the result that her self, which had been overwhelmed by the need to cling to defend against the abandonment depression, began to emerge and flower. She managed her parents in a self-assertive fashion during joint interviews, her improvement continued, and she was discharged to a local boarding school to continue in treatment with her therapist.

Follow-Up Two and a Half Years After Discharge

Marie was 18 when seen two and a half years after discharge. After leaving the hospital she had continued in treatment for six months, three times a week, at which point her doctor had to leave to go into the service. She was transferred to the author (JFM) who saw her three times a week for the next 18 months and then once a week for six months. She had functioned quite well without symptoms or much difficulty until her therapist left, at which time she went into a severe abandonment depression. She developed only mild anorexia but projected the withdrawing unit on her second therapist. Month after month interviews were filled with bitter recriminations towards him which did not yield to confrontation. Finally, towards the end of the first year, when she was finishing her junior year in high school, the projections began to yield, and she began to work through her severe feelings of loss of her first therapist's leaving.

Following that, she went away for the summer for three months and seemed to undergo profound individuation experiences. On her own for the first time in her life, she started to smoke and drink, and she had her first sexual relationship with a boy, including intercourse. She did not enjoy it and was strong enough to turn down the boy's further overtures. On her return, the old clinging compliance had disappeared, and she seemed to have a better feeling about herself.

She returned to school, where she was elected president of her senior class. She was now able to distinguish between what she wanted and what her parents, school or peers wanted and to use self-assertion to follow her own wishes. In the spring of the next year, she fell in love for the first time, had her first menstrual period and her first enjoyable sexual experience.

A short time later she found the boy to be inappropriate for her and was able to drop him without an abandonment depression. She had done very well in school, as well as socially, and was looking forward to going to college in the fall. In anticipation of this, she requested that the sessions be reduced to once a week. They were, and she tolerated it extremely well.

Parents of Marie

After Marie was hospitalized, both parents entered private psychotherapy in addition to the casework therapy at the hospital. Their treatment helped both to clearly see their own involvement in Marie's difficulties. The mother said, "My husband had five children and no wife at that point." It was clear to them that the purpose of their treatment was "to get our house in order."

They felt that previously Marie had really been the target of their own projections, while their other children were spared. At follow-up the mother viewed herself as less like a child, happier and content with herself and her marriage. She felt confident that Marie had the ability to cope. She was, however, anxious about her ability to socialize with boys. She added that she knows what problems she had and feels Marie is in far better shape than she was when she went off to college. The father was less optimistic, going so far as to say he felt Marie will always have trouble relating to men. He was, however, unable to give any basis for this beyond his own hunch.

Both parents did cite incidents to illustrate their feeling that Marie was attempting to shock them into some type of a restrictive response. They noted, for example, that they knew she had smoked cigarettes and felt somehow she wanted them to lay the law down—take over responsibility or test them to see how they would respond.

The mother at this point did not know when she would be ready to terminate her own treatment. The father said his treatment was now winding down. Neither, however, seemed very clear about what they were striving for or had accomplished in their therapy. This may be due more to a reticence to discuss it with the social worker or in each other's presence than a lack of understanding.

Another explanation may be found in Marie's view of her parents. Though she felt both had made gains, she felt both were extremely dependent on therapy, viewing it as the answer to everything. They wanted her younger sister to see someone "because maybe Marie's hospitalization had an effect on her," despite the fact that Marie's sister functioned well and reportedly had no symptoms. An older brother had some trouble around the time Marie was discharged. He was smoking a lot of pot, arguing and fighting with the parents. "He met a girl then and straightened out," according to Marie.

Marie viewed her mother as having made more significant gains than her father. Her father, she sensed still had a tendency to view her as vulnerable and different. He "showers" me with so much praise," it sounds "phony." Also, she sometimes felt that somehow she must continue to perform well for him (this may be projection). Although her mother also had high expectations, Marie felt that the mother was more ready to accept Marie's views if they differed from the mother's. Her mother returned to school, "doesn't lose control of her feelings anymore," and generally seemed to be relaxed.

Clinical Impression

Marie's self had been overwhelmed by her abandonment depression and her mountainous need to defend against it by clinging. She was not able to invest the self representation or be assertive.

The extreme difficulty that she must have experienced as an infant and child were probably signaled by the difficulties she had in the hospital with a dramatic intense struggle to avoid the feelings of anger associated with her individuation.

However, when she did begin to move she moved quickly and established a secure self representation, a perception of her parents as wholes both good and bad, a capacity to de-idealize them and deal with them in an independent manner, to give up her clinging and complying, to use her own self-expression as a guide for her own adaptation, to distinguish between her needs and those of the parents and environment, to support herself through self-assertion, and to persist towards her own goals.

She had had several relationships and tolerated their ending without abandonment depression, was prepared to experiment further for intimacy. Her creativity was evidenced by a plethora of interests such as dance, gymnastics, sports, yearbook, and many causes, none of which seemed to jeopardize her excellent school work. Although she had been somewhat anxious about leaving treatment and starting school, she was eagerly looking forward to these changes—another clear evidence of the emergence of the self, the disappearance of the rewarding-withdrawing units and the application of the self through adaptive mechanisms to cope with reality. Her pathological defenses of clinging and helplessness are gone, and there is ample evidence of creativity, autonomy, and a beginning capacity for intimacy.

The mother, in particular, seems to have made substantial gains since entering therapy, now providing support for Marie's continued growth. The father boasts of gains, but these are less evident, at least in his attitude toward Marie.

FRED

Follow-Up Five and a Half Years After Discharge

History of Illness At Admission

Fred, 17, a senior at boarding school, was admitted with a one-year history of a change in personality, truancy, running away from school and a suicidal attempt by scratching his wrists. Fred had had a long history of school difficulty, despite the fact that he had a relatively high I.Q. At the beginning of the year, his school work had begun to improve, but he underwent a drastic personality change from being extremely quiet, compliant and conservative to rebellious, hippie-like behavior. He developed sudden obsessive interests in the Beatles and in Russia and Communism.

Past History

Fred had a domineering mother who tried to oversee and control his every action and a distant, compulsively overworking but successful father. He responded with passive-aggressive behavior. He did poorly throughout childhood, and when he first went to camp, he had to be returned because of separation anxiety. This was followed shortly by a transient period of a fear of the dark.

On admission examination, he denied the existence of any feelings whatsoever, including depression. He also denied any content to his suicidal attempt. When razor blades were found in his luggage, he admitted placing them there to use in case his hospital treatment didn't work.

Fred's pathological defense mechanisms consisted of avoidance and denial of feelings, a façade of overcompliance which made a caricature of expectations, passive aggressiveness, marked avoidance of any aspect of individuation or self-expression, intellectualization and emotional withdrawal.

Hospital Psychotherapy

When the therapist confronted Fred with the destructiveness of his behavior, the patient would deny any affect and, as a resistance, comply with what he perceived as the therapist's instructions. The resident therapist, who had similar defenses of intellectualization and passive aggressiveness, developed an intense countertransference, and patient and resident colluded to present an illusion of psychotherapy based on instructions and compliance, devoid of affect.

This impasse lasted eight months, until the supervisor helped the resident to become aware of and contain his countertransference and thereby stop resonating with the patient's transference acting-out. The resident was then able to confront the patient and integration of the confrontation led the patient back to his terror of individuation, which related to his fear that, if he expressed any anger to his mother, she would abandon him. From time to time, when his transference acting-out was blocked, to manage his depression and rage, he would resort to the splitting defense by turning to the nursing staff. When this was confronted, he would resume working through his depression and anger. He managed a family conference extremely well, despite the fact that he was savagely and bitterly attacked by his mother for self-assertion, but he continued to improve and, after months of hospitalization, was discharged to attend college.

Follow-Up Five and a Half Years After Discharge

Fred, 25, continued in psychotherapy with the same therapist for four years throughout college and had stopped about eight months before follow-up. He graduated cum laude and had been an executive in his father's business for several years, living in his own apartment, supporting himself. In the intervening years, he had coped with the breakup of two love relationships and his father's stroke without an abandonment depression. He reported no symptomatology. He was dating but not seeking a close relationship at the moment.

He had many interests—camping, tennis, bicyling, arts, music, ballet and creative writing. He hoped to publish some short stories. He had a close relationship with his father, who had continued in treatment, and with his brother, but felt that he had to avoid his mother, who was still trying to run his life.

He had taken charge of his life, was able to assert himself, to activate his thoughts and wishes in reality in work and recreation, to reguate his self-esteem and pursue his objectives.

There was no evidence of the former predominant pathological defense mechanisms of intellectualization, suppression and denial of affect, overcompliance, passive aggressiveness and various forms of acting-out of his dependency. He seemed to have achieved whole object relations with a whole self and object representation, with full emergence of the self. There was much clear evidence of creativity and autonomy, but he still might have problems moving towards intimacy, since at the moment he was playing the field. He might be avoiding involvement by keeping himself busy.

Parents of Fred

The parents viewed their involvement in treatment as ancillary and felt that the major purpose of their sessions was for them to provide information to the social worker, who in turn would keep them up-to-date on Fred's progress.

The father was particularly affected by the parent's group therapy, viewing the other parents as poor excuses for adults and feeling that it was no wonder they had children with problems. He would often leave feeling that he was healthier than he thought—when seeing how crazy everyone else was. Though he viewed Fred as a competent adult, he felt it had nothing to do with his own involvement in treatment. "Fred grew up—that's the only difference." He was indebted to the hospital for Fred's improvement.

The mother did believe she had changed since treatment in relation to Fred. She described herself as "flying off the handle" with Fred at the slightest provocation before treatment. Now she felt in more control of her own anger.

Both parents viewed Fred as quite exaggeratedly touchy about his independence, to which they grudgingly acquiesced.

Fred saw no change in his mother and described her as rigid, controlling and intolerant of his independence. He had for the most part avoided being in her company. He felt that he changed as a result of treatment but that his parents didn't. However, he felt quite relaxed now with his father and enjoyed working and discussing business with him. "His strength doesn't scare me anymore."

Clinical Impression

Fred presents a good example of the inverse relationship between the emergence of the self and the rewarding unit—pathologic ego alliance of the borderline. Only when Fred was able to sense in therapy that his therapist could tolerate his anger was he able to begin to express the anger and depression in the sessions and thereby allow investment in an emergence of the self. As the anger and depression were removed, the self emerged and began to take over the patient's life.

There was evidence of minimal external separation trauma in his early life, the main influence seeming to be the overcontrolling mother and distant father. He had good intellectual endowment, stayed in the hospital for 18 months, and was discharged not to home but to college where he continued therapy with his same therapist. He did do it on his own with little help from his parents, who showed little change except a grudging acquiescence to the patient's insistence on independence.

HELEN
Follow-Up Seven Years After Discharge

History of Illness at Admission

Helen, 15, was admitted with a chief complaint of feeling like a misfit most of her life and depression and fears of committing suicide. She had dropped out of school six months prior to admission. She had been seen briefly in psychotherapy and was then sent off to a boarding school, where she befriended a delinquent girl and began using hash, pot and methedrine to defend against her depression. She ran away from school and was reutrned home to begin intensive psychotherapy. However, within a few weeks, while her mother and father were away on a three-week trip, she appeared for an interview stoned on pot, and her therapist recommended hospitalization.

Past History

Helen was the third of four children of an extremely disturbed mother, who perceived all her four children as one symbiotic unit and therefore could not distinguish one from the other. She had perfectionistic expectations for all her children, while at the same time, she exerted a severely regressive influence on them. The father was very distant and spent most of his time away from the home working.

Helen gave a long history of conscious feelings of deprivation and of being a misfit. Throughout childhood, she had frequent ear infections and sore throats which were used as pretexts to stay home from school. When Helen was 11, her sister attempted suicide. At 13, Helen feigned having poor eyesight, which was nevertheless diagnosed as a degenerative disease which would eventually cause blindness.

Helen always had adjustment problems at school, acting out provocatively with peers and teachers and often feigning illness. Her grades were just average.

Hospital Psychotherapy

Helen's hospital course was characterized by dramatic manipulative acting-out, in which she projected the withdrawing unit on the therapist, threatened her or cajoled her, or insulted her into providing regressive satisfactions. When this was not forthcoming, she would villify her.

At first she refused to attend school. Then she agreed to go, and almost immediately the content of her interviews shifted to extreme rage at her parents, sisters, herself and her doctor. This gave way to feelings that she could not get attention from the mother unless she was sick, and she started to feign illness. She expressed her feelings of rivalry with her sisters, whom she felt got most of the attention.

After a therapeutic alliance had been established, her therapist went on vacation, and Helen asked to be put on a more restricted floor to deal with her fear of her anger. This event was repeated several times. There was enormous anxiety about independence and fear of being abandoned for being independent, which were handled by passive-aggressive manipulative acting-out with her therapist, peers and staff. When Helen was confronted, she became extremely angry, which led to working through the enormous rage at the mother for infantilizing her and the father for his distancing.

However, Helen's therapist had an extreme countertransference problem, often colluding with Helen's manipulations. The countertransference was difficult even for the supervisor to control, so that the long period in the hospital resulted in a minimum of working through.

Follow-Up—Two Years and Seven Years After Discharge

Two-Year Follow-Up

Helen had been discharged to live at home, attend a local tutoring school, and see the same therapist three times a week. In retrospect, it would have been better to have transferred her to another therapist.

Helen's initial defense against the first crisis was to repress feelings in order to function. After discharge she went to school every day, where she did quite well. She denied any feelings of depression or conflicts at home. The issue of the conflict with the mother, that is, the mother's wish to hold on and the patient's temptation to go along with it, arose several months after discharge, when the mother and her private therapist wanted the patient to join that therapist's group therapy. Helen's therapist interpreted that this meant Helen was going along with her own and her mother's wish for reunion and that the group therapy was only a suitable vehicle. Helen had almost decided against going into the therapy, when the mother's doctor and the mother made the arrangement without telling Helen's therapist. This issue occupied therapy for the next four weeks. Helen reported that the kids in the group had no idea what was going on, and she was getting nothing out of it for herself. This clarified for her that she was doing it strictly to comply with her mother's wishes. She stopped, and her mother became very upset.

Concurrently, she was planning to leave home and looking for a place to stay in the city. She spoke about the fact that, although this was not the best thing for her to do, the idea of being on her own and not having her mother to care for her was very depressing, and perhaps she could not bring herself to do it. This was illustrated by her going through the motions of finding a place to live rather than actually following through. During this time, she began to take driving lessons and went out with a boy several times—who then broke up with her; this initiated a depression. However, she did fairly well in school, finishing the year with a B+ average.

Let us turn briefly to Helen's report of the mother's reaction to the planned move. Helen: "I don't know why my whole family is just a mess. They've gone the wrong way, and they're a bunch of sick people. I don't know how my mother feels about it. She has gone along with it. I think she's trying to hold me back. I was supposed to move earlier, and she seemed very pleased that I didn't. I guess she's just like a mother. She wants her little girl around." When asked how she felt about herself, Helen replied: "I feel like a person. That is the only way I can sum it up. I have things to do and places to go. I care about people. People care about me. I don't know when I decided I wanted to grow up, that I wanted to be a person and wanted to work in every area, but it was at some point in the hospital."

Helen graduated from the tutoring school and moved into her own apartment. She then worked for a year before leaving her original therapist to attend college. Two years after discharge, she was doing well, seeing a therapist once a week.

Seven-Year Follow-Up

Helen was 24 when seen again for follow-up five years later. She is a good example of the enormous variations in the course of treatment. She received inadequate working-through at the hospital, continued with the same therapist and struggled over the next six years before finally achieving individuation.

After discharge to her home, Helen continued with the same therapist for 18 months, during which time she graduated from high school.

After working for a year, she left treatment to go to college. She then dropped out of college due, probably, to abandonment depression, drifted for a year, was hospitalized for three months and then sent to another therapist for one year. During this time, she lived in her own apartment and attended college; after one year, she mutilated herself by cutting her arms, at which time her therapist threatened to send her to a state hospital if she was unable to control her behavior.

She decided to pull herself together, started an affair with an older man, left New York City and cut off all contact with the regressive influence of mother and father. As she reported it, she felt very much better, felt herself for the first time. At the time of the interview, she was in nursing school, studying to be a registered nurse.

In the interim of seven years, she reported recurrent experiences of depression and pangs of separation anxiety, but at the time of evaluation she was functioning well, was quite active and self-assertive, seemed to have a good image of herself and most of the pathologic defense mechanisms, such as the manipulative, dependent acting-out, had disappeared.

She was able to assert herself, was taking charge of her life, was able to regulate her own self-esteem, was coping with reality, had given direction to her life.

In addition, she had a more whole image of her father and mother and now was able to manage her relationship with her mother better than her relationship with her father. Creativity and many interests had replaced her lack of interests in the hospital. For example, she enjoyed pottery making, camping, ice skating. She is an avid reader, likes sports, is eager to try new things and gets satisfaction from new pursuits. Clearly, her autonomy is much improved, there is continuing growth of creativity, but possibly a difficulty with intimacy. Although she was having a relationship with a man, there was evidence that there might be fear of engulfment in a close relationship.

Parents of Helen

The parents expressed a great deal of anger toward the hospital treatment program. They felt that Helen was treated as if she were all that mattered and that other family members' needs were disregarded. They were particularly angry that the social worker shared information with Helen about a younger sister, which they had told her in confidence. They felt Helen should have been spared this. Their tendency to maintain secrets and control continued at follow-up. The father wanted to finance Helen's trip to New York but would only do so if we promised not to tell Helen. The mother was still upset by Helen's cutting off all contact with the family and still confused all the girls' names. Both, however, had grudgingly given in, since they had little or no choice.

The parents did feel that prior to treatment they had lived in a "fantasy world," denying any problems existed in their family. At follow-up the mother tended to obsess about the problems and give multiple vignettes of continued separation problems, particularly with Helen's two older sisters. The mother did seem aware of her own difficulty when she described her past tendency to define herself in terms of her children alone. This she felt had now placed her at a disadvantage. Her contemporaries were mothers but also developed themselves. This helped them, now that their children had grown and left. She had nothing. It would seem that rather than addressing her own problems now, she had instead convinced one daughter and her family to rejoin the fold. The parents had opened a new business with their sister-in-law in an executive position and looked forward to "all being together again."

Helen felt the only way she could have made it was cutting off all contact with her parents. She was visiting her parents for the first time in several years at the time of the follow-up and already had picked up on the father's attempts to infantilize and control her. She viewed her father as detached. He attempted to control by showering the girls with material possessions which she resented and repeatedly rejected. Helen felt the treatment had no positive effect on him. She felt her mother had made some gains in that she seemed more tolerant of her daughter's independence and less entrenched in maintaining a fairy-tale image of the family and the world.

Clinical Impression

It evidently wasn't until Helen had no other course but a state hospital that she began to turn around and try to take care of herself. Prior to that, her need to manage her abandonment depression and separation anxiety by regressive acting-out had remained in control. In other words, she finally overcame both a long experience with a therapist who had countertransference difficulties and the constant regressive pull of the parents to achieve individuation.

Although the mother appeared to be more aware of the difficulties she had in allowing her girls to separate and individuate and had an increased intellectual understanding of the etiology of her own difficulties, it had not enabled her to behave any more appropriately. Individuation appeared to occur in Helen only by cutting herself off from the mother. If Helen were willing, the parents would still eagerly welcome her return to a dependent and attached relationship to the family. The father seemed to show no change.

SUMMARY

These four patients with the best clinical outcome illustrate how widely the clinical course can vary, even with effective psychotherapy. In a case such as Betty, the relatively straight-line progress of treatment was challenged by severe post-hospital separation stress from her parents. Her overcoming this stress and her regression was testimony to the success of the psychotherapy, i.e., the work had been internalized. Fred's case was complicated by a severe countertransference problem and, again, by a mother who had difficulty letting go. Marie's course was burdened by her severe regression and transference acting-out to deal with her original psychotherapist's departure. Helen endured both a severe counter-transference on the part of her first therapist and a prolonged period of regression, lasting years, before the treatment finally took hold. Despite these various obstacles, the treatment worked and helped these patients to protect themselves and grow. The strong-est confirmation of that growth was the flowering of individuation that accompanied successful separation-individuation.

7

Mild Impairment (Group A)

The minimal and mild groups differ little in impairment of functioning, but there is a chasm of difference from the perspective of ego development and object relations. Although they function well, the 13 patients in the mild group have not separated from the symbiotic relationship with the mother, and therefore they have not achieved whole object relations. Consequently, they require pathologic defenses against separation anxiety and abandonment depression to maintain an entirely adequate level of functioning. Within this mild impairment group, we were able to select two subgroups (A, with six patients, and B, with seven patients) based on the intensity of that need for pathologic defenses as well as on the degree to which there had been consolidation of the self, i.e., the degree to which the patients had increased the capacity to assert themselves, to regulate self-esteem, and to activate their wishes in reality.

Subgroup A (Six Patients)

Although only four of these six patients will be described, all have shown at follow-up an improvement in self-representation, a feeling of the self being worthwhile, which is more realistically based. They are more open to their own feelings, have a greater capacity to identify their own individuated wishes and thoughts and express them in reality, to regulate their own self-esteem, as well as to assert themselves and to a certain extent to take charge of the direction of their lives.

However, although their self-representation is better and their adaptation is improved, they have not fully separated and do not have whole self or object representations. They have made one or another environmental arrangement—usually a relationship—which acts out the RORU and the WORU to defend against further separation anxiety and abandonment depression. There is a mild to moderate persistence of one or more of the original pathological defense mechanisms. As a result, they remain vulnerable to separation stress and further experiences of depression, and there is not the flowering of individuation or self-expression seen in the minimal group

LESLIE

Follow-Up Five Years After Discharge

History of Illness at Admission

Leslie, 17, was admitted to the treatment program after an overdose of No-Doz tablets at boarding school. The present illness began in the seventh grade at age 13, when Leslie switched to junior high school and lost her best friend. She began to miss school because of vague somatic complaints. At 14, she became rebellious, fought her teachers and skipped school. She was then changed to another school, but her rebellious behavior and increasing social withdrawal finally impelled her parents to send her to a boarding school, where she became depressed, did poorly in class and finally made a suicide attempt.

Past History

Leslie had an alcoholic father with a violent temper and an oversolicitous and infantilizing mother. The youngest of four children, she had no notable separation stress in infancy and early childhood but was overweight throughout childhood.

Hospital Psychotherapy

Her hospital course was characterized by a rapid and unusually easily established therapeutic alliance, leading to the identification of her anger and depression and the use of the clinging defense with her mother. For example, five months after admission, in response to recognizing that she would have to grow up and leave her mother and become responsible, she made a suicidal attempt, lacerating her wrist with a light bulb. This was the turning point in treatment, although there continued to be a good deal of procrastination about the issue of being on her own throughout her hospital stay.

Follow-Up Five Years After Discharge

Leslie was 23, recently graduated from college. She had begun a course of study in Librarian Arts for a Masters Degree. Five years earlier she had been discharged to live in a residence for girls and finish high school. She continued in outpatient psychotherapy twice a week with her own hospital therapist who had gone into private practice. She graduated from high school, worked during the summer and then started at the college from which she had just graduated. She has not lived at home since discharge.

Leslie is presented first because she is a good example of a patient who functions quite well with the assistance of environmental arrangements to deal with her anxiety about autonomy, rather than through the expression of her autonomy. For example, she described what sounded like an abandonment depression on discharge—feeling terribly lonely and depressed. When she started college, she again had another abandonment depression: "I clung to my roommate and didn't want to leave her for about six months."

However, she got involved in the school, thought she might want to go into pre-med, dropped out of this program and then began to major in history. At the same time, in her junior year, she moved into a new co-ed dormitory and again felt an abandonment depression, "alone, bad." This time, however, she felt she coped with her feelings, probably with the assistance of a conversion to the Episcopalian religion: "It takes away the nothingness that was frightening; it gives me a routine, something that is constant." Her obesity continued through college.

In her senior year she began to date a man, age 30, whom she is now planning to marry. She idealized her prospective husband: "He is solid, always there when I need him, sensitive and perceptive." She spoke similarly of her mother.

She saw a great change in her self-representation: "I used to think I was unattractive, not capable of much, basically incompetent. Now I am amazed at what I can do; my image is much stronger. I don't give in to my feelings, I recognize them and don't let them take over. I'm ninety percent more independent. I'm probably still dependent on my parents somewhat, my fiancé and the doctor." In the last year, in the setting of her relationship with this man, she converted again from Episcopalianism to Catholicism. She had a number of interests such as reading, singing, swimming.

Parents of Leslie

The mother's present relationship to Leslie was captured by an incident which occurred the day of the parents' interview. The parents, prior to the interview, had stopped unannouced at Leslie's apartment. The mother was very disappointed that Leslie and her husband-to-be were going out to a play. The mother had been planning all week to spend the day with them after their interview. However, she had not discussed it with Leslie.

Although both parents felt Leslie had been helped by the program, they proceeded to criticize it, deny that they or Leslie had any problems and point out what they thought was continued evidence of her difficulty. The mother said: "Leslie's biggest problem was with peers. . . . She was a product of the sixties. The program didn't seem to be very good, but at that point we had no choice." The mother felt the social worker was wrong to say that she was overprotective of Leslie. She felt she was no more protective of her than of the other children in the family. Later she conceded that perhaps she was a little more so with Leslie, since she was the youngest.

During the interview, the mother dominated the discussion, focusing primarily on the achievements of her children, repeatedly denying that the hospital was helpful and avoiding any discussion of herself.

The father was obviously preoccupied with his own concerns, which he made several efforts to discuss. Each time, his wife ignored his wish to talk and changed the subject back to her children.

All of the children have had separation problems. Even now Leslie is able to acknowledge that her closeness to her mother was unhealthy for her, but she enjoyed one part of it and hopes that it will last forever.

Leslie basically felt that little change occurred in her parents. Her view of them became more realistic, but they continued to relate to her in the same manner.

Clinical Impression

On the surface Leslie has had a good adjustment. She is doing well in school, living in a dorm and planning to be married, and has a career planned for herself. But when you look beneath the surface, it appears that a good deal of this functional capacity is because she has made environmental arrangements to provide her with structure which she is unable to provide herself. She has not fully separated—note, for example, the three episodes of abandonment depression.

I suspect that she is clinging to the prospective husband to deal with the anxiety about the autonomy involved in graduation. There seems to be a persistence of pathological mechanisms of splitting, probably somatization, clinging, and acting-out. For instance, she still does not have a realistic whole perception of either mother or father and continues to idealize both husband and mother. She is still overweight. However, her self representation is dramatically improved, as is her capacity to assert herself and to cope.

She has been in treatment the entire five years since discharge from the hospital. One wonders whether her therapist may have promoted this clinging to the rewarding unit by insufficient confrontation. There seems to have been no serious separation stresses. I would suspect that autonomy is greater, but she still has a long way to go. There is some creativity but little capacity for intimacy, her relationship with her prospective husband being on a dependent level.

JEAN

Follow-Up Six Years After Discharge

History of Illness on Admission

Jean, 16, was admitted with a ten-month history of an anorexia, weight loss, hyperactivity and body-image distortion. She had begun to use LSD and hash.

Past History

She changed residences at ages two, four, and six. Her maternal grandfather died when she was eight, and her maternal grandmother when she was 14.

Hospital Psychotherapy

Her course in therapy was fairly typical of a borderline anorexic with clinging, rituals around food, and intense transference acting-out of her symbiotic wishes, which required much confrontation. This finally led her to become in touch with her depression and rage at the mother's infantalizing behavior towards her.

Follow-Up Six Years After Discharge

At age 24, Jean lived alone in her own apartment, worked as a secretary and was supporting herself after a rocky five-year course characterized by gaining and then losing 40 pounds after discharge, trying college and dropping out because of dyslexia, and having difficulty saying no to men. She had been involved in two unsuccessful relationships with men and was currently seeing an older married man. Her functioning at work seemed adequate.

Since discharge her principal symptom had been sexual acting-out. There was no mention of anorexia or obesity. She had dealt with breaking up with the two men without abandonment depression. She continued in treatment with the same therapist until age 22, and had not had treatment since.

Her self-image had shown substantial improvement. She was more aware of her feelings, felt good about herself, was more assertive, and recognized her problem with sexual promiscuity. However, she did have difficulty identifying her wishes and actualizing them in reality and also in regulating her self-esteem.

There was a persistence of the pathological mechanisms of splitting and acting-out; however, the anorexia and obesity had not returned. Her object relations were indicated by a persistence of an idealization of her doctor, the acting-out of her anger at her grandmother and sister and the need to avoid her mother. It would appear that the doctor was the rewarding unit and her mother the withdrawing unit.

As to autonomy, it seemed that she had switched her dependency from mother to men through her acting-out. Although she had had sexual relationships, they seemed more like acting-out through clinging than true intimacy. Although making a concerted effort to involve herself in other activities (she had recently taken up tennis and taught herself to sew and was trying drawing), she was having trouble.

Parents of Jean

The parents showed striking detachment, denial and lack of spontaneity. Though they were cooperative and verbal, they seemed devoid of affect and involvement. At the time of follow-up they took no initiative in approaching with Jean but always waited for her to get in touch with them. Although at first this seemed motivated by their respect for her independence, it appeared that they could not take initiative with anyone. The father remembered, for example, that though he was very aware that Jean had problems and needed to be hospitalized, he was glad she said she wanted to go. Even now, he said, he could not have taken responsibility for hospitalizing her.

The youngest daughter, Margaret, 17, presented the most serious difficulty for the family, except for Jean. She had acted out since 13, with drinking and shoplifting. Though the shoplifting had stopped, Margaret began dating a boy on probation. The parents responded by first asking the boy's parents to keep them apart, and when that didn't work, they took the family to court. At the interview they said that they didn't think their daughter saw him much now, and that they were not worried. They felt her underachievement was because she was not a student. The parents acknowledged that Margaret and Jean didn't get along. The parents felt it was because they hadn't been together much; Jean felt it was because her sister was narcissistic, spoiled and self-centered.

The parents described their involvement at the hospital in positive though painful terms. They sounded like observers rather than participants. They thought the weekly interviews were one of the costs they had to pay in order for the hospital to take over Jean. The mother described feeling as if she had the flu every time she left a session. They both said they learned a lot, that it was "educational," but neither could be more specific than that.

Both parents bemoaned Jean's refusal to visit any of the family other than her parents and siblings. They felt she was coping and didn't think she would ever be out of control again, but felt like they were walking on eggs in her presence.

Jean has three siblings. Besides Margaret, who attends high school and lives at home, there are two older boys enrolled in college away from home. The parents described problems with all three and then denied they were having difficulty. The oldest, a college junior, was described as being disenchanted, considering quitting college and having no idea of what he wanted. (Jean noted that he had a severe drinking problem and had been dealing with cocaine.) The next boy was described as "absentminded," low-keyed, having no drive until he decided to be a farmer. (Jean described him as withdrawn, a loner, spending most of his time alone.) Both parents said the boys had minor drinking problems that were nothing to worry about.

Jean felt her parents made minimal gains. She added that they had never once talked about her or their experiences after she was discharged, beyond asking about her treatment. Jean felt her mother was jealous of her relationship with her therapist. Her mother did say that she thought Jean was too dependent on the therapist.

Jean felt her mother had at least tried to be more available to her children. She commented that at least she told Margaret the facts of life. In general, though, Jean believed her parents were incapable of providing more than food, shelter and clothing for their children or each other. "They don't know what feelings are. . . . I feel closer to my mother—she'd help anybody—somehow she's got a big heart—but she's frightened, stoic. She denies things and avoids a lot."

The father was reportedly frightened to drive. Jean reported, "My father is closed, a workaholic and detached, but his temper has mellowed. . . . They never grew up."

Clinical Impression

Five years after hospitalization, there is no anorexia. Jean has a better adaptation. There is an improved self representation and absence of observable abandonment depression, probably defended against by clinging, splitting and acting out the rewarding unit with men; although she has a good adaptation, she remains vulnerable to separation stress. There is a persistence of pathological defense mechanisms and a failure of autonomy and creativity to emerge.

The parents, though concerned and involved, gained little from their own treatment experiences beyond an intellectual awareness of their own difficulties. Their extreme denial of the manifest difficulties of the other siblings reflects the shallowness of their awareness of their continued problems.

GRACE

FOLLOW-UP SEVEN YEARS AFTER DISCHARGE

History of Illness on Admission

Grace, age 14, was hospitalized with a one-year or more history of running away from home, failing in school, excessive use of drugs, including pushing of drugs, sexual promiscuity, and socializing with rebellious, antisocial peers.

Past History

Grace had enuresis until age eight, and was shoplifting at age six, after the birth of her brother. There is a history of frequent family moves at ages five, seven, and 12. Also, Grace had a fear of insects as a child.

Hospital Psychotherapy

Grace's hospital course was characterized by a rather rapid control of her acting-out behavior. This was probably on the basis of compliance and was followed by a long spell of intellectualized compliance with little awareness of affect and with acting-out of the RORU with her therapist. This behavior was so marked that we considered the possibility that Grace might be an as-if character and that she was relating to her therapist on the basis of imitation, not clinging. In addition, her therapist, who also used intellectualization as a prominent defense, was ingenious at providing the intellectual substance of treatment without the feeling component so that it became difficult to break through her countertransference. The supervisor was left with the nagging suspicion that the result for the patient was part working-through of affect and part intellectual simulation. Grace was seen in follow-up two years and seven years after discharge.

Follow-Up Two Years After Discharge

Grace, age 17, had been discharged two years before this follow-up to resume the eleventh grade at a local boarding school, where she would live five days a week and go home on weekends. She continued to see her therapist three times a week. Upon discharge she became quite depressed. Her first defense was to project the cause of her depression on dissatisfaction at school or with the girls, but after several weeks of working on this, she could say, "I started to think that it can't all be the school, the externals; part of it is me and facing up to being alone. Being independent means being alone. I see that it's not going to be easy. It's not going to come all at once." She now started to deal with her depressive feelings as a reflection of her difficulty in separating from the hospital and making it on her own.

All through this time an endless push-pull existed with her parents, who were constantly creating situations which would encourage Grace to regress. When Grace came to a therapy session with little affect and obvious depression, it was an indication that something was going on at home. After several months, she talked about feelings of emptiness and whether it was really worth the struggle to be on her own. Nevertheless, she functioned very well in school and at midterm made the honor roll.

The parent's "hamstringing" efforts reached a climax over the planning of a trip out West for a family wedding. At an extra family session, Grace told them she did not want to go. Her therapy was more important. The issue then went undercover for a while, but it surfaced again to become a constant theme for several months.

The mother again used all the mechanisms she had used before —first, outright attack, then withdrawal and the silent treatment, and then angry arguments trying to provoke guilt. Grace, with the aid of therapy, was able to sustain her own wishes with regard to the Western trip, but soon after this the parents suddenly took her to Portugal for two weeks.

Four months after leaving the hospital, she met a boy named Ted who was a drifter. He spent his time sitting around the lobby of a local girls' college. He tried hard to get Grace out of therapy. She, on the other hand, was desperately looking for some relationship that she could hold on to. He told Grace that psychiatrists were not any good; they made you very dependent on them and they took over your life. He said that if she had any guts she would get out of it. Grace, terrified of her own dependence, recognized what was going on with her parents and was terrified that it was also going on with her therapist. Grace worked this through with her therapist and told Ted that she was going to continue in therapy; he then left her. After Ted left, Grace's mood again improved, and then the family brought up the Western trip again. When Grace stood firm, the parents decided that the father would stay home with Grace while the mother went on the trip. This was particularly interesting because it recreated the interaction before hospitalization; the mother was again using Grace as the pawn to deal with her sexual conflict with the father by pairing father and daughter together. The father said he needed to stay home to take care of Grace, but at the same time he gave her little attention and used the week to go out with his friends. He was happy to be away from his wife.

As summer approached, Grace decided to take a photography course in which she was very much interested. The parents, again threatened by this move toward individuation, sabotaged it by refusing to pay. She did, however, manage to get a job that paid her $100 a week. This money gave Grace some independence because previously she always had to go to her parents for everything. However, predictably, the parents again attacked her individuation. Her allowance was dropped. She had to pay for everything she did—her train ticket, her clothes, and every phone call she made; most glaringly, one morning the father decided to drive to the city rather than take the train and informed Grace that she had to pay her share of the drive as well as for parking the car.

Throughout this period of time Grace continued to function well at school, where she finished the year on the honor roll. She planned in the fall to return for her senior year and to continue treatment with her therapist.

Let us see how Grace viewed her treatment: "Well, I think I got an insight into my problems with myself but then the hardest part is after you find out about the whole thing—getting out after knowing all this and doing something with it. It's still hard because when you are in the hospital, you can say this is wrong or something is the matter and you can concentrate just on that, but when you get outside and there's all this stuff going on, it's much harder."

After a traumatic summer with her parents which she managed without too much inner turmoil, Grace moved into her own apartment in the city and returned to boarding school where she was elected president of her senior class.

Follow-Up Seven Years After Discharge

Grace, 22, was a junior executive in an advertising agency. She lived in her own apartment and supported herself. After successfully finishing high school, she went to an art institute for a year to study art and then transferred to a school of design where she stayed for a few years, graduating a year prior to the interview.

She continued private therapy with her therapist for four years after discharge, stopping two years before this follow-up, the frequency varying from three times a week to once a week. She had a very difficult time during her senior year in high school, when she began to act out again and was rebellious at school. At this time she formed domineering relationships with dependent girls.

When she graduated, she became involved with one man with whom she spent some time in Europe. In addition, she was also promiscuous and on drugs. When the acting-out disappeared at the end of her senior year, she got colitis which had persisted to the follow-up and required her to be on an ulcer diet.

Grace was angry, self-assertive, had no close relationship with either men or women, acted out in homo- and heterosexual one-night stands, and still formed and quickly broke off dominant relationships with dependent women, seeing them as quite weak.

She pursued her own life with autonomy and self-assertion and was remarkably improved from the time of admission. She had been exposed to a number of separation stresses. The father divorced the mother. She was happy at the divorce, but when he remarried, she was furious at him and still probably felt that he had abandoned her.

There was remarkable improvement in her self-representation; she described that before, she had no self, no regard for herself; she was two steps away from being a vegetable. Now "I feel good about myself, I can deal with my self-destructive patterns," which showed her denial. "I am still a perfectionist, have high standards for myself and others."

If anything, Grace showed an excess capacity for self-assertion. She could pursue her own interests and could actualize many of her wishes in reality. However, there was a persistence of splitting, avoidance, denial, and acting-out, particularly of the rewarding and withdrawing units in relationships with men and women. It would almost appear that Grace had now become the object. At the time of admission, we thought Grace had completely invested in the object, with little investment in the self, and it would appear that at follow-up this had reversed, with complete investment in the self and little in the object. She played out the role of the object, possibly projecting her self-image on needy others, both men and women.

The pathological mechanisms of avoidance, denial and projection and acting-out persisted. Grace functioned in an autonomous fashion but feared being taken advantage of, necessitating her excessive self-assertion, and saw all women as being weak. She felt the need to deal with her fears of being engulfed in a close relationship by avoidance and by acting-out. She might have been acting out a combined separation-individuation oedipal conflict with her father. Intimacy seemed to be a chief problem. There was evidence of creativity, since Grace was an artist by career who also did freelance work; she did not, however, have other outside interests.

Parents of Grace

The mother adamantly refused to be interviewed. Her anger had evidently held over from our original contact years ago. The father, however, was eager to be involved in the follow-up. He expressed a great deal of gratitude to the treatment team, not only for helping his daughter but for helping himself as well. The father felt that prior to the treatment he had denied marital difficulties and attempted, through the patient, to compensate for what his wife couldn't provide for him. He felt both he and his wife depended too heavily on their daughter. The counseling he received helped him to begin to evaluate his marriage and ultimately to divorce his wife.

Though he credited the hospital experience with his mobilization, he made no move to act until several years after Grace was discharged. One might also suspect that Grace's becoming unavailable as a substitute object forced the father to move, but not without what seemed to be some anger at Grace for individuation. The latter was manifest in his viewing her as having become "demanding, intolerant, always independent, very selfish." He added that he did not fault the hospital for this but only Grace. This anger toward Grace had particularly surfaced since his remarriage. The father felt that Grace disliked his new wife. Though he believed his new wife was "bitchy" to Grace and her brother, he felt that they should be more tolerant. He postulated that Grace resented the fact that his new wife was both an excellent homemaker and a successful businesswoman, whereas her mother was a failure at everything.

The father also felt that he had mellowed. He reported that prior to Grace's treatment he had difficulty with his temper, which jeopardized his business relationships. At follow-up he felt that he was in better control. It should be noted, though, that he later talked of serious problems with his boss which could lead to his dismissal. It was later learned that he left his job but the circumstances were unknown.

The father spent some time bemoaning Grace's long dependency on her therapist. However, on several occasions he asked to see the therapist about his own problems and frequently called for advice about Grace. For instance, if Grace asked him for something and he had reservations about getting it for her, he would call the doctor for support. Often the father questioned Grace's judgment, but when she was supported by the doctor, he would acquiesce. The father seemed to know almost too much about Grace's social life; he even said he knew she was promiscuous for a time following a break-up with a boyfriend.

Grace felt her father did what was best for him by leaving her mother. She felt, however, that he was more detached since his remarriage; she missed their closeness and blamed it all on his new wife. Grace believed she was "picky, bitchy, and possessive" of her father. Although she felt he had made his choice, she wished it could be more like it used to be.

It was unclear whether the mother had gotten worse since treatment or whether the father and Grace viewed her differently at follow-up. Both said that she hated being involved in treatment and found it unhelpful and unproductive. Grace felt that her mother wanted her to take care of her and tried repeatedly to "suck" her in. The most recent attempt was the mother's proposal that she sell the house, rent a loft in Manhattan and have Grace move in with her. Though Grace toyed with the idea for some time, she decided, the week of the follow-up interview, that it would not be good for her.

For the most part, Grace avoided her mother, because she feared loss of her own autonomy if she became involved on even a casual level. "My mother wants to be taken care of by anybody she can find and refuses to do anything for herself. . . . I can't afford to get involved."

In spite of Grace's appraisal of her mother's present state, she felt that she (mother) had made gains in treatment; at least, her mother listened now, which was something that didn't occur before. Behaviorally though, she described her mother as relating to her brother in the same way she had to her.

Grace viewed her brother as having the same problems she did at that age. She described serious acting-out and inappropriate behavior on the part of both parents in relation to him. They denied his difficulties, used him to vent rage at each other, blaming each other for his trouble, and repeatedly tried to pull Grace in (especially the mother) to somehow make the brother shape up. Grace did say that at first she felt a responsibility to her brother, but that she knew he had to pull it together himself—for his sake and her own, she had to stay out of it; it was not her responsibility.

Clinical Impression

There is obvious dramatic improvement in self-representation. The self has emerged and is able to operate in the career area, but has become so dominant in interpersonal situations to deal with her fear of engulfment that there seems little room for the object.

The father did begin to check his own behavior with Grace and also to face the difficulties in himself and his marriage. There are indications that the "hands off" with Grace was more of a function of her growth and her doctor's support. Although his new wife provides some further insurance, this marriage is not without major problems. Somehow the father's expectations and criticisms of Grace seem to reflect his fantasy that he could maintain the closeness he had with Grace before he remarried. Every criticism of her related to some facet of self-expression, self-assertion and independence.

The mother is more blatantly disturbed now and continues to want to rely on Grace—at Grace's expense. This apparently has intensified since the divorce. Grace seems to have a better understanding of this in her mother but seems less aware of the continued attachment to her father. The latter appears to create more anxiety for her.

BILL

Follow-Up Two and Seven Years After Discharge

History of Illness on Admission

Bill, 15, a model student at school, had begun at about age nine to have outbursts of anger and aggressiveness at home, usually when his father, a successful Broadway producer, was away and he was left with his permissive, indulgent mother, on whom he made excessive demands. In the beginning, his tantrums were mild, occurred about once every several months and did not involve destructive behavior. By age 11 or 12, however, he began to smash his own possessions, for example, a telescope that he valued highly. These destroyed possessions would later be replaced by the parents. On occasion, if Bill had an outburst when the father was at home, the father would expel him from the house for the night, forcing him to sleep in the garage or at a friend's house.

The conflict with the mother and father exemplified by the outbursts gradually escalated. Six months before Bill's admission to the hospital, the father again left home for a period of a month. The patient's anger increased to the point where he began to threaten his younger brother and talk about killing his mother. In an outburst of anger, he accidentally fractured his mother's finger. The poignant thing about this history was that this patient's behavior was a plea for help. The mother's lack of firmness and the father's inconsistency forced the patient to escalate his plea. Having received no help, he finally turned from destroying his own property to destroying the property of others, such as the phone on the wall or his father's possessions. A psychiatrist diagnosed Bill as a paranoid schizophrenic and advised a state hospital.

Despite this history of acting-out, the patient's basic defenses were obsessive, schizoid, and paranoid. For example, on examination, his facial expression had the quality of a Greek mask—a superficial smile with almost no emotion underneath. The defense of intellectualization was manifested by his obsessive interest in spending large amounts of time on science projects—at which his performance was excellent, although his meticulous attention to detail consumed endless hours. The schizoid quality of his character was illustrated by the fact that although he was a good student and had no behavior problems in school, he either became the class clown to get attention or had no friends at all. He had fantasies of retreating to the North Pole, where he would have no contact with humans and could become like a machine—a task at which he seemed to have almost succeeded. He idolized Mr. Spock of the television show 'Star Trek," because Mr. Spock was devoid of human feelings. His clinging and paranoid defenses quickly became apparent after admission to the hospital, where he adopted the same clinging, demanding relationship with a nurse that he had had with his mother. He had difficulty relating to his peers. The minimal role of acting-out as a defense was confirmed by the fact that his aggressive behavior never became a problem during his entire hospital stay.

Hospital Psychotherapy

In his 15 months of hospitalization, the patient projected the rewarding unit on the nursing staff, picking out specific nurses who would permit him to cling and from whom he would angrily demand attention. He projected the withdrawing unit on his therapist, whom he would constantly attack for not taking responsibility for interviews, for not asking questions or directing interviews, not giving him enough attention, etc. In addition, his rage was handled through a projection that his peers would attack him. There was also intellectualization, social withdrawal, isolation, and almost detachment of affect. He had fantasies of becoming the commandant of his own concentration camp and torturing inmates. At the same time, he had dreams of the Holocaust and his own death. It was necessary to have interviews increased to four times a week instead of the customary three, in order to help him get in touch with his anger and depressive affect.

Follow-Up Two Years After Discharge

After discharge, Bill lived at the local YMCA and attended a private high school for his junior and senior years. He graduated at the top of his class and was accepted at college. He was seen for six months, three times a week, until his therapist had to leave, at which time he was transferred to the author. Bill's home had now been moved to the West. At the time of discharge, his father was receiving psychiatric treatment, as was his mother. His 12-year-old brother was exhibiting the same symtoms that Bill had had.

Bill's defenses against his first crisis—the abandonment depression that occurs with discharge—consisted of excessive activity—for example, running all over the city, going to plays, attending the opera, trying to find people to do things with, and forming brief, dependent, clinging relationships with girls. In the interviews with the therapist, he first handled his feelings by denial and taking the rage out on himself: "The past is over and I don't want to talk about it. I don't have any character. I'm junk. I'm an ape. I'm subhuman."

However, the underlying pressure would suddenly burst through and "he would crash" one evening and suddenly feel depressed and suicidal. This phase, which had lasted four or five months in the hospital, lasted approximately four weeks in outpatient treatment— a testimony to the groundwork done on interpreting and attenuating the defense of denial while he was still in the hospital.

When Bill mentioned to his therapist that he had not gone to school, the therapist confronted him with his defenses against the abandonment depression. Bill responded: "I'm pretty angry at you. I guess I'm directing it all against myself. I guess I better talk about it."

The next night the therapist got a panicky call from Bill: "I'm suicidal, I need to talk with you. Can I see you tomorrow." Bill talked about his fear of expressing anger at the therapist and became aware that he was in a regression similar to those he had experienced in the hospital.

Bill then moved into his second defense, which was the symbiotic fantasy of an exclusive relationship with his therapist: "I want a protective relationship with you. I'm getting tinges of what it's like to have a straight head. I realize I'm pretty dependent on you, and I don't like that."

He then began to work through his feelings about separation from his therapist, crying in interviews as he expressed feelings of loss and as he projected his rage on fear of violence and of being harmed. He then explored the loss of the exclusive relationship with his mother in the setting of the loss of the exclusive relationship with the therapist. At one point, glaring at the therapist, he said: "Damn it, why don't you take care of me. I want you to!" After expressing these feelings, he became frightened and compliant, seeking the therapist's approval.

In the middle of a session he reported the following fantasy: He was getting very small and the therapist was getting very large with huge, long fingernails, and was standing over him—a fantasy repetition of the father's attacks on Bill. He verbalized his fear that his therapist would attack him and might call him a "punk kid" just as his father had. He then spoke of taking his rage out on himself through self-deprecation—that he was a "shmuck," subhuman. He would deny any feelings associated with this and then several days later would call the therapist: "I feel suicidal. What can I do? Can I see you?" He began having fantasies of knifing a woman, which were repetitions of the feelings he had worked through during his abandonment depression in the hospital. He would then attempt to make the therapist omnipotent: "I don't want you to be human. I don't want to have these feelings about you. I want you to be Superman, but you're telling me you're not Superman."

Bill then revealed that he had been frustrating himself by masturbating and stopping short of orgasm with a fantasy of knifing and killing. The therapist pointed out that he was frustrating himself and suggested that masturbation was a normal physical outlet. Before the next session, the patient masturbated to orgasm and arrived smiling and happy.

His mother clung to Bill in many ways, frequently calling him on the telephone. Bill would come to a session and say, "Damm it. I want to break away from her. Why doesn't she understand that?" Then he would turn to the therapist and say, "You don't understand me either. There are all sorts of things about me you don't know." Following this expression of anger at the therapist, he would become anxious and suicidal, and later call his therapist. After several of these instances, the therapist interpreted that the calls were for reassurance. Bill then would wait out the suicidal episode until the next session, when he would again express his rage and fear.

About six months after discharge, he had sexual intercourse for the first time. Bill said, "It was a very freaky feeling, but somehow or other it was a big turning point in my life. It does a lot inside you; it's sort of a turning point from being a little boy to becoming a man. It's a really freaky feeling. I feel manly. I belong with the guys now. A very good feeling." Bill then went on to say: "I haven't been crashing lately. Because I know you are leaving, I've been quiet, I've been depressed. I think I'm handling it quite well. I've been afraid of facing up to life but now maybe I will."

At this point, he might delve into three areas, any one of which would have previously produced a panic—anger at the therapist or mother, depression, and fear. Then, near the end of his sessions with his therapist, he reported a fantasy which he had first reported right after hospitalization: "A little kid in knickers, four years old, is shoved out the door. He turns around looking back at the door slammed in his face, feeling very alone." The fantasy had now changed; the door was closed behind the kid but this time he turned around and looked at the world, knew he had to go out there, and wanted to, even though he was afraid.

He finished the school year with a 94 average and received an award for outstanding achievement.

Let us now hear how Bill viewed his first six months of outpatient therapy when he began therapy with the author.

Therapist: "How do you see yourself as compared to when you first came in the hospital?"

Bill: "When I came into the hospital all my thoughts and feelings were jumbled up so I couldn't face what was really happening inside me as well as what was happening around me. I can put all this knowledge together and act on it. I think that's the biggest difference. I'm aware and I can handle my awareness. I don't know how it happened but actually I think it was a slow gaining of trust with my therapist and being able to slowly just peak around the corner of what was there. I'm going to Europe for the summer and I'm very excited about it. I feel it will be another turning point. I'd love to be free to roam the country. I don't want to be home. My whole family is in a hassle. They're all seeing psychiatrists and having a lot of problems. I'm enjoying school, both the work and socially. I'm having ups and downs with people, but I'm doing quite well. I have three or four close friends I can talk to and do things with and I know a lot of other people casually. I feel fairly comfortable and when I'm with friends I don't think as I used to here in the Clinic. I was always thinking about whether or not I was equal or is this right or is that right, but now I can be with others and be pretty comfortable and feel equal and not act impulsively. I have one girlfriend whom I like very much and she's the only girl I feel close to, but the relationship isn't on the romantic level I wish it to be. However, I have another girl on the sort of mistress level."

Therapist: "Where do you stand right now?"

Bill: "Well, I think one of my biggest feelings is a sort of fear. I've been getting more independent in facing the outside, doing more and more things on my own, but I've always felt that my therapist has been able to understand what's been happening inside my head and I could convey my thoughts when needed and he could grasp what I'm trying to say, which I never felt anybody else could do. Now that he's leaving, I feel I'm going to have to deal with all these thoughts a lot more on my own and a lot stronger and have to handle them and face the outside. I'm scared. Next year, you know, I will be living on my own. I'm going to school in the city and it is frightening to be alone, and I have a sense of aloneness. It's very hard to say goodbye to my therapist because a lot has happened. I got very close to him."

Bill spent the summer traveling through the hostels of Europe on his bicycle. He had a brief love affair which he terminated without an abandonment depression when he found out the girl was deceiving him. He enjoyed his summer thoroughly and returned to New York City in the fall to live alone in an apartment house and attended school. He saw the author three times a week in treatment. With resumption of therapy, he first worked through his feelings of abandonment at leaving his previous therapist and then his clinging defenses against further individuation. Eighteen months after hospitalization, he graduated from high school at the top of his class and was accepted at college. At that time, he separated from the author, spent another summer in Europe and then began college in the fall. Two years after discharge, he was doing well in college and seeing a therapist once a week. The depressive and paranoid features were gone.

Follow-Up Seven Years After Discharge

Bill was seen at age 24, seven years after discharge, in his second year of professional school. At this point, he was functioning well in school but was undergoing an abandonment depression of a much milder degree with feelings of loneliness, depression and anger since graduation from college and leaving his prior therapist.

Bill attended college for four years, graduating cum laude. During college, he was seen by Dr. R, who did not confront Bill to enable him to continue to work through the rest of his abandonment depression. Rather, as Bill reported, "We worked on every day issues; he became a father to me; he was fulfilling my fantasies of being taken care of." Under this therapeutic approach, as might be expected, Bill's depression and anger decreased, and he seemed to flourish, with many outside interests and several short-term relationships with girls, who, however, dropped him because of his demanding and possessive behavior.

Upon leaving college to enter professional school, Bill became quite depressed, lonely and angry. Much of his anger was projected and acted out on the school. During his first year in professional school, his father died, which deepened his depression. He felt that he dealt well with the father's death. Afterwards, however, he reentered treatment, where he was at follow-up being seen once to three times a week, again tending to project and act out his anger on his therapist.

His description of his new therapist resembled a projection of the WORU, i.e., cold, quiet, distant, not giving.

Bill said, "The anger, depression and wish to be cared for are still there, although I cope with them much better." There had been two serious separation stresses, i.e., leaving his therapist and the death of his father. Mastery and coping were much improved. He still used avoidance, denial, splitting, projection and acting-out. However, the paranoid phenomenon, the intellectualization and detachment of affect had not returned.

His self-image was dramatically improved. "Before I felt blind about myself—blind, angry, scared. I would grasp at anything to avoid feeling and would have killed myself without treatment." He could identify feelings, liked many parts of himself, thought he had great potential, was able to do more and to cope better. In addition he had a more realistic perception of his parents and did not project as much on his peers, although he was "not one of the boys." He had close friends and did socialize.

Relationships with girls had continued to be difficult. He had had sexual intercourse with quite a number and, in addition, had had two long-term relationships which were terminated because of his demanding and possessive behavior. As far as independence and autonomy, Bill had more or less been living on his own and managing his own life since his senior year in high school. He had much better autonomy in coping with the external world, but still lacked intrapsychic autonomy. He had intense fears of abandonment about intimacy, with demanding and possessive behavior as a defense. Bill had always been creative and since discharge pursued many interests avidly—marine biology, classical music, scuba diving, motorcycles, and travel.

Clinical Impression

Bill is presently and temporarily suffering from an abandonment depression at leaving his therapist of four years' duration; otherwise, his functional impairment would be much less. However, like the other patients in the mild impairment category, Bill's adaptation throughout college was based on transference acting-out with his therapist a projection of the rewarding unit. There were dramatic symptomatic, functional improvements based on this transference relationship with, however, little intrapsychic structural change. There was marked improvement of his self-image and a more realistic perception of both parents, along with an increased capacity to be assertive and to take care of himself and pursue his own interests. A good deal of the passive-aggressive compliance, isolation, intellectualization and paranoid defenses did not return.

There remains a reliance on the old rewarding part-unit—pathological ego alliance defense, which happened to be reinforced by his therapist. He dealt with separation from his therapist by splitting, seeing his new therapist as the withdrawing unit and the old therapist as the rewarding unit. However, he was still in treatment, and I suspected, that if the treatment was successful, it would go far towards resolving this intrapsychic problem.

To summarize, there was dramatic and consolidated improvement in his self representation; he took charge of his life and himself. There was a dramatic increase in coping and mastery. However, there was an underlying persistence of the split object relations unit, with a fair amount of separation anxiety and abandonment depression being managed through transference acting-out. Thus, he remains vulnerable, as is demonstrated by what happened when he left his college to go to professional school.

It is important to note, however, that his defenses against the abandonment depression were much less intense and were much more adaptive: He did not retreat into detachment, paranoid projections, isolation or withdrawal. Despite the fact that impairment persisted, this was no small improvement for a boy who, at age 14, was diagnosed as having paranoid schizophrenia.

Third Follow-Up Nine Years After Discharge

After the study was completed, Bill, age 26, suddenly dropped in to see me. He was in his senior year of professional school, had changed his interest from clinical to industrial psychology and had been going with a girl for a year and a half. His depression and acting-out had disappeared, and his perspective had improved with treatment. For example, he was now aware of the regressive effect of his college therapist's treatment and of how he had acted out to defend against the depression on leaving for professional school. He felt more "grown up," had a "better sense of reality," still got depressed on occasion, but felt he would be able to conclude his treatment in the near future.

SUMMARY

These patients resemble the minimal impairment group in the dramatic improvement in functioning, but they differ in the continued need for a defense against separation anxiety and abandonment depression and the consequent failure of the flowering of individuation to occur. They were all able to handle work or school without difficulty. It was in the area of relationships that their need for defense showed up most prominently. Each patient had his or her own unique style of defense: Leslie through marriage and religion, Jean through sexual acting-out, Grace through avoidance of intimacy with sexual acting-out, and Bill through transference acting-out in therapy. Should fortune smile upon them and not visit them with separation stresses, they could adapt at this level for long periods of time, and their underlying vulnerability would remain hidden. However, the passage of time itself would eventually reveal the power of the need for defense through goals not reached, relationships never experienced, interests untapped and unfulfilled.

8

Mild Impairment (Group B)

Four of these seven patients are described in this chapter. All seven were rated mild impairment because, although their surface functioning was adequate, when one looked beneath that surface at the psychodynamic basis responsible for that functioning, it became apparent that there was less improvement in self-representation than the subgroup A patients and a more intense need for defense against separation anxiety and abandonment depression. Although they felt better about themselves and were somewhat better able to assert themselves, this change was mild compared with the subgroup A patients. They could not take direction of their lives. They could not identify what they wanted and activate and pursue their interest in reality. There was moderate pathology in the self-representations as well as in object relations.

ELLEN

Follow-Up Six Years After Discharge

History of Present Ilness

The case of Ellen, 16, is a good example of the clinical and developmental aspects of the splitting defense mechanism. Eighteen months prior to admission, Ellen, at age 14½, came into intense conflict with her father who disapproved of her socializing with a girlfriend who wore low-cut dresses. He called the friend, Amy, a whore. Fights between Ellen and her father increased in frequency and intensity because she continued to associate with friends her father disapproved of, broke curfews, and dressed in a manner to which he objected. If her father forbade her to wear dungarees, she would sneak them out of the house in her purse. Ellen began to smoke marijuana and occasionally to act out sexually. During this period, Ellen and Amy were sent home from school for smoking.

There were increasing confrontations between Ellen and her father, during which he accused her of being a slut and a whore, and at times slapped her. He objected particularly to her association with Amy, whom Ellen described as being "all screwed up and taking all kinds of drugs."

On one occasion, two weeks prior to her admission, Ellen's father picked up the phone extension and could hear that Amy was talking to his daughter. He told Amy to stop talking to his daughter and not to call again. The next morning Ellen sneaked out of the house and ran away to Chicago with Amy, where both girls stayed with a friend. Ellen's father traced them, got in touch with the Chicago police and arrived there himself six hours later. After this episode, Ellen was hospitalized.

The history of present illness, as well as the initial interview, was inundated by Ellen's rage at her father and by unremitting conflict with him. Her mother was portrayed at that time as a positive, supportive figure: "My mother is the opposite of my father, very giving and understanding. I could see nothing good in my father—my mother and I had a good relationship. I know

I could go to her and talk. With my father, I'd go berserk—yelling, screaming and talking about killing him."

Ellen dealt with her anxiety about her rage at the frustrating mother—the negative WORU—by splitting and projection: She retained and projected on her own mother the image of the good mother (RORU), and she projected the image of the frustrating mother (WORU), with the associated rage, upon her father. This projection was fostered by the father's behavior, most of which was unconsciously prompted by the mother and by the fact that the father was the unconsciously sanctioned target for the hostility of the entire family.

Past History

Early evidence of the splitting defense was revealed in Ellen's past history. She was the second of four children. When Ellen was eight, the mother became depressed over severe conflicts with the father. At the same time, she gave birth to a deaf child, who required most of her time and attention. Ellen felt abandoned by her mother, withdrew from her and displaced her RORU on her next sister, Ann, age 18, while continuing to project the withdrawing side on the father: "I guess Ann was the only person who really cared for me and really showed it."

Hospital Psychotherapy

As soon as Ellen was admitted to the hospital, the therapist began treatment by setting limits to her acting-out. Ellen further revealed her defense of splitting by becoming angry and demanding—not with her therapist who ordered these restrictions but with the nursing staff who carried them out. She maintained that her doctor, like Ann and her mother before him, was the RORU, i.e., "the man on the white horse who takes care of me."

The nurse, on the other hand, received the WORU projection: "I just really got mad at that nurse; I thought about ripping her up and stomping on her. She's just so cold and impersonal. You're the person I'm closest to, doctor." Ellen preserved her feeling of receiving emotional supplies by splitting the RORU and the WORU, projecting the RORU on the doctor and the WORU on the nurse.

Ellen's projection of the RORU earlier in life on Ann, as the caring mother, was interpreted during the working-through phase as a defense against her hostility toward her mother for the abandonment. It was further interpreted that she was now substituting a similar projection on the therapist for the previous projection on Ann and that the nurse was receiving the projection of the WORU that the father had received in the past. These interpretations overcame the splitting defense, as evidenced by the fact that Ellen immediately became severely depressed and angry and, prompted by guilt feelings, made a suicidal attempt, saying: "I guess I felt Ann was one of the only people who really cared for me. I latched on to her, and I didn't want to let go."

After the suicidal attempt, Ellen, still unable to face the anger at her mother, shifted the projection of the WORU from the nurse to her therapist: "I just realized where I was. I couldn't turn to Ann anymore, and I was finally on my own, all alone. I couldn't take that. Nobody else was there but me. First I hated you, my doctor, and then finally my parents and everybody." When the therapist finally confronted her with her last splitting defense, the anger returned to the original object from which it had been split, the mother. The patient could now work through her suicidal depression and homicidal rage at the mother's abandonment.

Follow-Up Six Years After Discharge

Ellen was seen for evaluation at age 22, six years after discharge. Her father had died. She was married and living with her mother, who supported Ellen and her husband. She had recently returned to college.

She had been discharged from the hospital to live at a boarding school and continue with her own therapist. She did well until her therapist had to leave. Rather than continue with another therapist, she discontinued therapy altogether and returned home to live, while continuing as a day student at the same school. She did not do well in school.

She then started an affair with an ex-patient who was quite emotionally ill and got involved in obtaining drugs for him "because I was afraid he would reject me."

Following the simultaneous break-up of the affair and graduation from high school, she impulsively (probably to defend against abandonment depression) went to Puerto Rico, thus avoiding a prior plan to go to England to study. Here she met a man whom she impulsively married. They eventually did go to England. She became depressed, gave up school, returned home, and finally made several half-hearted attempts at school. She was now back in school on her junior year, lackadaisically studying history.

She felt that she took her father's death much better than she expected, that she did not feel as guilty as she did when she was 15. She continued to idealize her mother as well as her husband, describing him as aggressive, strong, domineering, but also "gentle and soft." She denied any difficulties. She was not "ready" to have a child. There was evidence in the interview of massive avoidance of individuation, denial, splitting, and acting-out. The patient had had no prolonged periods of symptomatology except that mentioned above. She had very few interests outside of school and few peer relationships outside of home and school. She had been exposed to the separation stresses mentioned.

There had been improvement in her image of herself. She described herself before as meek, afraid, unsettled. She described herself at follow-up as assertive, more aggressive, less anxious, less guilty, more settled, more able to take care of herself. There was some increased autonomy since hospitalization but not very much. Her marital relationship seemed to represent an acting-out of the rewarding part-unit projection rather than true intimacy. There was little, if any, creativity.

Mother of Ellen

The mother denied and projected as much if not more than Ellen. She felt that Ellen probably hadn't needed treatment, that her major problem was minimal brain damage, that this in turn created self-confidence problems which could have been avoided had remedial work been afforded her at a younger age.

She continued to project on her husband, feeling he was responsible for Ellen's difficulties in adolescence. "He wanted her to be beautiful, dumb and dependent. He was intrusive—tapping the phone and always accusing her of acting like a tramp." Later she restated the problem by saying that if she learned anything in treatment it was that the father had to be more than a financial supporter for his girls. "He had to be more involved."

The mother described the period Ellen was in the hospital as being the worst time in her whole life. She was severely depressed and worried constantly about Ellen. She saw these feelings as being quite nautral and in no way indicative of any problems. She said that if she had known then how long it would be before she'd get to see Ellen again, she never would have allowed "them" to hospitalize her. She also felt the other patients were far sicker than Ellen.

The mother felt that any changes that occurred took place in the father and Ellen, not her. She felt that the father realized his mistakes and was forced to see that he had to look at himself. Ellen became less withdrawn and more confident and was able to try new things.

The father died two years after Ellen's discharge. The mother's description of her life since his death reflected her own lack of individuation: "Before my husband's death, I had no idea of money, bills, managing. My husband did everything." The mother was forced to take courses so that she could manage her affairs. She felt the experience was good for her. The mother had made no efforts to socialize since her husband's death. "I still have my house and my girls to take care of, I'm closer to the girls now than ever. I don't have time for a social life. Anyway all my old friends are married; they don't want a widow around."

At the time of the interview, Ellen and her husband lived with and were completely supported by the mother, though the mother resented the fact that she was putting her son-in-law through school. It was not the dependency that bothered her. She was angry that his family wasn't paying for it.

The mother idealized her relationships with all of her girls. There was only one girl who caused her any concern, Jennifer. The mother described Jennifer as being different—detached and cold. "She was always very independent, capable—she didn't and doesn't come to me for help. I know she has problems, but she won't share them with me." It seems that Jennifer is the only one who has been able to individuate. She is presently in her junior year at college. The problems and conflicts that arise focus on Jennifer's objections to her mother's trying to run her life.

Ellen, on the other hand, was viewed as a loving, close daughter. She lived at home and was not uncomfortable with the arrangement.

Clinical Impression

After Ellen's discharge, when her therapist had to leave, rather than deal with the abandonment depression that this produced, Ellen regressed and returned home, probably to use again the relationship with the mother as a defense. She did not resume treatment.

Ellen's next defense against the abandonment depression was the affair, where she acted in a compliant, self-destructive manner "so he won't leave me."

After he did leave her, Ellen, after graduation, made a very impulsive marriage, also probably to avoid autonomy and the abandonment depression it would bring. This notion is reinforced by the fact that when she went to England, she felt depressed, was not interested in school and finally had to return home.

Ellen's father died, and she ended up living with and being supported by her mother. Although there has been some improvement in the emergence of the self and a better self representation, as well as a better capacity to assert herself, she still is unable to identify her real interests and pursue them in reality or to autonomously regulate her self-esteem. There is a persistence of pathological defense mechanisms with a heavy emphasis on splitting, especially in regard to the mother and acting out of the rewarding part-unit. This failure to fully deal with her abandonment depression and individuate is reinforced by the lack of flowering of self seen with individuation, the lack of autonomy and the lack of many interests. She is able to function in this fashion, propped up by her defenses, but remains vulnerable to separation stress.

LINDA
Follow-Up Four Years After Discharge

History of Illness on Admission

Linda, 16, first showed signs of illness two years prior to admission, when she was sent away to a catholic girls' high school which required two hours of commuting. She failed all her subjects. The next year, age 15, she repeated the year and began in the spring of that year to come into increasing conflict with her mother over rules and restrictions.

She began to seek out rebellious peers, fought with the mother, became depressed and withdrawn, spent more time alone, and had an increasingly difficult time relating to peers as well. The mother finally gave up efforts at discipline and control. Linda became more depressed, hated the rules of the school, began to skip school and take drugs, slashed her wrists, was referred for private therapy, developed a fear of leaving the house and cut her wrists again, at which time she was hospitalized. Linda denied the need for the hospital, and the mother was torn over the need to hospitalize her daughter; as can be seen, she had myriad pathological defenses.

Past History

The father deserted the mother when Linda was 13 months old, and the mother had to go to work. Linda was cared for by a series of substitute figures, but the mother remained tied to the patient. From ages two to five, she lived during the day with a foster mother so that her mother could work. She clung to the mother each evening on the long walk home. When Linda was five years old, the mother was hospitalized for a hysterectomy; when she was nine, the father died; at age 12, the mother was hospitalized for a thyroidectomy; and when she was 15, a neighbor taking care of Linda died. Past school and social history was good, with the patient, however, not living up to her potential in school.

Hospital Psychotherapy

Her behavior was characterized by intense splitting of staff and doctor, intense clinging to them and demanding, transference acting-out with denial of affect, projection, projective identification, and avoidance of individuation. Confrontation eventually led to the depression, but the biggest obstacle was when the patient awoke to the reality of her rage at her mother, followed later by her extreme anxiety about autonomy.

Follow-Up Four Years After Discharge

Linda, age 21, was living with her mother and husband at the time of follow-up, supporting herself with a job. The first year following discharge, Linda stopped treatment: "I wanted another fling with babyhood, I didn't want to grow up." Linda had great difficulty adjusting and felt lost, not knowing how to manage all her freedom. She was unable to hold a job and became caught up in a constant round of promiscuity and drinking.

Approximately one year after discharge, she moved back into the home with her mother and gave up the drinking and promiscuity. She then met a boy "whom she fell in love with, because he did not push sex," got married and became increasingly dependent on him and resentful of him. She found him in an affair with another woman, walked out on him, and then had a reunion with him. She was not on drugs, nor was she promiscuous at follow-up.

Linda continued to idealize her prior therapist, her mother and her husband and complied with both mother and husband, subjecting herself to abuse, splitting and projecting her anger on others so that there was less acting-out but a persistence of avoidance of individuation and denial.

Though she said, "I don't feel helpless anymore; I can protect and assert myself," there was evidently much denial in this as she described her relationship with mother and husband. Object representations were split and idealized or devalued as in the rewarding or withdrawing unit. She still seemed unable to tolerate the separation stress, as evidenced by the reaction on discharge from the hospital and the continued living with the mother while married. There was little autonomy, as she seemed to vacillate in dependency between mother and husband, although she no longer acted out destructively. She still described herself as not feeling very worthwhile much of the time. The relationship with the husband was based on clinging rather than real intimacy. She had few interests and little creativity.

The Mother of Linda

The mother described herself as gaining a lot from her treatment. She noted that when Linda was hospitalized, she had come to the end of her rope. She felt responsible, guilty and despondent. She felt that she had difficulty helping Linda become independent: "The social worker helped me to see 'you not only have to rear them, you have to release them too.' She also helped me to see I wasn't just a mother; I was a person."

Following Linda's discharge, the mother felt Linda went crazy with the freedom. At one point, she was so distraught she called the therapist for help. "The therapist told me it was up to Linda now." The mother provided partial support but beyond that let her alone. "I didn't intrude, I waited for an invitation, even though I worried. I knew she had to get through it."

Linda returned to live with her mother at 19 to get away from the drugs and promiscuity which she felt would kill her. She remained at home until her marriage, kept a steady job and helped defray expenses.

Linda also returned to live with her mother following her separation from her husband. She had been with her six months at the time of the follow-up. There was a reconciliation two months prior to the follow-up, and following this, the husband moved in as well until an apartment in the building was to become vacant.

Neither Linda nor her mother was comfortable with the situation and both seemed to be looking forward to the move. Linda felt like a guest and therefore not free to act as she would in her own place. The mother felt that the couple needed to be on their own to work out (if possible) whatever problems they had. She added that she felt their earlier problems were due to over-involvement from the boy's family.

Linda agreed with her mother about the gains from treatment. She added that she felt they could relate like adults now and that she was glad to see that her mother now had more in her own life. The mother was involved in doing volunteer work with retarded youngsters, taught religion and had been taking nursing courses. She said she would like to pursue the latter more seriously in the future. The interest in a new career was partially motivated by the fact that she feared she might lose her job.

The mother said she didn't know if Linda and her husband would work out their problems, but she was confident that Linda was capable of making the decisions that were best for her.

Clinical Impression

This patient has clearly some better self representation, at least seeing herself sometimes as not being helpless, being able to assert herself, being able to hold a job, and for that matter to be married. It is also evident that there is a fair amount of denial in this self-observation.

Through acted-out environmental arrangements, clinging to the mother and to the husband, the patient is able to deal with her failure to individuate and thereby perpetuates her problem. Though there is some improvement in the self representation, it is minimal; the object representations remain the same; there is the same vulnerability to separation stress, with persistence of the same pathological defense mechanisms of denial, avoidance, splitting, clinging, acting-out, etc. There is very little independence, intimacy or creativity.

Linda's functional adjustment is achieved through the use of environmental arrangements, i.e., avoidance of true individuation at work and acting-out through clinging with husband and mother to deal with her separation anxiety and abandonment depression, thus leaving her vulnerable to future stress.

At best, one can say that the destructiveness of the acting-out has decreased and the self representation has improved somewhat. One wonders how long this would hold up under stress. A question can also be raised whether the patient is unable to internalize or whether the key event was the failure to follow through on outpatient treatment with her therapist, where the separation-individuation failure would have been treated effectively.

Linda's mother's capacity to let her daughter go is in marked contrast to Ellen's mother's continuing attitude of taking care of her daughter. Linda's mother is aware of her past tendency to overprotect and live through her daughter. The history reflects conscious efforts on her part to let Linda work out her own life. She has also made definite efforts to expand her own interests to substitute for her interest in her daughter.

Ellen's mother, on the other hand, saw nothing alien about Ellen's being home with her husband and being supported by the mother. She liked it that way and viewed her other daughter Jennifer's autonomy in negative terms.

BEN

Follow-Up Five Years After Discharge

History of Illness at Admission

Ben, 16 years old and a tenth grader, gave a history of passive-aggressive response in conflicts with his parents from early life. Until the age of two, he clung to his mother, followed her around, and cried hysterically whenever she left him. Otherwise, his early development was reported to be without incident, and he showed no separation anxiety when starting school. However, following a bout of infectious hepatitis at age seven which caused him to be kept in bed at home for a number of months, Ben, previously a good student, became an "underachiever."

Perhaps the physical illness, which reinforced his physical dependence on his mother, promoted an emotional regression to the clinging, symbiotic bind of his first two years, from which he was then unable to emerge. He felt strange in class, did little homework, daydreamed, and was preoccupied with staring out the window. He dreaded bringing home his progressively bad report cards, due to the 15-minute lectures they involved from his mother.

When Ben was five, his mother, a piano teacher, began to give him piano lessons which he enjoyed: "They were the high point of my day." Was it the lessons or the symbiosis he enjoyed? At age 10, in the fifth grade—perhaps spurred on by an inner maturational spurt—he became rebellious toward his mother and the piano and gave up practicing. In the sixth grade, he had psychotherapy once a week for six months, stopping because he felt no change. At age 11, he began to teach himself to play the electric guitar and played in a dance band. He almost failed the seventh grade, and he resumed playing the piano on his own in the eighth grade.

By the summer of the ninth grade, at age 14, depressed and apathetic, he began experimenting with drugs. He used marijuana daily, as well as LSD and mescaline. These drugs did away with his "bad feelings" and allowed him to get closer to people. His course over the next two years prior to hospitalization was progressively downhill. His passive-aggressive behavior increased and caused him to be expelled from several different schools. He started psychotherapy but it was of no help because he failed to attend or to participate when he did attend. Ingestion of drugs continued unabated. His behavior deteriorated further so that for a number of months prior to admission he would spend more than half the day in bed and get up just before his parents came home (they both worked) to go out and acquire his drugs.

When he was admitted to the hospital, his physical appearance broadcast his state. He was of average height with extremely long hair, had braces on his teeth, and wore glasses. He appeared almost catatonic; his affect was flat; he was withdrawn, almost mute and extremely passive. He talked in a distressingly slow manner, as if retarded. The extent of his passivity became readily apparent shortly after admission. In interviews he would only speak when asked questions, and on the floor he remained aloof with his peers. He only attended activities upon direction, and he then quickly demonstrated his passive resistance by oversleeping; he was unable to control his oversleeping for several months.

Hospital Psychotherapy

The principal problem was Ben's severe passive-aggressiveness, manifested by procrastination, oversleeping and being late for school and activities. Eventually, extreme restrictions were necessary to bring this to his attention. This led to the next defense of compliance with detachment of affect, which had to be worked through. There was always some question as to whether the patient was having a true affective experience or a simulation.

Follow-Up Five Years After Discharge

At follow-up Ben, 22, lived by himself and supported himself by giving piano lessons while he practiced to become a concert pianist.

Ben was discharged from the hospital to his home, where he attended local high school and continued with his own therapist. After high school graduation he moved away from home, got an apartment with a friend and started college.

At this time his therapist had to leave. Ben reacted with a profound abandonment depression, from which he had probably not fully recovered at follow-up. He managed to continue on in college, taking private piano lessons. He continued to complain of mild, recurrent depression and once, when jilted by a girl, had a severe depression "which he pulled himself out of without drinking or drugs." He showed great inconsistency and had problems with passive-aggressiveness when trying to pursue the practice of his piano.

When he was 20 and in college, he lived with a girl for one year, became disillusioned with her, though childishly attached, and she "dumped him," but he recovered after a few months. He still slept late, arose late, smoked pot almost every night, had a big problem with procrastination and felt very distracted and doubtful about himself.

He had continued to see a therapist once a week for the last four years and felt he had made some improvement, but not much. He felt that he was more detached from his parents' values now that his own were established. He used to see his parents as hazy and foreboding, and now saw them as depressed, with no vitality in their lives. As to himself, he felt he was more himself, more discriminating and more independent, but still needed external structure. Self-assertion was still a problem: "I still drift; I still go with the flow." He had had two long-term relationships with girls with no sexual problems, but he responded to the "liveliness and spark of the girls." Evidently, his dependency caused one girl to reject him. He had very few other interests outside of his piano.

Parents of Ben

The parents felt the program helped Ben in that he "went in a vegetable and came out a human." They expanded on this and seemed to view Ben quite accurately. They were cognizant of his continued difficulties, but at this point there was little they could do—he had to do it.

They were quite negative about their own treatment experience. The mother felt that she was never able to achieve rapport with the social worker. She felt she was not understood—"put into a niche." "I felt so guilty and responsible for Ben's trouble, but I didn't know what to do about it. . . . We were so grateful they took him, we would have done anything, but we never understood or felt understood."

They were particularly hostile toward the group therapy, felt one of the fathers acted in a crazy manner and made therapy into a circus. They felt nothing in common with him and asserted that only the "talkers" ever got the floor. They became "participant observers," feeling it was a waste of time.

The father felt that he thought very differently than the social worker. He described wanting an intellectual understanding—wanting books to read—and feeling unable to connect. "They told me not to read." Obviously, the father's defense of intellectualization was challenged and he resisted it.

In spite of their negativism, the mother, in particular, appeared to have made gains. The heavy costs incurred by treatment forced her to increase her time at work. She obtained a substitute teaching job in special education, became interested, finished a Masters degree in Special Education and was considering going further. She worked full-time at follow-up. She felt her success in the field had increased her self-confidence and ability to assert herself. If she were involved in treatment now, she believed she would be less passive and probably would have voiced her objections more easily.

Both parents viewed themselves as tired—tired of being parents and impatient with Ben.

Both of the younger siblings were reported to have difficulty in adolescence, especially the boy, who was on soft drugs for a while. He appeared to have straightened out and was presently attending an electrical engineering school. The youngest child, a girl, married at age 19 and was reported to be doing well.

Ben felt that his parents tended to be conventional, rigid and "products of their generation." He described them as having set down their goals and being content to settle for them—house, good job, a few friends. His father was viewed as tight—little communication occurred because he could not see Ben's life as productive. It should be noted, though, that Ben only felt antagonistic to his parents and their life-style when he was depressed. When he was feeling good, they related well: "Sometimes it's hard for me to separate what is my problem and what is their problem."

Clinical Impression

Ben, similar to the two previous patients, has a better sense of himself, a little better idea of his values, some ability to articulate them and support them, and a more realistic image of his parents.

However, his pathological defense mechanisms persist to a high degree; he lacks motivation; he still has a problem with passive-aggressiveness, denial and avoidance. He is unable to regulate his self-esteem autonomously or to pursue his wishes in reality. For example, whenever he meets anger, frustration and depression, he again becomes passive and gives up.

His object representations show no change. He acts out through clinging in heterosexual relationships. He has better capacity to deal with separation stress without hopelessness and helplessness, but there is very little autonomy, very little capacity for intimacy and very little creativity except in playing the piano. It seems clear, however, that Ben was doing well until his doctor had to leave, and rather than persist and work through his abandonment depression, Ben "fell apart." He did not and still cannot mourn, but tends to react with detachment. He had not internalized the treatment enough by the time his doctor left. He returned for treatment once a week to another doctor for the last four years, where it seems as if he acts out the rewarding unit in the transference.

BART
Follow-Up Two Years After Discharge

History of Illness at Admission

Bart, 17, had a history since age 1 of being demanding, stubborn, and always wanting his own way. He had trouble in school because of temper tantrums and lack of cooperation. His father had died when he was 10, and two years prior to admission, there was a gradual escalation of difficulties at school and truancy. Although Bart was previously a good student, his grades now fell, he began to have trouble with his temper, and at one point he had to change schools after assaulting a teacher. His grades continued to deteriorate, and there was truancy, extreme temper outbursts and physical assaultiveness. He assaulted both the mother and the siblings and finally withdrew socially. The patient retreated to his room and threatened anyone with a bat if they approached him. He also had a history of belonging to an antisocial gang.

Hospital Psychotherapy

Bart was hospitalized for only nine months. His initial testing behavior was not, as one might expect, aggressive, but rather passive-aggressive. When confronted, he would express his rage at the therapist, at times expressing his fear of loss of control and saying that his alternatives were to be helpless or in an uncontrollable rage. Bart's passive-aggressive acting-out behavior was a defense against his terror lest he lose control of this homicidal rage at his father who had left him and at his mother for her infantalizing attitudes. He tested his therapist to see if this therapist could control him and therefore relieve his anxiety about loss of control of the rage. His therapist was, however, never adequately able to do this, and when the patient got into the working-through phase and got closer to his feelings about mother and father, he signed out against advice.

Follow-Up Two Years After Discharge

Bart was seen at age 20, two years after discharge. Following his discharge, he returned home to live with his mother. He was shocked by his former friends, one of whom was killed by another gang and one of whom was alcoholic; the rest were on drugs. He avoided them but had a dream-like episode when they slipped LSD into his drink. He began to do handyman work for his grandparents and continued living at home with his mother.

At follow-up he was subject to recurrent episodes of depression, was somewhat seclusive, had very little social life, and tended to avoid his mother. He had a relationship with a girl, age 19, whom he was planning to marry and who had moved into the house with his mother. He felt that now when he got depressed he could pull himself out of it by being active. He had much better control of impulses—for example, "I no longer punch holes in the wall, and I think before I act."

There seemed to be a persistence of the pathological defense mechanisms of avoidance, denial, splitting, projection and acting-out, despite the fact that his impulse control had improved.

The image of himself had improved: "Before, I didn't like myself or anyone. I couldn't figure out what I wanted to do or do it. Now I like myself better and talk about myself with others, and I can to some extent figure out what I want to do and then do it."

There was better self-control and a better self-image but still considerable difficulty in actualizing his wishes. Conflicts with the mother continued as before, and he saw her as aggressive and pushy. He handled her by avoidance. Object relations were the same as before. He had very few friends and very few interests. When not working, he was either shooting pool or drinking beer. There seemed to be little autonomy, little capacity for intimacy or creativity.

Mother of Bart

The mother's participation in the follow-up was motivated by her concern about her son's continued difficulty and her feeling of being overwhelmed. She was extremely anxious during the session and appeared to hope the follow-up team would in some way provide both her and her son with additional help. She felt she gained tremendously from the treatment. She felt particularly indebted to the social worker whom she continued to feel made it possible for her to cope better generally. She felt in retrospect that she had been too overprotective of Bart on the one hand, while on the other leaning too heavily on him to provide a model and father figure for her other two boys.

When he signed out, she felt in better control of herself but at follow-up she felt that both she and Bart lost what they had originally gained.

Though the mother harbored resentment that Bart had remained at home, she had made no demands upon him to make plans to find his own place for himself and his fiancée (who moved in six months prior to the interview) or even to contribute to the running of the house with money or work.

Though she consciously said she wanted him to be autonomous, she spent a lot of time discussing her own poor health and inability to provide for the two other boys, and found fault with every plan Bart had thus far presented to leave.

Following the interview, the mother called and inappropriately wanted to know what Bart had said about her and how we felt he was doing. She did note that in the past her interference with his therapist caused him to quit shortly after. The mother seemed aware of her increased inability to control herself and, when it was suggested, said she would call the social worker.

Clinical Impression

Although he has better impulse control and has overcome destructive acting-out, Bart is unable to go further. He continues to act out the rewarding unit through clinging to his mother and girlfriend and to deny and avoid individuation. He is somewhat seclusive, has very few interests, is not sure of what he wants to do with his life and is probably getting married to act out the rewarding unit. However, as Bart says, if it had not been for the treatment, he would be dead now. In spite of a short hospital stay and an inadequate therapist, inadequate management of his testing, and finally his signing out, there resulted a partial improvement of destructive behavior plus some improvements in self representations. He feels better about himself and is able to identify his wishes, but is unable to actualize them. His acting-out is controlled, and when he gets depressed, he no longer feels hopeless and helpless.

Though Bart said his mother had made gains, he felt she continued to interfere in his life. He spontaneously noted that he thought she would probably be mad at him when he did leave home. Bart also felt that "she has a mental block about me. She keeps saying I'm going backwards. She's never happy with what I do and is always pushing me. The thing she doesn't know is that when she pushes, I just won't do it." Bart said he had missed his first scheduled appointment because she had pushed by reminding him about it and he just wouldn't do it.

Bart entered treatment at one time with his mother's therapist.

He explained that she had said he had to go or he had to leave the house. Bart went but quit a short time after because: "All the therapist wanted to do was talk about my mother. . . . I wanted to understand myself, not my mother."

Bart indicated that she does get "under my skin," but he finds that if he withdraws, ignores or regresses, he doesn't get mad.

It would seem that as long as the mother was in therapy, she was able to control herself and function more appropriately in relation to Bart. Since her discontinuation, though, she has been less and less able to contain her anxiety. It would also seem that, as Bart makes any effort to separate, the mother becomes increasingly inappropriate.

Bart continues to be quite passive and tends to deny and rationalize the continued effect his mother has on him.

CHAPTER SUMMARY

The four patients included in this chapter, representative of the seven patients in Group B, have improved their ability to function, but even that seems compromised by their need for defense, i.e., their need to avoid the anxiety associated with individuation impels them to avoid higher levels of functioning. All four had clinical episodes of abandonment depression. All stopped treatment, and three of the four are still living at home with their mothers. The demands of adult life may well foreshadow further clinical episodes of abandonment depression for these patients, unless they are able to continue to defend against these demands by perpetuating idiosyncratic life-styles. Even so, their vulnerability to separation stress is great.

9

Moderate Impairment

These patients were helped very little by treatment. Four representative cases will be described in this chapter. They have continued to suffer from severe symptomatology and moderate impairment of functioning. Their clinical pictures were dominated by the need to defend against the abandonment depression at the cost of adaptation to reality. There was little or no autonomy, intimacy or creativity and no change in intrapsychic structure.

However, within this dismal picture, there were some positive aspects which may have been due to treatment. For example, one patient finished the second year of college, another graduated from high school and a third was able to graduate from college. The destructiveness of the acting-out of three patients was markedly decreased, and one patient, after living the life of a junkie for five years, was able to overcome his drug habit through the help of Odyssey House. This patient recently (after the study was finished) graduated from college and started professional school. It is entirely possible that without hospital treatment none of these achievements would have taken place. Consequently, although the treatment made very little dent on their defenses against the abandonment depression, it did evidently increase to some extent their capacity to cope with reality.

JILL
FOLLOW-UP FOUR YEARS AFTER DISCHARGE

History of Illness at Admission

The present illness of Jill, 14, began around age 10, when her sister, age 17, began severe acting-out against the parents. About the same time, her stepbrother attempted to sexually molest Jill. The mother became more and more preoccupied with the sister's problems, and Jill began to cut classes, take and push drugs, steal and act out sexualy. She became involved with a 19-year-old criminal who pushed drugs. She often ran interference for him, because she felt that she would be spared because of her young age. Jill was first placed in a reform school and then hospitalized. On admission, she denied any difficulties. "All I want to do is drink, take drugs and have a good time," she said.

Past History

Jill was adopted at age two and one-half. Her adopted mother died when she was four. From four to six, she was taken care of by the grandmother and several housekeepers. When she was six, her father remarried, and she became a model child. At seven her older sister became involved in drugs, having Jill hold the tourniquet for injections. School and social history was good until age 10, when the patient matured physically before her peers and felt embarrassed about it.

Hospital Psychotherapy

Her acting-out was readily controlled. She began to work through her anger and depression, which was accompanied by much regression and acting-out. She seemed, however, to work through some of her abandonment depression. She finally started family sessions, where both she and the family showed great resistance to separation. The discharge planning was complicated by the patient's reluctance to give up her reunion fantasy about the parents and the parents' resistance to supporting Jill's individuation. This resistance was further reinforced by a local family psychiatrist. Nevertheless, Jill was discharged to a local boarding school near home to continue in treatment with her doctor.

Follow-Up Four Years After Discharge

Jill, 18, did well her first semester, continuing with her hospital therapist as an outpatient twice a week. She then dropped out of therapy and returned to live at home. Her clinical condition had gone downhill ever since. She had chronic and recurrent acute depressions, intense mood swings, temper outbursts, overeating and, increased drug use. She smoked marijuana every day. She occasionally stole from her stepmother and, when confronted, said that she was entitled to it.

She became reinvolved with the same criminal as before hospitalization, an involvement which became sadomasochistic with intermittent beatings. She finally terminated this relationship a few months before the interview, after she had had a pregnancy and an abortion.

Throughout this period, she was seeing a private therapist once a week, but the treatment was finally stopped by the therapist when she would not or could not control her behavior. She had been on the honor role at school and then, after a fight with her mother, dropped out of school and starting tripping on LSD, and pot, holding only temporary jobs.

She recently returned to work again, but now she was beginning to think about college. Part of her status at follow-up was due to a relationship with a new boyfriend whom she idealized "because he doesn't want to have sex." She continued to handle separation stress poorly with the need for destructive acting-out as a defense against abandonment depression. Her original pathological mechanisms of defense continued more or less unchanged. Her self representation, although a little better, was quite infantile and unrealistic; for example, she said would like to teach but had no high school diploma and was unsure about college.

Parents of Jill

When Jill was hospitalized, the father said his family was like an "amalgam"—"a lot of people living together with very little communication." Everyone was on his or her own track and incapable of hearing anyone else. He also believed that both he and his wife wanted to deny the existence of problems and viewed the world through "rose colored glasses." He felt that much of the time he wanted to maintain a view of Jill "as a child, to protect her and to see her only as a completely loving daughter."

His individual treatment forced him to view Jill more comprehensively and realistically. For the first time, he sat down and talked with Jill about her mother's death. Previously, "his efforts had been to spare her by hiding all remembrances of her." He also felt that he had subsequently been more comfortable in expressing and acknowledging feelings with his second wife.

In spite of this, the father appeared to continue to have a blind spot when it came to Jill. He was most responsible for her quitting boarding school and returning home. Later he made it even more appealing for her to stay home by buying her a car. Both the parents and Jill viewed this in retrospect as having been a mistake. The father continues to have difficulty setting appropriate limits for his daughter. Jill described her father as easily manipulated into overindulging her. Each time it occurred, she became furious, because she knew he shouldn't give in to her and she knew she shouldn't ask.

Jill was seen several months after her parents had been seen and reported that her father had told her she had to leave by the end of the month. She felt that her father "has reached the end of his rope, has given up on me and feels I am a lost cause." Jill felt that it was probably the best thing he did. Even though she was scared, she felt that it was the only way she was going to get her head together.

The adoptive stepmother was grateful for her experience in the hospital treatment. "I learned that I had to look for my own happiness." I couldn't base my happiness or unhappiness on what my children did or did not produce." She felt that, as a result, her whole attitude changed. She could view things more realistically— didn't need to expect reward from the children to feel good about herself.

She credited this experience with ultimately helping her to return to work. She had been working full-time for over a year as a civil servant. She loved her work and felt her life was more balanced. She described how it was difficult at first because Jill resented her not being home and her expecting Jill to assume more responsibility.

She did not feel that the relationship with Jill was good but felt it was better. Jill resented her replacing her prior mother, went from acting more mature to tantrum-like behavior in seconds, and repeatedly tried to get both parents to take over for her. For example, when Jill began seeing the same man she had dated prior to being hospitalized, the parents initially became very involved, going so far as to obtain a court order forbidding the man to see her. In spite of this, they continued to see each other. Then the parents set limits on the hours they spent together. At this point, the man began to physically abuse Jill, necessitating a doctor's care. The parents pressed charges but made it clear that, from then on, they would refuse involvement beyond providing medical care. In addition, the mother began confronting Jill with her own self-destructiveness and her subtle attempts to induce her parents to take over. It was at this time that Jill stopped seeing the man.

Although Jill often wished the mother were out of the picture, she at the same time respected her. Jill also felt that both parents were far more realistic since the treatment and that she herself provoked most of the communication difficulty. She described feeling sometimes that when things were going too well—she was getting too close to them—she deliberately became "bitchy, mad or anything obnoxious, because I cannot stand the closeness. I guess I am always afraid that if I get close, they'll leave—die."

The other children in the family had their share of problems as well. The only one spared was the youngest girl, age 10, the only product of this marriage. All agree she gained the most from her parents' maturity. A son, age 19, weighs over 300 pounds and spends most of his time alone, watching television cartoons (according to Jill). A daughter, age 22, was apparently off heroin for the last six months and was living with the natural father in Michigan. A son, age 18, never took drugs, but he, too, had adjustment problems when he left for college. He was described as always having academic problems, as well as depression and loneliness once off on his own at college.

Clinical Impression

Perhaps Jill says it best: "After I left the hospital, I felt better about myself, it was different. Then other things overwhelmed me, and I didn't care about myself. When I get close to anyone, I get angry and bitchy, and I must be afraid they will leave me." The severe early trauma, the early onset of acting-out, as well as the severely conflictual family, the pronounced wish for reunion with the family's resistance at discharge, all combined, when she was faced with the abandonment depression always associated with discharge, to impel her to give up her efforts at working-through and go back to her regression with her family, which has persisted to this day.

Although this family has made some gains, particularly the mother, unfortunately the father continues to deny reality and thus has interefered with Jill's development. Jill views his recent "throwing me out" as the best thing he could have done for her. Whether or not he or Jill will be strong enough to sustain the separation and work it through is yet to be determined.

LEE

Follow-Up Five Years After Discharge

History of Illness at Admission

Lee, 14, was always socially withdrawn and did poorly in school. Two years before in the seventh grade, she began to truant and avoid her homework or try to get her parents to do it for her. Over the next two years, treatment, including brief hospitalization, did not work, and finally she was hospitalized for truancy and school failure, stealing, temper tantrums, fighting with her sister and malicious behavior toward her mother. For example, Lee destroyed several of her mother's papers, some of her dresses and poured out her perfume when she did not get her mother's attention. She withdrew to her room for long periods of time.

Past History

Lee's mother returned to work when she was two months old. When she was three, her sister was born; when she was five, her mother's first nervous breakdown (diagnosed as psychotic) occurred. The mother was hospitalized at that time for six months. She had a second breakdown when Lee was 12. She was diagnosed as a manic-depressive disorder. Lee's maternal grandmother was also hospitalized with a nervous breakdown when Lee was five. Her schoolwork was always poor, and she repeated second to fourth grades. She was rated a minimal achiever.

Hospital Psychotherapy

Psychotherapy in the hospital was focused on her passive-aggressive acting-out, failure of school attendance, failure of school performance, poor personal hygiene, and poor socialization. Gradually, through confrontation, her behavior was brought under control, and she began to deal with her feelings about her mother. However, she was always extremely sensitive to her separations from her therapist, with severe regressions each time. She would then recover and begin to make progress. However, when home visits were begun, the parents' resistance increased. Then her therapist had to leave for a prolonged period. At this point, she managed to manipulate her parents into signing her out against advice.

Follow-Up Five Years After Discharge

Although Lee, 20, had graduated from boarding school, she remained locked in the same hostile, dependent relationship with both parents, who verbalized disappointment but nevertheless encouraged and supported her continued dependency. Lee was sent to boarding school, perhaps because she was making her parents' lives miserable. She resisted returning after weekends at home, socialized poorly and did poorly academically, but managed to get through because, in her senior year, when she refused to do homework assignments, her father did them for her.

The mother reported that Lee stole money from her to buy clothes, stayed up late at night watching television, still had a constricted social life with no dating, and no job other than a summer arts and crafts program and occasional babysitting. Lee had refused therapy since discharge. However, because of her interest in clothes, she was willing to spend her money, travel and shop alone, in order to maintain a wardrobe.

On examination, she still appeared much younger than her age and behaved in a constricted, unspontaneous, guarded fashion, denying all difficulties. She still clung to her family to avoid separation stress; there was a persistence of all pathological mechanisms with the improvements being, it seemed, finishing school and being able to manage her wardrobe. She exhibited very little change in self representation or object representations and very little autonomy, intimacy or creativity.

Parents of Lee

This family's situation was, if anything, worse at follow-up than at the time Lee was hospitalized. It was not as explosive, but the pall of apathy and resignation at Lee's poor functioning was depressing. The parents expressed only mild resentment about their daughter's living as a "vegetable" and quite openly said they didn't think she would ever improve. It was this acceptance of a bad situation which seemed highly pathological.

The father was quite candid about his pulling Lee out of the hospital program against advice. Though he rationalized his behavior by saying her change in therapists was the straw that broke the camel's back, he also spoke of his own inability to sustain the separation, his guilt over hospitalizing her to begin with and his strong negative reaction to the recommendation that she be placed in a boarding school. The father said he did not think hospitalization was helping Lee and she didn't seem happy, but she was never involved in the decision. After the parents made the decision, the father felt like "I was being excommunicated by the staff."

The parents tried unsuccessfully to have her remain at home and attend day school. This broke down within months, and Lee was enrolled in boarding school on Long Island. It would seem that much of the parents' behavior was motivated by rage and guilt. They provided no limits, allowed Lee to behave like an infant in a demanding way, and then became so angry that they wanted her out of their sight. This in turn stimulated guilt and a return to their indulging her again to salve their own consciences.

In Lee's last semester of high school, she refused to return. Assignments were sent home and done by the father and copied by Lee. The father felt his behavior was inappropriate but "I didn't want to see the money go down the drain and felt it was important that Lee graduate."

The father was quite aware of her not making any effort to improve herself. She did nothing at home beyond sleeping, watching soap operas and occasionally volunteering to do some of the housework. The only area she had sustained interest in was clothes.

She was allowed to buy whatever she wanted; this was rationalized with not wanting to stifle her interest. The father acknowledged that he would like to confront her but didn't to avoid hassles. Though she attended her aunt's modeling school for several weeks, the father noted that she did nothing afterwards. The only job she got was through her aunt, who offered her a two-day job passing out free cigarettes on the street. The father didn't think Lee would ever work, marry or leave home. He felt that things were more harmonious without her but actually contributed to her living a limited, stagnated life.

The father felt he gained little from treatment. He never seemed to get beyond the separation from his daughter, to get involved. The entire time, he focused on her ultimate discharge.

The mother was, at least consciously, more disturbed by Lee's functioning—or lack of it. It was she who initiated three different efforts to re-engage Lee in outpatient treatment. What was so striking, though, was her sabatoging of one effort. Lee did become involved with a family agency. The agency insisted that the mother be involved also, but the mother withdrew after several weeks, saying that she "was working, it was a waste of time, I had to take a bus to get there." Lee withdrew shortly after.

Lee had also expressed interest in getting her driver's license, but the mother had said she couldn't until she was 21. She explained that Lee was diagnosed as having perceptual problems as a child, so she couldn't trust her. The mother also reported that Lee had been stealing money to buy clothes. Lee had been confronted but said she felt she had a right to take it, as they were her parents and obliged to clothe her. (Lee had 25 pairs of slacks.) The stealing continued, but the mother felt she couldn't confront her all the time, because she had no proof.

The mother commented that the major benefit from treatment for her and her family (with the exception of Lee) was the respite and peace experienced while Lee was hospitalized. She felt that she was misunderstood as an individual by everyone at the hospital. The mother believed that everyone saw her as a "bitch." She felt that maybe if she had been less open, like other parents, she would have been liked.

In spite of the mother's animosity to the program, her involvement in the follow-up was motivated by her desire to be eligible for help for Lee in the future. She expressed repeated concern about her being told when she and her husband took Lee out of the hospital against advice that they could not return. She hoped that, if the program reopened, her daughter could be considered for treatment.

The mother also expressed her belief that Lee had made positive gains from treatment; though still a "vegetable," she was actually in better control than she was prior to treatment. "She can at least pass for a human being now." Her bouts of "hysteria" had also lessened.

Clinical Impression

The history of a psychotic grandmother and a mother who was hospitalized twice during the patient's early development, poor school and poor social achievement almost from the very beginning, together with the fact that in the hospital she managed to improve until the point of separation came, which she was unable to tolerate, suggests that she could not internalize enough in order to get the strength for autonomy. In other words, she could not separate no matter how much therapy was used.

This family brings to mind the studies on formerly hospitalized schizophrenics—oftentimes these patients function no better, but their families accommodate and become resigned to the pathology. Although hospitalization is avoided, it is at a tremendous cost.

The other factor which cannot be discounted is the way in which Lee's illness serves her parents' own needs. Although it is speculative, one must wonder about the fact that since Lee was discharged, the mother has not had to hospitalize herself for psychiatric reasons, despite the fact that she has had a colostomy and is maintained on lithium. Functionally, she looks good in comparison to Lee. Everyone is also candid about Lee's tie to her father. The father prides himself on his rapport with Lee, commenting that his wife does not enjoy the same rapport. These parents seem to need Lee sick and have provided a protective environment where she can "comfortably" remain so.

HARRY

FOLLOW-UP EIGHT YEARS AFTER DISCHARGE

History of Illness at Admission

Harry's present illness began at the age of nine, when the family moved to New York City. The parents had difficulty in adjusting, drank heavily and withdrew from both their children and each other. Harry had trouble adjusting to his peers. By age 14, in the ninth grade, he began to associate with an antisocial group, and communication with his parents practically ceased. His acting-out escalated in all areas: all sorts of drug use including addiction to heroin, trouble with the police, failure and truancy at school. At age 16, he was arrested for robbery and given the choice of hospitalization or going to jail.

Past History

Harry had frequent colic as an infant. His mother found him demanding and had trouble satisfying him and setting limits. At age three, the family moved to Florida, where the mother became depressed and started drinking.

Hospital Psychotherapy

Harry was hospitalized for 10 months. His principal defenses were passive-aggressive acting-out and emotional detachment. Despite the fact that the acting-out was brought under control and he worked through some of his depression, the staff had the impression that there was more compliance than actual working-through.

Follow-Up Eight Years After Discharge

When seen at age 25, eight years after discharge, Harry had been at a country facility of the Odyssey House drug program for the last 20 months for treatment of drug addiction.

Harry had been discharged from the hospital to live at home and continue at the local high school—in restrospect a mistake—and to see his therapist regularly. Within a short time, he became depressed, started taking drugs and was recommended to the Odyssey Program, where he managed to do well and get off heroin, until he had to assume some program responsibility, at which point he collapsed, stopped his treatment and resumed taking heroin.

The next six years were an almost uninterrupted story of drug use (barbiturates, heroin), as well as various arrests for armed robbery and possession of narcotics. Most of the robberies were to get money for drugs. At age 22, after several years of this behavior, Harry said: "My girlfriend threw me out after I cheated on her. I was arrested for attempting to rob a drugstore. I lost my car license for not paying a fine. I got scared I was going to jail. I hit rock bottom. I was tired of the drug life, and it started to get hard to be a dope fiend. I turned myself in to Odyssey House, where I have learned to be honest and responsible for myself and others and am now responsible for the whole place: groups, counseling, services, etc."

He had been returned to the city, where he was in charge of local program, was more active and had his own apartment. However, he was still on an allowance. His affect was that of being bored. He stated that instead of taking drugs for his anger and boredom, he talked it out with his supervisor. He felt that there was an improvement in his self-image. He felt he could do things and meet people and hold a regular job. However, he still had not held a responsible job except in the Odyssey House program. His relationships with his parents was better since his involvement in Odyssey House. He felt that because his siblings had moved out of the home, he looked at them more as people. Harry's condition

—in terms of symptoms, functioning, pathologic mechanisms of defense and separation stress—remained about the same as when he left the hospital, as did his intrapsychic structure. There was little capacity for autonomy, intimacy or creativity.

Parents of Harry

There had been dramatic changes in the family structures since Harry left the hospital which, however, cannot be credited in any great degree to the treatment. After leaving treatment, Harry began acting out again. He lived at home and got very involved in drugs and illegal activities, with his parents bailing him out each time. Harry credited his hitting rock bottom— i.e., being jailed for armed robbery with imprisonment being inevitable, being rejected by his girl, and finding he could no longer "con" himself or others —as "forcing" him to face up and change his ways.

The mother saw her own changes beginning prior to treatment, when she entered Alcoholics Anonymous. This, in addition to her individual work with the social worker and subsequent therapy with a local psychiatrist, facilitated her growth, particularly as an individual. She felt that she had previously been a leech on her husband and children and unavailable as a parent: "The only time we ever functioned as a family was in a time of crisis, and there were many." The mother felt that Harry suffered from this, and even after treatment, she felt incapable of setting the limits necessary: "We should have made him face up earlier and not bailed him out." The mother felt she was more available for the other children after she stopped drinking herself, but she still believed her greatest growth was personal.

Although trained as a nurse, the mother had not been able to work for 25 years. Three years ago she went back to work and continued at follow-up in a mid-management administrative positive at the Council of Art. She felt it was a big step for her in that, prior to this, she was chronically depressed, withdrawn and unable to function even at home. She loved her work and felt better about herself in general. She admitted, however, that her return to work was "forced."

The father quit his job to free lance in 1971. He had since not been able to support them adequately, so that the mother felt she had no choice but to work. It was amazing that she now functioned and her husband didn't. The mother seemed delighted by her own growth and productiveness and did not seem particularly upset that her husband was deteriorating.

The father described his own views of treatment. He initially welcomed the respite when Harry was hospitalized. At the same time, he noted that he naively believed the treatment would solve Harry's problems. (The hospital would take over for him— assume his responsibility.) When Harry wasn't cured, he was angry, disappointed and frustrated.

The father noted that he did learn about himself in treatment. He recalled having a terrible temper which he had trouble controlling and often inappropriately vented on Harry. This he learned to keep in better check. He also felt that the latter became an asset in relationship to his other children, in that he tried not to control them as much and did not displace onto them his own problems.

Another significant event occurred several months after Harry entered the Odyssey Program. The father went into a serious depression (he cited no connection with Harry but credited his depression to "mid-life crisis"). He entered treatment but quit after six or seven visits. He described again feeling that, if he went into therapy, the doctor would have all the answers—make him better. This didn't happen, and he felt cheated and left, believing therapy was useless. Since then the father had been in a chronic depression and had not worked. I might add that there was an effort on his part to cover this situation with a lot of esoteric, philosophical discussion.

Harry felt his parents had grown. He believed they tried very hard to communicate and trust him after treatment but that he was unable to use this to his advantage. He viewed them now as more content but believed that this was a function of not having children around to worry about. At the same time, he did not seem at all aware of the depth of his father's depression. The latter may in part be due to the infrequency of seeing his father since his entry into Odyssey House.

All of the other children manifested problems in separating and becoming autonomous. What was common among Harry's three siblings was that they left home as soon as possible. The youngest, a girl now 19, married a 25-year-old man when she was 17 and moved to Florida. Another daughter, 23, ran away from home about four years ago: "I wanted to be independent—have a life of my own." For three years she had been living with a man but didn't want to be tied down through marriage. She was attending a local college. A son, 21, "traveled awhile" and ended up in San Francisco, where he was studying photography and art. The parents believed that all three children had their problems but would never turn to drugs because of what they saw with Harry.

The father wanted to believe Harry was "over the hump," noted that he "conned us so much," he didn't trust him. He criticized his son for what he felt was his tendency to want to "feed off the fat of the land," referring to his continuance in Odyssey House and his desire to get his education funded through the government. He felt he should get a job and pay his own way (one wonders how much is a projection).

The mother hoped Harry had put his life together but believed that now *he* had to manage his affairs and that they, as parents, were no longer important and really shouldn't be involved. "He has to find his own way."

Clinical Impression

It would appear that the auxillary ego support of Odyssey House, which has decreased the necessity of the patient to function on his own, has been a great help, enabling him to take up some responsibility and face some of his feelings.

On examination, though, he shows a flat affect, the burned-out emotional quality of the ex-addict, a flat facial expression with little variation, eyes empty. The whole impression is of inner emptiness and lack of drive. I wonder, when he leaves Odyssey House supervision, how well he is going to do?

It is anybody's guess whether Harry will make it. His father is no longer able to "bail him out" and he has trouble holding himself together. His mother has grown and seems content in mothering her husband, and the family dynamics certainly continue to center on separations and dependency, but the children really seem to be out of it.

The parents will remain in the symbiotic tie to each other, but my guess is that the children will not be pulled back in—the damage is done. If there's to be reparative work and/or resolution, Harry will have to do it alone, i.e., without parents. They don't need him anymore—they have each other.

TED
Follow-Up Four Years After Discharge

History of Illness on Admission

Ted's present illness began approximately at age 13, when he let his hair grow and became rebellious at school, arguing and balking about rules and regulations. He was thrown out of summer camp for the use of drugs, and later out of school. At age 15, he threatened to kill his father, who had had a heart attack the previous year, with a knife, and was admitted to the hospital.

Past History

Ted's mother was over-solicitous and infantalized him. His father was the sole survivor of a group from a German concentration camp and had had two heart attacks. His maternal grandmother and grandfather had attempted suicide.

Ted's school history was good until the seventh grade. His social history was always poor.

Hospital Psychotherapy

Ted was hospitalized for 18 months, during which time there was great resistance to treatment, manifested by acting-out requiring many restrictions. He exhibited a tremendous amount of passive-aggressive behavior, as well as detachment of affect. None of the pathologic defense mechanisms was ever fully brought under control; for example, after he had worked through some of his depression, discharge had to be postponed three times because of his passive-aggressive defeating of specific plans. As a result, unsatisfactory discharge plans were for him to attend a private school and live with a friend of the family near the family's apartment.

Follow-Up Four Years After Discharge

When seen at follow-up, Ted, 20, had finished his second year of college. However, he was markedly depressed and frequently suicidal, was constantly taking marijuana and cocaine and was frequently not working at school and dropping courses. He lived at home, had no heterosexual relationships, felt close to no one.

Four months after discharge, in an abandonment depression, he returned to live at home and stopped treatment. He felt strongly that the hospital stay had been debilitating, had stripped him of whatever strength he had, whatever connection he had had with life. The pathological defense mechanisms of avoidance, denial, projection, acting-out, clinging and splitting were unchanged. He had no capacity to deal with separation stress. He saw his parents the same as before: "My mother is still unsuccessful, overprotective, the same as always; my father a tired old man. . . . I respect him a little more but don't get along any better." On examination, he had the same long, straggly hair, seemed depressed, intellectualized, with much passive-aggressiveness, acting-out and projection. There was no change in self or object representation; no capacity for autonomy, intimacy or creativity.

Parents of Ted

This family reminds me of what many of the family situations looked like when the patients were first admitted. The only difference is that the parents were resigned to their situation while fully aware of its pathological effect on all of them.

Ted spoke of the situation being essentially the same. His parents "make believe it's better, but it's not." Both parents were quite aware of their son's constant use of drugs, isolation from peers and alienation from life. Though the mother felt it was bad for him, she continued to literally finance his demise. It also seemed that Ted got a perverted sense of accomplishment in reminding them daily of their utter failure as parents.

The situation appeared to have been further compounded by the father's loss of his job. He apparently was pushed out of his position as partner several years ago and was forced to take a far less prestigious position for half his original salary. Both Ted and the mother described him as depressed, apathetic, having gained a great deal of weight, having difficulty sleeping and spending most of his time alone.

The mother felt that in some ways the misfortune had enhanced Ted's relationship to his father: "He's no longer that all-powerful man who was so critical of Ted." The mother noted that now both Ted and the father enjoyed knocking her, i.e., her traditional beliefs, "superfluous concerns over such things as cloth napkins." She accepted this, saying it was worth it because "now at least they communicate even though it's at my expense."

The mother did feel that her treatment with the social worker often confronted her with her constant concern about Ted and her husband, with complete omission of her own needs. "I guess my only justification in life was taking care of them. . . . I am a person and I'm entitled to having things for myself."

It was this awareness which the mother felt enabled her to return to school and earn a Masters degree in Library Science. She continued to work part-time and enjoyed the autonomy of having her own money. At the same time she bemoaned it, as her independence had in no way facilitated what she wanted most. Her husband "doesn't care about taking care of me—he only thinks of himself—otherwise he'd do the things that he knows are meaningful to me" (lose weight, dress well, not put his elbows on the table). She went on to say she had often thought of leaving but couldn't. "I have a responsibility to Ted; he can't handle it without me." She then immediately added that if the social worker heard her say that, she would blow up. I asked her about it, and the mother explained that the social worker said that was her whole problem—she made Ted dependent and that if she didn't expect more from him, he'd never be anything but dependent. The mother then rationalized her behavior but at the same time made it clear she needed him to be dependent to avoid facing the same issues in herself.

Clinical Impression

The severity of Ted's disorder suggests the diagnosis of psychopathic personality. However, it may be that the treatment helped him finish two years of college. He remains as depressed as before, acting out his rage at the mother's "mindless optimism" through passive hopelessness. Since the age of approximately 12, when adolescence brought with it the first requirement that Ted give up his symbiotic dependency and function on his own, he has tenaciously fought this move in his own passive-aggressive way. (Is he another example of being unable to internalize?)

This is a good example of how borderline parents clearly sacrifice their children to avoid dealing with their own problems with individuation. Ted stays around to get revenge by confronting them with their failure and also to avoid dealing with his own problems.

SUMMARY

There is a striking clinical consistency to these patients who did not respond in an appreciable way to treatment. Their parents, more seriously disturbed, seemed to have a greater need for the pathologic regressive behavior of their adolescents and therefore less capacity to perceive and respond to the adolescents' individuative needs. The adolescent patient also seemed to have less capacity to handle his own separation anxiety associated with his individuation. This came to a head clinically near the end of hospital therapy, when parent and adolescent banded together in joint unresolvable resistance to individuation. This led us to the concept that these adolescents lacked the capacity (perhaps constitutionally) to internalize the object, and therefore they were unable to separate. Nevertheless, one cannot help feeling somewhat shocked and dismayed at observing the truly extraordinary way in which these families remained locked in their mutually linked, symbiotic, dependent ways, absolutely inured to the destructiveness of their behavior.

10

Severe
Impairment

The two patients who committed suicide are described below.

KAREN

History of Illness At Admission

Karen, age 15, had a five- to six-month history, following the start of boarding school in the tenth grade, of severe acting-out, sexual promiscuity, truancy, stealing and taking drugs such as heroin, speed and pot.

Past History

Karen's maternal grandfather was committed to a state hospital. Her mother had asthma from age five to 15 and was severely depressed when the patient was 18 months old, requiring hospitalization. The mother had another depression when Karen was four. She started drinking, became an alcoholic and was again hospitalized. The patient started stealing at age four. Attention-getting behavior at school, as well as provocative behavior with peers, feeling lonely and unaccepted, was prominent.

Hospital Psychotherapy

Karen was hospitalized for 17 months. She had an acting-out resident as a therapist who colluded with her against the program to achieve only a simulation of therapy.

Follow-Up Four Years After Discharge

Karen was seen at age 20, four years after discharge. Since discharge, she had shown a progressive history of severe acting-out with addiction for several years to heroin. She had had an abortion. She had moved around from place to place, unable to succeed at school or at a job. She complained of her inability to be alone, of confusion, of lack of direction, and of desperately searching for someone to hold on to—very often a male drug addict. She showed little awareness or insight into the dynamics of her behavior. Separation stresses could only be handled with severe acting-out. There was a persistence of all pathological defense mechanisms, little change in self or object representations, very little autonomy or capacity for intimacy or creativity. Three weeks after this interview, Karen committed suicide with an overdose of a sedative.

Parents of Karen

(This is based on a short telephone conversation with the mother and an interview with Karen.)

The day Karen was interviewed, her mother was scheduled to be seen also. Karen came alone, however, because her mother didn't feel well. Karen was obviously disappointed, as they were to have spent the day together in the city, but she tried to cover the disappointment by saying it didn't matter. Karen did say that her mother had periodic attacks and had to take cortisone when they occurred.

Karen felt the treatment did her mother a world of good. "Prior to the treatment, she was an invalid in every way." Karen described that after treatment her mother divorced her father, went into Alcoholics Anonymous, and began working as a companion to an elderly person part-time.

When I spoke with the mother after Karen's death, she verified Karen's report and added that she felt guilty that she had gained so much from treatment and Karen hadn't gained enough.

Karen felt her father had received no benefit from treatment. She described that even during the treatment program he knocked it constantly, cancelled as many appointments as he could and acted like he knew it all. In spite of Karen's continued animosity to the father, she had invariably gone to him over the years when she was "down and out." Karen moved in with him, called him when she needed an abortion, and, when she went off drugs, lived in the same city with him. Karen felt that all of her contacts, though, were disappointing because "nothing I did was right, he always puts me down, he still checks me out to see if I'm clean" and "criticizes me for getting dependent, right now on welfare." Karen also felt anger toward him for acting as if he supported her since her discharge, when she declared she repaid every penny he ever gave her.

Karen felt her relationship with her mother had improved. Though she noted that their contact had been sporadic (sometimes none for a year or more), she felt "absence makes the heart grow fonder." At one point, she said she could no longer tolerate the life of a drug addict and called her mother to ask if she could come home. Her mother said she couldn't, because she feared her own sobriety would be at stake. Karen went to her father instead and denied any ill feeling toward her mother. She did feel respect for what her mother had been able to do in pulling herself together and viewed her as a model.

The two younger siblings were described as having difficulties but not of the same gravity as Karen. Karen felt that they suffered socially from her reputation. "They had to pay for my problems." Her brother, 19, had been failing in tenth grade and spent a year in a farm school (sounded like a residential placement) because "my father wouldn't pay for private school." The boy was graduating from high school the following Saturday and planning to enter college in the fall.

A sister, 13, remained at home and attended seventh grade at a local school. Karen reported she was a "slow learner" who worked hard and, though sensitive, had fared much better than either she or her brother ever did.

Clinical Impression

Karen's clinical history is strikingly like all of those patients with moderate impairment plus a mother who was quite ill and a father who himself had had many separation incidents early in life. She had a history of stealing from early age, and then severe acting-out with the use of heroin. Treatment was complicated by the fact that her therapist could not control her countertransference. Her evaluaters were very cautious about her seemingly improved status on follow-up, but she complained of being bored and desperate to find someone to hold on to. She was in contact with both her parents at the time. There would have been no way to predict a suicide, although the evidence would certainly indicate that the possibility of suicide could not be excluded.

One thing is clear—in spite of Karen's rage at her father and her belief that he had been unsupportive throughout and had made little gains from his involvement in treatment, he was the one she had been most consistently involved with since her discharge, for better or worse. Her contact with her mother was idealized and sporadic, and vignettes of their interaction involved disappointment, which was denied.

Although the mother certainly appears to have improved functionally since her divorce, one does not get the sense that Karen ever worked through her relationship with her mother or vice versa. The same would be true in her relationship to the father. The younger children, who appear to have thus far continued to function, may well have been spared parental immaturity.

PHIL
FOLLOW-UP FIVE YEARS AFTER DISCHARGE

History of Illness at Admission

Phil, age 14, had a six-month history, following transfer from a Yeshiva to a local high school, of increasing depression, loneliness, fear of being attacked by his peers and social isolation. Three weeks prior to admission, after a friend was attacked, he regressed and refused to attend school, staying at home. His behavior was angry and demanding with the mother; he punched her on occasion and kept a knife under his pillow.

Past History

Phil's mother was oversolicitous, engulfing, histrionic, manipulative and volatile, openly admitting to resenting responsiblity, feeling that the patient, the eldest of three children, had "fulfilled her life" and that she had treated him more like a peer as a child and used him to make up for the loneliness in the relationship with her husband. The father was distant, punitive and withdrawn. The patient's angry, demanding behavior began at age two, with the birth of his brother, when he would have long temper tantrums. He managed to do fairly well in early school, but after his second brother was born at age seven, the angry, demanding behavior returned, and he began to underachieve at school. He was rude to his peers and teachers, had difficulty concentrating and became socially isolated.

Hospital Psychotherapy

Phil was hospitalized for 15 months and had a good therapist There was a long initial period involving regressive, demanding, temper-tantrum behavior, refusing school, refusing to cooperate with the various activities and requiring many restrictions. This led into his depression, which was dominated by terrors of being abandoned and loss of love, should he grow—defended against by the expressed regressive wishes to return to the womb as the only way out. He felt that if he grew up, his mother would die. There was much splitting to manage his anger and much castration fear. As the treatment came to a close, it became clear that he could not return home, but no place could be found for him except a youth residence, to which he was discharged. Unfortunately, they required that he come completely under their auspices for treatment.

Follow-Up Five Years After Discharge

The follow-up is from the mother, who reported that after staying in the group home for three to four months Phil left and returned home—a fatal mistake—and stopped his therapy. He attended the local high school and did graduate. Following this, however, he seemed to fall apart. He could not hold a job, was not able to sleep (slept all day and was up all night), seemed to be chronically depressed with suicidal preoccupations, had very few friends and outside relationships, and seemed to have no idea of a career. He left home for San Francisco, where he lived for six months having the same difficulties, came home for a brief two months and then went to Israel to live on a Kibbutz. Six months later, at the age of 20, he committed suicide.

Clinical Impression

Phil's not being able to find a place to live away from home and still remain in the treatment program was probably a key to the tragedy. Although he finished high school, my guess is that his abandonment depression overwhelmed him and he was unable to move, especially living at home as a target for the mother's regressive projections. His efforts at distance were perhaps a way of dealing with this, and certainly the trip to Israel to a Kibbutz was perhaps to find a better home, free of these projections, which did not require autonomy—but this too failed and ended in suicide. The problem was a fixation which seemed more severe and a need for defense which was greater than in many of the other patients.

ROY
Follow-Up Five Years After Discharge (Psychotic)

History of Illness at Admission

Roy, age 16, had an illness which began at 14, when he was sent away to prep school. During the next two years, there were isolated episodes of stealing, getting drunk and being suspended. Finally, when his girlfriend rejected him, he returned home, entering the local high school. Then during that summer he went camping out West with two other boys and became increasingly isolated, withdrawn and had strong feelings of union with plants, trees and the outdoors. He returned home rebellious, talked about living his own life, pitched a tent in his parents' yard, exhibited poor hygiene, and began to speak bizarrely with paranoid ideas. When the parents frustrated him, he assaulted them and threatened to burn the house down. He was then hospitalized.

Past History

A maternal uncle was hospitalized with psychosis. His mother and father were divorced when Roy was four, after much fighting and drinking. The mother remarried when the patient was four. Roy was described as having been stubborn, demanding and temperamental from birth. He was enuretic until five, and had frequent, difficult-to-control temper tantrums. Between eight and nine, he had frequent crying spells and several times ran away from home. In early grades in school, he was preoccupied, forgetful, daydreaming.

Hospital Psychotherapy

Roy was in the hospital for 16 months, where his treatment was characterized by severe regressive periods with paranoid thinking and acting-out, once physically attacking a therapist. He appeared to work through his depression and was discharged; continuing with his therapist, he attended college and lived in a dorm.

Follow-Up Five Years After Discharge

Roy, age 24, five years after discharge, had been psychotic and hospitalized at a state hospital for the last four months with delusions, confusion and apathy.

Following discharge, he continued in treatment and managed to complete two years of college with high grades. At this point, he inherited some money and, in a resistance phase of his treatment, he acted out and stopped treatment when his therapist refused to approve his dropping out of college to have his parents support him. There was continued violent conflict with the family, as well as very poor peer relationships. He dropped out of school and wandered around the state. He ran out of money about six months before being hospitalized in a state mental institution.

Parents of Roy

Roy's parents spoke with the social worker on the telephone. The primary focus of the interview was Roy's functioning, but the social worker did obtain some information regarding the parents' perceptions of their own involvement in the treatment.

The parents reported that their relationship with Roy had been either non-eixstent or highly conflictual since his discharge. During the first two years after discharge, the parents frequently argued over how and what monies should be given to Roy. The stepfather bent over backwards to be factual and fair with money while the mother was consistently "more understanding" of Roy, initiating conciliatory moves toward him and often acquiescing to his requests. Following the depletion of Roy's trust fund, there was little contact until he was finally hospitalized.

The parents were able to provide a full chronology of the boy's functioning following discharge, despite what they considered a lack of involvement. They questioned how much they wanted to be involved, even at the point when he arrived home psychotic, acting and speaking in a bizarre manner.

I was struck by how similar their response was to their statements when Roy was admitted to the hospital. At both times the parents watched this boy decompensate dramatically but were unable to mobilize themselves until their safety was jeopardized.

While involved in treatment, the mother focused on her relationship with all of her children and how often her over-involvement, infantilization and over-indulgence was a source of conflict in the marital relationship. The mother reported that she and her husband were "agreeing more," and the younger siblings were functioning more independently. A daughter, age 21, was briefly married and divorced and was now back in school and less angry with the family, especially the stepfather. Another daughter was away at school, and a son (the only child of this marriage) was in college and doing well.

The parents reported that they felt they and Roy gained from their treatment. They did express concern that the younger children were initially angry at them for hospitalizing Roy, but this later dissipated.

The mother was disappointed by her son's deterioration and wondered if all the treatment he got was worth it. She was feeling that Roy was becoming like her brother—the latter was in and out of psychiatric hospitals all his life. She wondered if the genetic/organic elements of Roy's difficulties were greater than was suggested.

Clinical Impression

Roy was either psychotic when we saw him and we missed it, or he became psychotic later. If he were psychotic at the time, we may have underestimated the paranoid thinking, the poor hygiene and the social withdrawal. Even the report of the Rorschach at that time did not mention a thought disorder. The chances are that he was not schizophrenic at that time, but that after discharge there was an emergence of a process schizophrenia. It is worthwhile to note that as long as he remained in treatment, he continued to do well.

It would seem that Roy's clinical picture is more schizophrenic than borderline. He functioned best following discharge when provided financial and therapeutic support. Once left to his own devices—or lack of them—he again decompensated.

In spite of this, it would seem that the same condition was further compounded by his parents' inappropriate or non-existent responses to him. The mother seemed to want desperately to reactivate her relationship with Roy via her being quite willing to inappropriately overindulge him. But when the need for involvement seemed imperative (i.e., when he arrived home blatantly psychotic), neither she nor her husband were able to mobilize themselves to get him hospitalized but provided him with money to "get out." The younger children, by inference, appear to have had some problems individuating. I would speculate that the children had better integrated internal structures which served them in the process of separation.

STEVE

Follow-Up One Year After Discharge (Psychotic)

History of Illness at Admission

Steve, age 17, had a two-year history prior to admission of increasing acting-out, beginning with getting high on drugs, LSD, daily pot, poor achievement at school, antisocial behavior such as shoplifting, fraudulently obtaining records through the mail, and wrecking his car twice. He took a high number of amphetamines and LSD, became psychotic, led police on a wild 100-mile-per-hour chase for 12 miles, attempted to have sex with his mother and was hospitalized.

Past History

The mother had an automobile accident when Steve was two and a half, and had to spend a lot of time in bed, so the sister took the nurturing role. When he was 10, the mother started working, and the patient felt neglected and became rowdy in school. He always had trouble socializing because of poor athletic ability.

Hospital Psychotherapy

Steve was hospitalized for one year. He had a poor resident who had difficulty controlling behavior, but nevertheless Steve did get into his depression, feeling empty, not wanting to live, but working through some of his anger at the mother's controlling and manipulative ways. He was caught in the midst of the closing of the unit and eventually was discharged to begin college.

Follow-Up One Year After Discharge

When seen one year after discharge Steve, 20, had had an abandonment depression and had gone back to drugs, including drug dealing when the parents took away his allowance. His conflict with his parents increased when they tried to set limits, and the patient projected more. His relationships with girls were clinging and dependent. He left psychotherapy and was no longer interested in therapy. There was persistence of all pathological mechanisms of defense, no change in self and object representations and minimal capacity to deal with separation stress. Six months after this interview, the patient was hospitalized again with a psychotic episode, again making sexual overtures toward his mother.

Parents of Steve

In spite of multiple complaints, both parents felt the program helped Steve, and the mother felt she had gained from it as well. The father "never found anything to hang his hat on," felt he was different from other parents who "liked baring their souls," and found he adamantly disagreed with the social worker. He cited still being unnerved that the social worker felt he was "unrealistic." This came up in relation to his being unconcerned about Steve's demolishing a $10,000 car. The father was consistent in that he bought Steve another car upon his discharge, which Steve again demolished the following year—on the anniversary date of his discharge. The father continued to financially support Steve for the most part. He resented, however, that Steve always said he didn't need his parents and could do it on his own. Out of spite, the father said he would like to withdraw support "to test him," but he really didn't think Steve could make it. The mother believed that he could.

The mother felt her relationship with the social worker was supportive, but not in relation to Steve. The father had open heart surgery while Steve was hospitalized. "I couldn't have made it through without her during that time. . . . She was a sounding board for me. . . . I guess seeing her made it more tolerable not to see Steve. . . . I didn't always agree with her, but she did help me see some things."

Since Steve's discharge, the parents described "walking on eggs" all the time with him. The mother felt she tended to be hyper-critical of Steve before and now tried to see "the good points." She also (as did the husband) felt that Steve tried to con them into giving him things. The mother said she usually felt she didn't know what to do. "If I give in, it may be the same old thing—he won't do for himself. If I don't, I'm afraid I may be being unreasonable."

On the other hand, the mother did continue to be quite involved. She noted, for example, that: "I never let more than a couple of days go by without calling him." She was also upset that, since Steve was discharged, they had not met more of his friends. The parents were also annoyed that they had not seen his apartment, but then credited it to Steve's idiosyncrasies and took a "hands off" approach. They seemed content that at least he visited home once a week.

Their criticisms about the hospital focused on the forced separation from Steve. Both parents felt "like patients," complaining that they should have known more of what was going on and that Steve should have been allowed home sooner. The mother couldn't understand why Steve's doctor got upset when she insisted on knowing what and how well Steve was eating.

One minute the parents attributed grandiose capabilities to the boy and the next they were highly critical. They noted his keen mind and ability to think. Later, they spoke of his "poor grades, crumby jobs and poor appearance." They had no doubt that he would be a competent banking expert, but noted that he probably could not survive without their continued financial support. They then heavily subsidized him via cars, trips, etc.

Steve expressed dislike for his parents—particularly his father, whom he viewed as "uncompromising, rigid and unaffectionate." He also felt that his father was "closed to new ideas, has a victorian set of values." At follow-up he felt they got along, i.e., "don't fight as much," but he wished he could "disregard them completely." Though on one level he said this, at the same time he visited weekly. Steve believed his parents were more accepting of him following his discharge. "I can yell at them when I feel like it—I can tell them, I don't want you in my life." He cited their honoring his not wanting them in his apartment as proof of their respect of his autonomy.

Steve spoke of his relationship with his sister. His view of her behavior toward her own child might reflect his feelings about his parents' behavior toward him. The sister was 28, married, with a seven-year-old boy, and living in Chicago. Steve believed his nephew had emotional problems but that these were the mother's fault. "She spoils him rotten—now he's a brat, and she feels guilty." The sister was taking the boy to a psychiatrist. Steve was furious about this. "There is no reason to put the boy at the mercy of psychiatry because of her guilt. She's more concerned about relieving her own guilt than she is about helping the boy."

Clinical Impression

It was our impression that Steve was most likely psychopathic. We may have minimized the history of sexual overtures to his mother, his poor social relationships and his original psychotic attack, which we thought was due to separation anxiety. It appears that the diagnosis should be schizophrenia with a psychopathic façade.

The most striking aspect of the parents' interaction and perceptions with and of Steve is the discrepancy between the parental view of Steve's functioning and his presentation of himself. The parents show little awareness of Steve's sociopathic behavior, tending to present primarily the positive aspects of his behavior. Though they do not have enough contact to know, they denied the severity of his difficulty, even when he lived under their roof. It is possible that Steve "continues to con" them, but it is also true that the parents also have a proclivity for denial.

The parents continue to overindulge the boy, view him as their "little boy" and understand his demands for autonomy as idiosyncratic rather than expectable attempts at individuation. The father seems proud of his disagreement with the ideas gleaned from treatment and continues to function as before. The mother is certainly more reflective about her behavior toward Steve and his needs, but states quite clearly her continued conflict over what her role as mother should be at this point.

SUMMARY

The follow-up of these patients illustrates some of the clinical traps and pitfalls involved in working with borderline patients. Both suicides can be related to therapeutic errors: In one case (Karen), the therapist's countertransference was never brought under control, and in the other (Phil), the post-hospital continuity of the treatment was interrupted. Although neither of these errors was the direct cause, they have to be viewed as contributory.

The third patient, who eventually became psychotic, illustrates the sometimes extraordinary difficulty in distinguishing between a borderline patient's temporary psychotic reaction to separation stress and a true psychosis.

11

A Guide for the Clinical Evaluation of Therapeutic Change

The spectrum of change is reviewed here to enable the reader to put the clinical details which he was just digested into a larger perspective. Careful study of this spectrum will provide a guide which the therapist can use to monitor or track the therapeutic progress or regression of his own borderline patients. The therapist should begin by tracking the slow, small incremental increases in self-assertive adaptation to reality and in self-image as seen in the moderate and mild (subgroup B) impairment categories. This progresses to full self-assertive adaptation to reality with a positive self-image but with the persistence of pathologic defenses against separation anxiety and abandonment depression as seen in the mild (subgroup A) impairment category. Finally, as seen in the minimal impairment category, the patient progresses

211

to complete separation of self representation from the object representation with the disappearance of splitting and the other pathologic defenses against separation anxiety and the resultant flowering of individuation.

The therapist who is able to "lock" the radar of his therapeutic perception on these fluid movements back and forth as they evolve in the treatment will himself develop a unique understanding of the process and be better prepared to help his patient. The usefulness of the scale is shown by the way it helps to differentiate changes in adaptation from changes in intrapsychic structure; for example, if the patient is functioning well without symptoms, and the therapist feels he may have separated from the symbiotic relationship with the mother, the therapist can check by determining if the patient exhibits whole self and object representations in the transference and if there occurs the resultant flowering of individuation (see Chapter 6). If there is not evidence of whole self and object representations and the beginnings of individuation, in all likelihood the patient has not fully separated.

MINIMAL IMPAIRMENT

These patients showed the most dramatic improvement. They had worked through the rage, depression and despair of their abandonment depression, separated from the symbiotic relationship with mother, and received the resultant benefits for ego development and the development of object relations.

Their object relations developed approximately to the stage of object constancy with whole self and object representations that were realistically based. There was strengthening of the ego, as splitting and other pathologic defense mechanisms (projection, acting-out, passivity, and avoidance and denial) were replaced by higher-level mechanisms. Regressive behavior gave way to self-assertive attempts to cope with and adapt to reality. The vulnerability to separation stress was drastically reduced, the capacities for creativity and autonomy developed, and, as individuation took place, the self emerged, to be consolidated and expressed in a flowering of newly found wishes and interests. Intimacy still posed some problems which were dealt with by experimentation rather than avoidance and denial.

MILD IMPAIRMENT

The minimal and mild groups differ little in impairment of functioning, but there is a chasm of difference from the perspective of ego development and object relations. Although they function well, the 13 patients in the mild group have not separated from the symbiotic relationship with the mother, and, therefore, they have not achieved whole object relations. Consequently, they require pathologic defenses against separation anxiety and abandonment depression to maintain an entirely adequate level of functioning. Within this mild impairment group, we were able to identify two subgroups (A with six patients and B with seven patients) based on the intensity of that need for pathologic defenses, as well as on the degree to which there had been consolidation of the self, i.e., the degree to which the patients had increased the capacity to assert themselves, to regulate self-esteem and activate their wishes in reality.

Subgroup A (Six Patients)

All have shown at follow-up an improvement in self representation, a feeling of the self being worthwhile, which is more realistically based. They are more open to their own feelings, have a greater capacity to identify their own individuated wishes and thoughts and express them in reality, to regulate their own self-esteem, as well as to assert themselves and, to a certain extent, to take charge of the direction of their lives.

However, although their self representation is better and their adaptation is improved, they have not fully separated and do not have whole self and object representations. They made one or another environmental arrangement—usually a relationship—which acts out the RORU (or WORU)—pathologic ego alliance to defend against further separation anxiety and abandonment depression. There is a mild to moderate persistence of one or more of the original pathologic defense mechanisms. As a result, they remain vulnerable to separation stress and further experiences of depression, and there is not the flowering of individuation or self-expression seen in the minimal group.

Moderate Impairment

These patients were rated mild impairment because, although their surface functioning was adequate, when one looked beneath that surface at the psychodynamic basis responsible for that functioning it became apparent that there was less improvement in self representation than the subgroup A patients and a more intense need for defense against separation anxiety and abandonment depression. Although they felt better about themselves and were somewhat better able to assert themselves, this change was mild compared with the A patients. They could not take direction of their lives. They could not identify what they wanted and activate and pursue their interests in reality. There was moderate pathology in the self representations as well as in object relations.

Subgroup B (Seven Patients)

These patients were not helped much by treatment, but although the treatment made very little dent on their defenses against the abandonment depression, it did evidently increase to some extent their capacity to cope with reality. They continued to suffer from severe symptomatology and moderate impairment of functioning. Their clinical pictures were dominated by the need to defend against the abandonment depression at the cost of adaptation to reality. There was little or no autonomy, intimacy or creativity and no change in intrapsychic structure.

However, within this dismal picture, there were some positive aspects which may have been due to treatment. For example, one patient finished the second year of college, another graduated from high school and a third was able to graduate from college. The destructiveness of the acting-out of three patients were markedly decreased, and one patient, after living the life of a junkie for five years, was able to overcome his drug habit through the help of Odyssey House. This patient recently (after the study was finished) graduated from college and started professional school. It is entirely possible that without hospital treatment, none of these achievements would have taken place.

SEVERE IMPAIRMENT

Two patients were still hospitalized, two became psychotic and two committed suicide.

12

Parents' Clinical Outcome

This chapter shifts the emphasis from the adolescent to the parents to describe how they responded to treatment. It details how their attitudes changed toward themselves, toward the adolescent, toward the spouse, toward their roles as parents and toward the communication patterns in the family. It also describes whether they supported or resisted the adolescent's individuation and what mechanisms of adaptation were used to manage the adolescent's emancipation from the family.

Both parents of each patient had casework treatment once a week throughout the adolescent's hospital stay, usually individually but sometimes jointly. In addition, they had group psychotherapy once a week and a period of several months of family interviews with their adolescent.

Fourteen of the 31 sets of parents improved, 16 showed no

change and one got worse. Among the 14 who improved, there were three themes:

1. Both mother and father improved (three couples).
2. One parent (usually mother) improved, but the other (usually father) did not (10).
3. One mother improved during treatment but relapsed on discharge.

An example of each group is given below.

1. BOTH MOTHER AND FATHER IMPROVED

Parents of Marie*

There were the only two parents who continued in individual psychotherapy after their daughter was discharged, which may help to explain the fact that they also were the only parents who were able to provide positive support for their daughter's individuation. They both became aware that they had projected their own emotional problems on their daughter, had scapegoated her and been unable to provide appropriate parental support. The mother particularly changed a great deal, felt less like a child, was happier and more content with herself and her marriage and more confident in her daughter. She was thus more able to let her go. The father had also improved significantly but had somewhat less confidence in his daughter. The mother had withdrawn her clinging projection on Marie, invested herself in her own life and had returned to school. Their continued joint investment in psychotherapy seems to have prevented any destructive efforts to compensate for Marie's leaving the family unit.

2. ONE PARENT IMPROVED

The most common theme was the mother's (in one case the father's) responding to treatment almost exclusively in terms of

---

* See pages 108 to 116 for patient's history.

herself and her own problems, which enabled her to pull back from the intense involvement with the adolescent, contain her negative projections and invest more affect in herself, achieving greater autonomy. These mothers' behavior became self-directed, often for the first time, with new or better jobs and new interests and activities outside the family. Despite this improvement in their own lives, the mothers were not able to extend themselves to provide maternal nurturing and support for their adolescents' individuation. Nevertheless, the withdrawal of the projection itself was helpful to the adolescent. They, too, paid a price for this change, as I shall describe later in this chapter.

Mother of Betty*

This mother was quite candid and aware of her own difficulties and how they related to and interfered with her daughter's development. She noted that before treatment, she had denied her difficulties with her detached and unavailable husband on whom she had given up, drank heavily and was dependent on her daughter.

She felt her therapy forced her to look at her own trouble. She had returned to work as a nurse and had difficulty starting because of her guilt about her other two children at home. She still became depressed and had difficulty with her husband. The father, on the other hand, had changed from being aloof and withdrawn to being unpredictable and intrusive, having rage outbursts at Betty. He often viewed her individuation as a problem. There was a possibility that the father and two remaining daughters were binding together in one symbiotic unit and projecting on and excluding Betty as the bad object for individuating.

3.   MOTHER IMPROVED BUT RELAPSED

Mother of Bart**

The mother felt she was helped by treatment to see her over-

---

* See pages 102 to 108 for patient's history.
** See pages 171 to 175 for patient's history.

protectiveness of her son and her need to lean heavily on him since her husband had died. But when Bart signed out and returned home, she unconsciously indulged his remaining at home and not making moves on his own. The cessation of treatment required her to again use her son to deal with her own anxiety.

EMOTIONAL ADAPTATIONS OF THE FAMILY TO THE CHANGES BROUGHT ABOUT BY TREATMENT

What happens in the system of communication in the family between parents or among parents and other siblings when one of the family members is removed or his participation is changed? Does the mother turn her projections onto the other children or onto the father? Do the mother and father come into conflict?

The kinds of adaptation were a reflection of the degree to which change had occurred in the patient. In the three families where both mother and father improved in continued treatment, there seemed to be no destructive adaptations. These families were buttressed by the fact that the mother had continued to receive support from treatment, generally had stopped her clinging projection on the adolescent, and had invested herself more in her own life, taking up activities of her own.

There were three divorces and three marriages in serious conflict. In five cases, the mother improved substantially in treatment while the father did not, while in one marriage the father improved and the mother did not. In two other cases, the marriages remained stable. In one situation, the mother improved and the father did not, and there remained three seriously ill siblings. In another family, the father improved but the mother did not and she clung to the patient's younger brother, who became seriously ill.

Where both parents improved under treatment, there were constructive adaptations to the change; where one parent (usually the mother) improved and the other did not, there was the risk of divorce, of severe conflict in the marriage, or of the unimproved parent clinging to the remaining siblings, resulting in further clinical illness. Although a few did better, usually the best one can expect is for the mother to give up her clinging, invest herself in her own life, and develop interests and activities of her own which reduce her tendency to cling to her adolescent. It is hoped the father will either improve with the mother or go along without combating her.

In those families that showed no change there was, of course, less need for any kind of adaptational change, since the pathologic tie remained. Clearly, the major theme would be denial of any pathology and continued pathologic behavior. In several, the parents admitted the continuing pathology, but, apparently resigned, accepted and indulged the patient's behavior. In six of the 31 cases, parents denied that siblings were seriously and clinically ill.

SUMMARY

Approximately half of the parents improved in response to treatment. By far the most common theme was the improvement of the mother (in one instance, the father); in three cases both mother and father improved. It appears that continued treatment beyond the hospital stay is necessary for the parents to be able to continue to grow and to allow the adolescent to grow. The fact that mothers improved more than fathers is further evidence of the vital nature of the mother's tie to the borderline adolescent, for when the tie is interrupted, the mother has no choice but to find some other source for this libidinal energy. The mothers invested it in their own selves and in their own development; they were able to develop new interests and activities which reduced their temptation to project and cling to their adolescents. They could not, however, function in a maternal way. It was all they could do to manage themselves and not cling, let alone make an effort to nurture the patient.

If the mother improved and the father did not, she ran the risk of severe conflict with the father and/or divorce. A father who improved without the mother ran the same risk. If the parents did not improve, as was the situation in 16 out of 31 cases, a number of themes emerged. The major theme was continued pathological behavior with denial of difficulty. In other cases, where an adaptation had to be made because the adolescent had left the home, there would be clinging to the next sibling, sometimes to a number of siblings, with clinical illness on the part of the sibling.

Why did the fathers not respond more to treatment? Was it because the therapeutic effort was not as intense? It seems to me that it was because the nature of the father's tie to the adolescent was not nearly as intense as the mother's; further, the father's defense often consisted of distancing and detachment, which served as a good defense in a treatment that occurred only once a week.

13

Clinical Outcome: Outpatient Psychotherapy Alone

The preceding chapters illustrated the range of improvement with hospital psychotherapy. Is it possible to achieve similar results with outpatient psychotherapy alone, without hospitalization? This is a pressing question in the light of current governmental and third-party payers' emphasis on community mental health centers and outpatient psychotherapy, which has resulted in the curtailing or closing of long-term inpatient facilities for adolescents.

Although our study was not designed to answer this question, two borderline adolescents, whom I had treated in my private office years ago and reported on at the time, returned serendipitously to see me ten years later. They are presented here, one in detail and the other in summary, to provide some evidence on this question and to add to the perspective gained from the study of inpatient psychotherapy.

FRANK

Follow-Up Ten Years After Treatment

Frank's case is presented in detail because it demonstrates well how this developmental theory sheds light on the transference and informs the therapist not only when and how to intervene, but what response to expect from the intervention.

History of Present Illness

Frank 16, a junior in high school, had been battling with his parents for several years, was performing poorly in school and taking methedrine, pot and LSD. He was shooting speed intra-venously and getting into violent fights with his mother, after which he would not come home but would wander the streets. He was active with an antisocial gang and was occasionally picked up by the police.

On examination, Frank was short, extremely pale, painfully thin, with long, straggly black hair. He wore a black leather jacket, black turtleneck shirt, blue jeans and sneakers. His expressions varied from a perpetual snarl or sadistic grin to an infantile, childish smile.

Past History

Frank, the oldest of three children, was a very bright, energetic, articulate and creative infant and child. His mother, a librarian, saw in him a perfect instrument for the belated fulfillment of her own frustrated ambitions, academic and otherwise. He was clearly the apple of her eye. She overindulged and rewarded his compliant, clinging behavior, failed to set appropriate limits, directed and dominated every aspect of his life. When he deviated from her wishes, she reacted with criticism and dramatic rage outbursts. On the other hand, the father, a businessman, was rather passive and inadequate; he also was dominated by his wife and took very little interest in his son. As so often happens in borderline families, Frank's poorly disciplined and self-indulgent ways, partially hidden behind his evident intellectual ability, as well as his ability to manipulate, were denied by both parents throughout latency and childhood. When he went away for three months in his twelfth summer, this separation initiated an abandonment depression and set the stage for the battle that began on his return. Unable to tolerate his mother's domination, he turned to intense and severe acting-out.

Intrapsychic Structure

Frank's RORU consisted of a maternal part-object which was omnipotent, providing total approval and supplies for compliant and clinging behavior. The rewarding part-self representation was of being a good, passive child who was also omnipotent and quite unique and special. The affect was of feeling good and being loved.

The WORU consisted of a part-object which was domineering, depriving, attacking, engulfing and powerful. His withdrawing part-self representation which he described in the interviews was of being a creep, an insect, a bug, having no suggestion or self-assertion, being a small and helpless victim. The most important component of his profound abandonment depression was rage. The pathological ego's defense mechanisms consisted prominently of avoidance, denial, clinging, splitting, projection, identification and severe acting-out.

The pathologic ego formed alternate alliances with the rewarding and the withdrawing part-units. These alliances functioned as follows. When the alliance was with the rewarding part-unit, the abandonment depression was internalized and clinging was the principal defense. When it was the withdrawing part-unit, the abandonment depression was externalized and projection and acting-out were the principal defenses. He would project part of the rewarding unit on his peers, who then became the maternal part-object, giving him supplies for heavy drug usage, for complying with their standards. At the same time that he would spend a great deal of time fighting with the mother, he was also able to project the rewarding object representation on her, and he would have long, reunion-type conversations with her.

The major alliance seen clinically was with the withdrawing

part-unit. He projected the withdrawing part-object representation back on his mother, as well as all authority figures in society; by acting-out his rage at being deprived, he seemingly solved his problem from the past in the present. Instead of being the small, helpless victim of his mother's wishes, he was the powerful victimizer. In therapy, the first question that was brought up by his behavior was: Would I, the therapist, resonate and respond, either with the rewarding unit projection or with the withdrawing unit projection or alternately with both?

Outpatient Psychotherapy

Four interviews with Frank and one with the mother and father were used to arrange for Frank to be seen three times a week by me, and the mother and father once a week by the social worker. In the fifth session, while denying his depression, Frank regaled me with glee about attacking his mother to see if I would resonate with his WORU projection and join him in attacking her. I immediately began the task of confrontation by casting grave doubts on his happy mood. I said that it certainly looked as if he was enjoying himself, but I couldn't believe that he was enjoying it that much. Nobody in so much conflict with his mother could be so happy.

I went on to further challenge him with the statement that underneath his superficial glee he was basically very unhappy but unable to admit it. I continued: "Perhaps you are expressing the anger at your mother this way, not only to get back at her but to also keep yourself from feeling badly." I elaborated that this unfortunately kept his feelings from coming to the surface in his interviews, and as a result their meaning remained elusive. I ventured to say that such expression might give him transitory relief but certainly seemed to me to do him much more harm than good. It might be to his interest to air his feelings in the interviews and make an effort towards controlling them at home. Actually, I added, if his thesis that it was all his mother's fault were correct, then he should move away from home, and he and I really had no business together. But I suspected that there was a good deal more to it.

Frank pushed his testing of the withdrawing image projection further. He said how poorly he did in school: "It's to get back at my mother—I don't care." "That's too bad," I said. He was taken aback by this and said: "What do you mean?" I replied: "It's always very sad to see a bright person's potential for satisfaction and achievement thrown out the window in the service of a battle from which he cannot escape unwounded." This brought to Frank's attention the reality destructiveness of his behavior, which he was denying. Having failed with the withdrawing image projection, Frank now wanted to test if I would resonate with his rewarding image projection. He said that if he should ever control his anger, he would feel so bad he would have to see me right away. I responded, "I'm afraid that you will have to maintain control over a period of time until you can get to see me; this is a long-term problem, and emergency measures are not going to solve it."

Each time he verbalized his self-destructive acting-out and attempted to make of it a virtue, I quickly countered by pointing out the reality that he had denied, i.e., that he had harmed himself, and I wondered why. The confrontation of the withdrawing image projection caused him to again change defense and to go back to testing if I would resonate with the rewarding image projection.

In the sixth session, after we had already agreed that he would pay out of his own money $15.00 a week for treatment, he stomped into the room saying he refused to pay. "Why should I give money to you? I need it for clothes and drugs and records. It's my money and I'm not going to be pushed around by you. My friends think I'm a patsy to pay you."

I said, "It seems to me that you want to have your cake and eat it, too. You may say you want to be on your own, but you don't seem to want to support yourself as much as you are able to. You want the results of the treatment, but you just don't want to do what it requires." I then elaborated that his payment of the fee was not forced on him but was proposed as part of the requirements of treatment to which he had agreed. I said that refusing to pay was distorting his relationship with me by denying our contract; he was attempting to see me as his mother and the $15.00 fee as being imposed upon him as my wish to push him around; therefore, he must rebel against me as he had rebelled against his mother. I pointed out that by so doing, he was possibly throwing out the baby with the bathwater.

He repeated that his friends considered him a sucker to pay a doctor this way. His own money should be used for drugs and records. "Let's see if I have you correctly," I said. "The only useful purpose for money is for immediate pleasure?" He said, "That's right, Doc," to which I responded, "It seems to me that people who do that end up nowhere, don't they?" He said, "Yes, but they have a lot of fun doing it." He then said that defiantly he would push drugs to get the extra money, and that when he was pushing drugs he got money and prestige, to which I commented, "Yes, you get everything but self-respect. Rather than finding pleasure and being on your own and supporting yourself, you take the easy way out and prey on other people's weaknesses, in order to make it easier on yourself. What kind of self-respect do you think that builds?"

This test having been passed, Frank integrated the confrontation and came in to the next interview with his $15.00. He slumped into a chair, looked at me angrily and, testing me again, demanded that I ask him questions, to which I responded: "I'm afraid you have it all wrong, Frank. I can *help* you out of this, but I can't do it for you. We will have to work together. Maybe we should look into the beginnings of some of these painful feelings."

The acting-out of both the rewarding and withdrawing image projections having been confronted, Frank for the first time was beginning to take a look at his intrapsychic problem. This led him to express his feeling that he was a carbon copy of his mother's wishes. For example, he went to an expensive camp of his mother's choosing. He disliked it intensely, but he refrained from telling his parents because they had spent so much on it. He recalled how he had asked for a musical instrument, not because he wanted it but because his mother wanted him to have it. This caused his depression and feelings of inadequacy to surface and required him to defend himself by going home and erupting, i.e., acting out the WORU in a rage. He saw his room as a visible symbol of the childhood compliance to his mother. Determined that his room should be an expression of himself, he wrote obsenities on the wall in chalk. Needless to say, this set off another battle with his parents, in which he twisted the contents of my remarks to use them against his parents, saying, "The doctor says that my problems are all your fault."

In the next session he told me what he had said to his parents and I reminded him how he distorted my views and that this way of expressing his anger was potentially very harmful to him. For example, he might actually provoke his mother and father into taking him out of treatment, if he kept using what occurred in treatment against them and this could not possibly be in his best interest; nor could I believe that writing obscenities in chalk on the wall was an expression of his real self. Somewhere between this old way of compliance and his way of rebellion was an expression appropriate to him, but he was unable to find it because he was devoting himself to being a sacrificial victim in the holy war with his mother. I mentioned, incidently, that in the previous interview he had talked more about why he had complied so readily with his parents wishes, and I wondered if his angry outburst could have been a response to this awareness. I was trying to link feelings to behavior. Frank responded hopelessly that there seemed to be no alternative to taking drugs; otherwise, he would be doing nothing and be out of it and bored. All his friends took drugs. I said that it was a very sad state of affairs that one either had to be on drugs or have nothing to do. I asked him what had happened to the potential he had shown only a few years before, when he had a number of interests and hobbies from which he derived a lot of satisfaction. I also wondered if these potentials had been drowned by the drugs. I then drew a contrast between the immediacy of the pleasure of the drug experience and other satisfactions which, however, required time, effort and self-discipline but offered a more abiding kind of pleasure and were not destructive.

Frank understood what I was saying and finished the session

with a sigh, saying: "I feel trapped between seeing the destructiveness of this urge and being unable to control it." I responded, "Perhaps you may feel trapped at the moment, but you don't have to remain so."

The next session he allowed that he was not straight yet, but he had given away his works for shooting drugs intravenously. He reported that he had taken mescaline for the first time and that it had made him very depressed. He spontaneously picked up the theme of the last session, saying that he was depressed afterwards. He then revealed for the first time what was bothering him about himself, the first indication that his testing of me was diminishing. He was beginning to develop confidence. Frank said, "I think something is missing inside me; I feel emasculated; I don't seem to be able to feel mad or strong or anything else, and a drive to do things is missing. I know I should face it, but I don't. I have no interest in girls, and I have no competitive feelings. I can't say no, and there doesn't seem to be anything I can do about it. It makes me feel terrible."

To this I responded, "I can see how these feelings would upset you. The purpose of the treatment is to deal with these feelings." Having faced his abandonment depression and the self representation of the withdrawing part-unit, he now turned again to acting out the rewarding unit as a defense. He got mad and said, "Well, you don't do anything about it." I said: "You mean if it's not an instant cure, I am doing nothing." I wondered aloud if maybe this was not why he was so tied up in drugs—they took his mind off how badly he felt. I wondered also if he was not being so daring and courageous with the gang to conceal the feelings of inadequacy he had about himself. He was actually acting this way to create a smokescreen, to conceal his lack of fire. His answer was: "It's really to force fire." Then he asked me what conflicts I saw and said, "I tried to fix the situation by acting independent and dominant; it doesn't make me feel that way, and it doesn't work." I mentioned that acting and feeling are two different things and that his efforts to act independent had so far been very destructive. I wondered why he couldn't be independent in a constructive way or if perhaps some of the reason had to do with the conflicts with his mother and father. To this he replied, "My mother forced her way, her planned desires on me, and I feel trapped with her; I disappointed my father. I had a strong inner urge to beat the insides out of her, but I'm afraid I wouldn't succeed. And now I have thoughts about killing myself as a way out, as a way to solve the problem."

In this interview, he was no longer talking about his acting-out, but had begun to get to the conflicts that lay beneath the acting-out. In the next session, predictably retreating to defense, Frank was silent for a number of minutes, after which he finally said, "It's marvelous to get an opportunity to sleep in an air-conditioned room for 30 minutes." I wondered why he was silent and then sarcastic and asked if he was upset about what he had talked about the last time and was protecting himself against resuming it. He said he couldn't remember the previous session. I recalled it for him—his feeling of being trapped by the mother, his disappointment in the father, his thoughts of suicide. He responded, "Well, I'm awfully glad I didn't remember all that; it would have been very depressing. At this point, he again went deeper into his conflict with his mother: "I flair up at her, but I still want to talk to her and that bothers me. I'm afraid of some power she has over me. As a kid my father told me that he was weak physically—I guess he was sickly. They both make me feel guilty that I am such a terrible person and killing them with my behavior. It makes me feel angry to feel guilty, and I think of the nastiest things I can say to them." I interpreted that his parents were expressing their anger and disappointment at him for failing their expectations. He then recalled how he had felt when his parents attacked him, saying, "They never stood up for me as a child; help was the last thing in the world I could expect from them. For example, they would bail me out of jail and never think that I was right, they always made me feel wrong and I felt cheated." I then suggested that he was disappointed in his expectations that his parents would support him, and he was expressing it by retaliating against their expectations. Unfortunately, at the same time, he was defeating himself. He agreed with this interpretation by describing an incident where his mother told him he must ask me if it was feasible for him to get a driver's license. He said, "She never thinks I can do anything right, she always expects the worst; and when she does, I give it to her. If I do get a car, I'll drive recklessly, just because she always predicts disaster."

This brief resume of Frank's treatment emphasized the actual verbal interchange to convey the flavor of the therapeutic confrontations, which seem to me to be the key to establishing a therapeutic alliance with the adolescent. Confrontation of the defensive acting-out and alternately of the alliances with the RORU and the WORU led to abandonment depression, which led to defense, which again was confronted, eventually leading the patient back to his intrapsychic problem, i.e., the abandonment depression. Treatment continued through the working-through phase for about two years, by which time Frank had graduated from high school, spent a year at college and a summer in Europe. At this point, he was entering the last or separation phase of treatment and, rather than work through his separation anxiety in the transference, he decided to act out a defense against it by leaving treatment and going to Europe once again.

Frank, Age 26—Ten-Year Follow-Up

Frank's acting-out provided the illusion of independence in behavior while, at the same time, he retained his dependence on the intrapsychic image of the therapist. The acting-out prevented him from giving up this image and becoming truly autonomous. He went to Europe where he joined the army and functioned well as a soldier for about eight months, until he became ill with colitis and received a medical discharge. He then returned home to live with his parents and attend a local college, where he earned a degree in Business Administration, graduating with honors.

He described his academic development at college as follows: The first year he coasted and took a lot of courses to find out what he wanted to do—a good description of individuation through experimentation. His second year he decided on Business Administration as a major, because he wanted a background in business, and on French as a minor, because he wanted a window on another culture.

He then got a Masters in Business Administration and was at the time of the interview working at a prestigious brokerage firm on Wall Street. He reported that he occasionally had colitis but that he had had no depression for several years, until very recently. He had no problem with anger or with acting-out and very little conflict with authority.

He described himself now as being quite content with himself. He felt that he had overcome his doubts about his self-assertion. He said things had been going very well for him, but that if they didn't go so well, he might have more trouble. His aggression seemed now much more channeled into constructive coping activity. He reported that he could be self-assertive without having to be destructive and that he had developed for the first time an interest in sports, not team sports but individual sports—jogging and tennis.

He described his relationship with his parents: "When I left home, they got scared that I wouldn't return. They decided to leave me alone. When they decided to leave me alone, then what I did was exactly what they wanted me to do."

He had returned to see me because of a depression brought on by the break-up of his first love relationship, which had lasted for about three years, with a girl of 18. He said the relationship had been fine except for what he felt was her possessiveness. There had been no sexual problems with the relationship.

Frank's view of the girl's possessiveness was belied by the fact that Frank had ended the relationship because she refused his demand that she live with him because she felt that she was too young for such a commitment. Frank's narcissism and projections are seen in the fact that he could see no merit at all to her argument and couldn't tolerate the feeling that she was rejecting him.

The change in Frank's appearance from age 16 to 26 was hard to believe. The sloppy, long-haired, blue-jeaned hippie adolescent had evolved into the very prototype of the conservative Wall Street businessman—close-cropped hair, clean-shaven, black pin-striped Brooks Brothers suit, blue shirt with button-down collar, etc.

He complained of depression and loneliness, anorexia, insomnia and weight loss, alternating with states of detachment where he felt nothing, and frantic periods of sexual acting-out to relieve his depression. He saw clearly how much better he felt and functioned when he had the relationship with the girl and that his difficulties in dealing with rejection were far beyond the normal. However, he felt these represented a basic genetic flaw in his character rather than an emotional problem. In interviews, the defense of detachment was profound. He denied any feelings about the relationship and said his memory of it was vague. He could remember no dreams. He had difficulty starting the sessions, resented my not stepping in for him and projected the WORU on me, which led to further detachment. In sum, the clinical picture he presented was of a patient undergoing an abandonment depression related to a separation experience, which he was defending against by distancing, detachment and acting-out. No amount of confrontation seemed to have an effect. As might have been predicted, after almost six months of therapy twice a week, Frank found the same pseudo-solution to his problem—i.e., he found another girl, moved in with her and immediately began to feel better and decided again to stop treatment.

JANE
Follow-Up Ten Years After Treatment

History of Illness At Admission

Jane, 18, the youngest of four children, complained of depression and obesity; admitting promiscuity, she said that she "would do anything for affection." The history of present illness began around age 11, when her mother returned to work and Jane's weight problem, previously under control, got out of hand, and she became obese. Her menses had begun early, at the age of 10, and by the age of 12, she was extremely attractive girl inspite of being overweight. She courted the attention of boys in her class throughout high school. She began "going steady" with an older boy with whom she had sexual intercourse, became afraid she was pregnant and told her parents. They were outraged and referred her to a psychiatrist, after it was found that she was not pregnant.

At her parents' insistence and despite her intense objections, she shortly afterward left the psychiatrist and enrolled in college away from home.

This separation proved too much for her. She was terrified at living alone and often would pick up a boy to relieve her fear of loneliness. Living alone, she became fearful at night, felt depressed, began to eat more, gained weight, and fell into rampant promiscuity, ending up in a "ménage à trois." She was anorgastic, preferring foreplay to sexual intercourse. She had returned from college and was overeating, socially withdrawn, and spending most of her time alone in her room at the time treatment began.

Past History

Jane's mother did not want her, tried to have an abortion before she was born, and felt she demanded excessive attention from very early in life. She was born with a hip deformity which required orthopedic care for the first six months. She had asthma from age two to age seven. She was in an almost continuous battle with her older sister. However, throughout grammar school, she was a good student, interested in designing and painting. She acted in various school plays and was a cheerleader and something of an athlete.

Outpatient Psychotherapy

Jane did well in the testing and working-through phases of her psychotherapy, but as she came to the last or separation phase of treatment, the temptation to resolve it by acting-out mounted.

As her separation anxiety came into focus in the therapy, she was under greater and greater pressure to act out to defend against it. She began a relationship with a boy and became depressed and confused by the conflict between her desire for fusion and her sexual conflicts. Her depression deepened as she became aware that she was using the man to deal with her fear of separation. Nevertheless, in the midst of Jane's vacillation between separation anxiety and defensive clinging to the man, they decided to live together. Jane's separation anxiety all but disappeared and she began to feel the therapy was a threat to her relationship with the boy. Confrontations fell on deaf ears and Jane stopped therapy. One year later she formalized the defense by marriage.

Jane, Age 28—Ten-Year Follow-Up

Two years after leaving treatment, Jane returned because of conflict with her husband, and in the next year, she got a divorce. She had graduated from college and obtained a job as a secretary while she took design courses on the side. Over the next two years, she managed to live in her own apartment and support herself through an interior decorating business, but in her emotional life she remained prone to recurrent bouts of anxiety and depression, which she continued to defend against by overeating or sexual acting-out. She always seemed to end up with inappropriate men. Discouraged by this, she again returned for treatment at age 28, after the break-up of a relationship with a particularly unsuitable man.

Clinical Impression

Jane could be rated mild impairment, subgroup A. Her capacity to function at work had greatly improved and persisted through the dramatic emotional storms of her affective life. There had been improvement in her self-representation and a greater ability to assert herself and articulate her wishes in reality, mainly in the area of work, where she showed substantial creativity. However, there had been little change in her intrapsychic structure. She still required a defense against separation anxiety and abandonment depression in the form of the alliance between the rewarding object relations unit and the pathologic ego. When under separation stress, she had to act out to defend by either overeating or sexually acting out. She had not achieved the stage of whole object relations, and there was persistence of the pathologic defense mechanisms.

There was little capacity for intimacy or autonomy.

The strongest precipitant of separation anxiety was the possibility of a real, intimate relationship, either with a man in her life or through the therapeutic alliance. She defended against the former by assiduously avoiding appropriate men, ending up in transient affairs and then blaming the men for it. In therapy, whenever the transference acting-out of the RORU—pathologic ego alliance seemed to be coming under control, she was impelled to act out outside the interview. Any real relationship so threatened the intrapsychic, symbiotic bond with her RORU that it triggered intense separation anxiety, which she had to defend herself against at all costs—as usual, at the cost of adaptation in life structure. This need for defense had defeated intensive therapy just as it had defeated the possibility of a real relationship with a man.

SUMMARY

Is it possible to achieve similar results with outpatient therapy alone? The answer is a qualified yes. Both patients, rated mild impairment, are functioning much better than before treatment. However, both cases illustrate the price that is paid for not working through the separation anxiety with the therapist in the last or separation phase of treatment. The patient does not achieve the necessary change in intrapsychic structure and remains vulnerable to separation stress.

14

Prognostic Factors

This chapter shifts the perspective from clinical description to systematic analysis. It begins with a review of prior follow-up research on formerly hospitalized adolescents as a prelude to presenting the results regarding pre-admission, admission, hospital and post-discharge variables which were found to be of prognostic value for this sample of borderline adolescents.

REVIEW OF THE LITERATURE ON PROGNOSIS

Review of the literature revealed that strict comparisons of our results with the results of prior studies were impossible because of differences in study sample, treatment models, follow-up strategies and methods of analysis. The following discussion provides an overview of these differences and then reviews the results of those studies.

237

Sample Composition

Most studies involved both male and female adolescents who had no prior history of psychiatric hospitalization. There were two exceptions—Hamilton's early study of an all-male population and the Menninger Study of a predominately adult population. The latter was reviewed because it included adolescents and emphasized borderline pathology.

None of the studies dealt exclusively with borderline adolescents, since most were done before this diagnosis was defined and accepted. Some used the APA diagnostic classification system which did not include a diagnosis of borderline personality. Those adolescents with borderline personality organizations would fall into a diagnosis of Behavior Disorders of Adolescence or Personality Disorders. In those cases where admitting residents were hesitant to make a diganosis on an adolescent, Adjustment Reaction of Adolescence was frequently used, a practice whose hazards were thoroughly documented several years ago (89). The APA's emphasis on symptomatology and its orientation toward adults made its classification harder to apply to adolescents. The clearest prognosis differences between diagnostic groups emerged when only the diagnoses of psychotic, neurotic and character disorders were used.

The predominant socioeconomic groups in our study were middle and upper-middle class. This was not generally the case in prior follow-up research, where there was a tendency for adolescents from middle-class families to predominate in studies from private institutions, while broader socioeconomic classes were represented in studies from public institutions.

Models of Treatment

One of the major weaknesses of most follow-up research is that the treatment model and its objectives are not defined. Treatment was typically described as educational (41), milieu (129), or psychoanalytic (61, 73, 89). Differential treatment for various diagnostic groups did not exist, at least by definition. Our efforts to define treatment goals beyond symptom alleviation and functional improvement and to develop a treatment model geared specifically to the need of the borderline adolescent are one of the strengths of this study. Without this knowledge, it is impossible in follow-up studies to assess how the treatment contributes to outcome.

In our treatment model, medication is rarely used, since it has not been found to be particularly effective with borderline patients. On the other hand, it is well accepted for psychotic patients, which may account for its heavy usage in those programs reviewed; for example, in the Hartman et al. study, 50 percent of all subjects received medication (42).

Follow-Up Strategies

Follow-up contacts in most studies occurred at least six months following discharge. For the most part, the investigators relied on personal interviews with former patients. When face-to-face interviews were not possible, relatives were consulted, telephone interviews conducted or questionnaires administered. The use of auxiliary or indirect sources of information was more the exception than the rule and did not present the major problem for comparison of results.

The criteria used to evaluate follow-up varied widely from study to study: Some investigators looked primarily at the severity and chronicity of the symptomatology (16, 61, 129); others reviewed the subject's improvement from admission status (2, 59); and still others focused on functional status at outcome. The definition of functional status also varied: Warren (129) used employment status and incidence of antisocial behavior, while more recent studies (29, 42, 73, 89, 108) used multiple dimensions such as symptomatology and quality of object relations. These latter criteria for follow-up evaluation came close to that used in the present study. The qualitative ratings themselves were in no way standardized and, therefore, required close scrutiny for the purpose of comparison.

Methods of Analysis

The level of analysis, a function of the type of data obtained, ranged from informal impressions and descriptive non-parametric statistics (41, 73) to highly sophisticated statistical procedures (124-127). The majority used levels of analysis similar to this project's and typical of this type of research.

Keeping in mind that direct comparisons were not possible, we nevertheless reviewed the prognostic factors found in the literature that were used in our study.

Pre-admission Prognostic Factors

Intelligence, academic performance and the quality of peer relations have all been found to have prognostic value. In a number of studies, patients who had below average intelligence and/or organic impairment were found to do poorly (2, 16, 42, 108, 129). In studies of subjects of average intellectual ability, a history of underachievement was a sign of a poor prognosis (42, 89). A number of studies also found that good pre-adolescent and adolescent peer relationships predicted a positive outcome (16, 42, 108, 124-127).

Life stress, as it is defined in the present study, was not conceptualized in former studies; yet, some dimensions of it were studied. Masterson (89) found the incidence of physical illness in early childhood had no relationship to outcome. The Menninger Study (124-127) found that "the incidence of stress and conflict triggers, degree of interpersonal and material support, mutability of the environment and availability of environmental opportunities" had no relationship with outcome.

Carter (16) found a relationship between familial mental illness and patient outcome; however, the level of pathology among family members was more significant than the incidence of mental illness alone.

Follow-up research has not demonstrated the degree to which parents reinforce their children's illnesses. Hartmann et al. (42), however, did find that when adolescents received secondary gains from their illness, they did poorly on follow-up.

The age of onset of illness was found to have a relationship to outcome which varied by diagnostic group—in schizophrenic adolescents, the later the onset, the better the outcome (3, 16, 89, 108, 131A). The relationship for neurotic and character disorder patients was indefinite. Although Masterson (89) found that adolescents with a character disorder did better with an earlier onset, Pollack, Levenstein and Klein (108) found the relationship at best equivocal.

Studies of whether the onset is acute or chronic have associated acute onset with a good outcome and chronic onset with a bad outcome (16, 42, 142A).

In summary, the adolescents who have at least normal intelligence, positive peer relationships, a good history of academic performance and an acute onset of symptomatology have the best prognosis. To date, research has not substantiated the role of intervening life stress and age in prognosis.

Hospital Prognostic Factors

The hospital prognostic factors most frequently studied have been the patient's admission status, the hospital setting itself and the patient's hospital course.

Adolescents diagnosed neurotic fared best; those diagnosed as psychotic fared worst; those diagnosed character disorders fared somewhere in between. There were no studies of specifically diagnosed borderline patients.

All studies measured how symptomatology impaired both psychic and social functioning. They found that the least functionally impaired at admission tended to do best at follow-up (42, 60, 108). In addition, those patients who showed aggressive, rebellious and acting-out behavior were better at follow-up than those who were severely regressed, withdrawn and passive at admission (16, 42, 89, 108).

When symptomatology was ego-alien (the patient considered it a problem) the outcome tended to be better (42, 124-127). In the Menninger Study (124-127), these same patients had a higher tolerance for anxiety. In addition, the Menninger study concluded that high initial motivation was not necessary for successful outcome. This seemed particularly true for those patients who entered the hospital with little insight into the role of emotions in behavior.

Another hospital prognostic factor of value related to the mastery of developmental tasks—specifically physical and emotional separation from parents. The more adolescents were physically and emotionally separated from their parents and involved with peers in age-appropriate activities, the more positive was the outcome (42).

Early research on adolescent inpatient treatment focused on the relative merits of mixing adolescents with adults or providing them with an exclusively all-adolescent unit. Beskind (42) has done a thorough review of this early work. It is sufficient to say that adolescents are best treated among peers, in a program which is structured to meet their unique developmental needs (4, 29, 37, 60, 73, 108, 124-127). With the exception of the Menninger Project, little has been done beyond this to specify the optimal treatment model for different diagnostic groups. Though it did not follow adolescents exclusively, the Menninger Project's emphasis and findings regarding borderline pathology are relevant. Borderline patients fared best at follow-up when they were treated with expressive-supportive treatment which utilized as much external structure as necessary. Also, patients with a highly skilled therapist tended to fare better at follow-up (42, 124-127). The Menninger group expanded on this, noting that this was particularly crucial for borderline patients. The employment of medication has also been associated with poor outcomes (29, 42).

The remaining hospital prognostic factors studied related to the patient's course in the hospital. Those adolescents who became involved in the milieux and evoked positive responses from other patients and staff tended to function better at follow-up (29, 73, 89, 124-127). This may again be tapping the quality of the patient's object relationships. Continued attendance at a community school (42) and rapid symptom improvement (16, 89) also predicted a better outcome.

Garber (29), one of the few who studied the relationship between duration of hospital stay and outcome, found that patients who were in the hospital less than six months tended to do poorer at follow-up than those who stayed over six months. This finding is quite congruent with the senior author's theoretical model, which stresses that longer periods of intensive involvement are necessary to achieve structural change. When symptom improvement alone is the goal, a shorter hospital stay may be sufficient, recognizing that this change may be superficial. If the patient has not internalized new and more effective self-regulatory skills, he may well regress and become symptomatic when again faced with inevitable stress (89).

The necessity of concomitant treatment of parents was cited as early as 1961 when Hamilton et al. (41) then published their impressionistic, non-statistical follow-up results. The "teachability of parents" was considered an important prerequisite for good adolescent outcome study. Much later, Garber (29) did find a relationship between concomitant parental involvement and successful follow-up.

In summary, the results of former investigations regarding relevant hospital prognostic factors would suggest that those borderline adolescents who are least impaired at admission aptly derive the most benefit from their inpatient experience and fare best at follow-up. Expressive supportive treatment with a highly skilled therapist would be the model of choice. In addition, involvement with other adolescents, attention to the specific developmental needs of this age group, a hospital stay of over six months, and concomitant treatment of parents would also enhance the prognosis.

Post-discharge Variables

Continued treatment after discharge was repeatedly found to be related to a positive outcome (4, 37, 42).

Garber (28) also reported that former patients frequently stated that the transition from the hospital back to the community would have been eased by the support of a transitional facility. They felt the move from a completely structured environment to complete independence was too dramatic and not eased by outpatient care alone. Though many of these adolescents were able to master the transitional phase, they believed additional supports would have made it easier for them. It was also noted that for those who regressed following discharge and had yet to regain their losses at follow-up a transitional facility might have offset the deterioration.

A summary of the outstanding good prognostic factors shown in the literature are presented in Tables 11 and 12.

TABLE 11

Factors Associated with Positive Outcome

Prognostic Factor	Study
History of Good Peer Relations	Carter (16), Hartmann et al. (42), Pollack et al. (108), Warren (129)
Early Onset of Illness (Character Disorder)	Masterson (88), Pollack et al. (108)
Acute Symptom Onset	Carter (16), Hartmann et al. (42), Weiss and Glasser (131A)
Least Functional Impairment at Admission	Hartmann et al. (42), King and Pittman (60), Pollack et al. (108)
Symptoms Ego-Alien	Hartmann et al. (42), Menninger (124-127)
Highly Skilled Therapist	Hartmann et al. (42), Menninger (124-127)
Positive Involvement in Milieu	Hartmann et al. (42), Levy (73), Masterson (88), Menninger (124-127)
Hospital Stay over Six Months	Garber (29)
Concomitant Involvement of Parents	Garber (29), Hamilton et al. (41)
Expressive Supportive Psychoanalytic Treatment	Menninger (124-127)
Program Attention to Unique Developmental Needs of Adolescents	Beavers and Blumberg (4), Garber (29), Gossett et al. (37), Hartmann et al. (42), King and Pittman (60), Levy (73), Pollack et al. (108), Menninger (124-127)
Continued Treatment Post-Discharge	Beavers and Blumberg (4), Gossett et al. (37), Hartmann et al. (42)

SYSTEMIC RESULTS

The remainder of this chapter will focus on the prognostic factors we found to be significantly related to the outcome status of the borderline adolescents we followed. The correlation coeffi-

TABLE 12

Factors Associated with Poor Outcome

Prognostic Factor	Study
Below Normal Intelligence and/or Organicity	Annesley (2), Carter (16), Hartmann et al. (42), Pollack et al. (108), Warren (129)
History of Academic Underachievement	Masterson (88), Hartmann et al. (42)
Use of Medication (in hospital)	Garber (29), Hartmann et al. (42)

cients and levels of significance of the prognostic factors and outcome indicies are presented in Tables 13 through 16. They are divided into pre-admission, admission, hospital and post-discharge factors. A discussion of these results will follow. Both life stress and

TABLE 13

Pre-admission Prognostic Factors

Prognostic Factors	r^*	p
1. Life Stress	.46	.01
2. Social Functioning Pre-onset of Illness	.39	.02
3. Academic Functioning Pre-onset of Illness	.15	.2 (ns)

* r—product-moment correlation—a value of .35 is necessary to achieve a level of significance at the .05 level for a sample of this size.

social functioning pre-onset of illness leading to hospitalization correlated at a significant level with outcome. There was no relationship between early academic functioning and outcome.

The final admission index, along with its components, correlated highly with outcome, supporting the hypothesis that the patients who were least impaired at admission fared best at outcome. The components of the final admission index with the weakest relationships were Symptom-Chronicity and Symptom-Social and Psychic Cost to Functioning. The remaining factors which tapped ego intactness, mastery of separation from parents

TABLE 14

Admission Prognostic Factors

Prognostic Factors	r	p
1. Age at Admission	.01	.2(ns)
2. Final Admission Index	.71	.002
3. Symptomatology Mean	.74	.002
A. Chronicity	.44	.01
B. Recognition	.73	.002
C. Social and Psychic Cost to Functioning	.39	.02
4. Ego Self-Regulatory Functions	.70	.002
5. Independence and Autonomy	.67	.002
6. Peer Object Relations	.51	.002

and quality of object relations, provided the highest correlations with outcome. There was no significant relationship between age at admission and outcome.

TABLE 15

Hospital Prognostic Factors

Prognostic Factors	r	p
1. Duration of Stay	.11	.2(ns)
2. Model Realization	.73	.002
3. Patient-Therapist-Supervisor Matching	.74	.002
4. Prognosis at Discharge (natural distribution)	.79	.002

Model Realization, Patient-Therapist-Supervisor Matching and Prognosis at discharge provided the strongest relationship to outcome of all prognostic indicators investigated. The value and reliability of these results were further enhanced by the independent procedures used to derive the model realization and Patient-Therapist-Supervisor factors and the natural versus forced distribution used for the Prognosis at Discharge factor. The hypothesis that patients who had the optimal therapeutic in-hospital experiences would fare best at outcome was therefore supported. The duration of hospital treatment did not correlate with outcome.

TABLE 16

Post-discharge Prognostic Factor

Prognostic Factor	r	p
Continuation of Treatment Post-Discharge	.65	.002

The Point Biserial Correlation technique was used to determine whether there was a relationship between continuation of out-patient treatment and outcome. The resulting correlation was significant.

Other Nonsignificant Findings

Since a Chi square between patients' perceptions of the effectiveness of parental counseling and outcome was not significant ($\chi^2 = 2.6$, $p < .9$) a correlation coefficient was not calculated.

Impressionistic Findings

Patients also reported their perceptions of the strengths and weaknesses of the program. The quality of the individual therapy experienced was spontaneously cited by 96 percent of the respondents as crucial to treatment success. Although no other factor was cited with such frequency, the weight of patient's remarks was enhanced by the fact that they were spontaneously offered. Other positive features of the program mentioned were the protective aspects of hospitalization, the control of self-destructive acting-out and the facilitation of the patients' becoming more autonomous. The most frequently noted weakness (46 percent) was the lack of a post-discharge transitional facility.

DISCUSSION

The findings support the hypothesis that borderline psychopathology in adolescence exists on a continuum that is demonstrable (36, 38, 48, 84). In spite of common but varied difficulties during the separation-individuation phase, patients clearly differed

in their subsequent childhood years in developing social relationships, in the degree to which they were able to master age-appropriate developmental tasks and in the establishment of ego autonomous functioning. Those patients who were most successful in
all of these areas were less impaired both at admission and at follow-up. Though structural deficits, faulty object relationships and
failure to individuate were the hallmarks for diagnosing borderline
psychopathology, a deeper, more detailed assessment of these
various areas was essential to determine the actual individual prognosis. The aim of this study was to explore those factors which
might account for these differences in severity and to identify
prognostic factors in the following areas: pre-admission, admission,
hospital and post-discharge.

Pre-admission Factors

The pre-admission prognostic variables which did relate to outcome were life stress and the quality of social functioning prior to
the onset of the illness. It was hypothesized that patients who were
exposed to repeated life stress (see Appendix III for definition)
would have greater difficulty coping, would appear more impaired
at admission, would be less able to take advantage of their hospital
experience, and would fare worse at outcome. On the other hand,
the reverse would occur in patients who had more benign environ-
ments in early childhood. The hypothesis was supported for outcome $(r = .46, p = .01)$, but not for severity of illness on admission
$(r = .30, p = .10)$. This lack of relationship may be explained theoretically. Patients may be able to cover up the effects of early
traumas on their ego development by maintaining surface functioning, other compensatory behaviors, and relying on substitute
figures. The surface functioning later gives way when the ego development is not adequate to and becomes overtaxed by later
developmental expectations. This becomes particularly stressful for
borderline patients in adolescence in that they must now eman-
cipate from their parents and function more autonomously,
despite the fact that, not having separated, they lack the under-

lying ego development which facilitates the normal adolescent's mastery of the latter developmental task of emancipation.

The borderline adolescent's foundering before this task of emancipation contributes so much to the acuteness of the clinical picture on admission that it tends to mask the effect of earlier life stress. At follow-up, however, its effect is again discernible.

The significant correlation between the quality of early social functioning and outcome $(r = .39, p = .02)$ agrees with the findings of prior investigators (16, 42, 108, 124-127). This suggests that adolescents—regardless of diagnosis—who are able to establish successful, gratifying peer relationships are in advantaged positions, both at admission and at outcome. For borderline patients, this finding raises a question. Does success in social relationships imply less psychopathology or a capacity to compensate for the same level of psychopathology? If the former were the case, one would expect a very high correlation between the social relationship variable and the final admission index. Though the correlation coefficient was significant $(r = .45, p < .01)$, it was not sufficiently strong to imply that assessing successful relationships was an indirect way of measuring the severity of pathology. It should be noted, however, that since the final admission index was not solely a measure of the severity of illness, its lack of a higher correlation with early social relationships does not negate the possibility that one is a function of the other. The question really requires further investigation.

Early academic functioning did not correlate at a significant level with outcome $(r = .15, p = .2)$ but did with the final admission index $(r = .57, p < .002)$. This finding differs from earlier research, where successful early academic performance did relate to a positive outcome (42, 88, 108). The unique aspects of the borderline pathology and the fact that all subjects in this sample had at least normal intellectual ability may explain the differing results.

Adult borderline patients typically manifest difficulties in cognitive functioning. Though cognitive deficits do exist, adult borderlines are generally able to sustain themselves in both employment and academic areas. Our knowledge of normal development also tells us that a maturation of cognitive functions occurs in adolescence. This would suggest that borderline patients are able to profitably benefit from the maturation of cognitive skills in adolescence. Thus, early failure need not necessarily predict a poor outcome with this diagnostic group.

Early academic failure or underachievement did, however, correlate highly with the final admission index ($r = .57$, $p = .002$). While early academic failure may not necessarily predict a poor adult outcome, it certainly has developmental implications during the elementary school years. It has even greater meaning for this group of patients because all had at least normal intellectual ability. It is likely that early academic failure for this group reflects symptomatic behavior and a failure in age-appropriate functioning. It becomes, therefore, a measure of the severity of the illness and should provide a sign to both parents and educators that something is wrong. Unfortunately, many of these patients' early pleas for help went unheeded until a crisis situation occurred.

Admission Factors

The final admission index ($r = .74$, $p < .002$) and all of its component variables were significantly related to outcome. The healthiest adolescents at admission were also healthiest at follow-up —a finding that corresponds to the findings of former studies (42, 59, 108, 124-127). The component factors of the admission index which were particularly relevant were Independence and Autonomy ($r = .67$, $p = .002$) Ego Self-Regulatory Functioning ($r = .70$, $p = .002$), Object Relations ($r = .51$, $p = .002$) and Symptom Recognition ($r = .73$, $p = .002$). Though the symptomatology mean provided the highest correlation, this result is deceptive. The symptomatology score was obtained by averaging the scores on symptom chronicity, symptom recognition and the symptomatology's social and psychic cost to functioning. The recognition component of this mean, in restrospect, seems to be more a measure of ego functioning than a measure of symptomatology. It taps the patient's ability to view himself and his behavior realistically, the degree of ego alienation from his symptoms and the degree of motivation for change. This component of the symptomatology mean carried the bulk of the numerical weight and was, therefore, responsible for the strong relationship with outcome. If the recognition component were taken out of the symptomatology mean, the resultant correlation would have been substantially lowered ($r = .37$, $p = .02$). Though still significant, the symptomatology mean provided the weakest correlation of all variables investigated.

While significant, the symptomatology variable thus has the weakest prognostic value, while ego functioning, object relations and the mastery of developmental tasks have the strongest prognostic value. Hartmann et al. (42) also found that mastery of development tasks was a significant predictor of outcome. The severity and chronicity of patient symptoms do measure the degree of pain a patient is experiencing, but their assessment does not enable one to measure the underlying strengths of the patient. One might, therefore, question the value of using symptomatology to assess prognosis. Also, the lack of a strong relationship with outcome makes one question the value of using symptomatic improvement as a measure of treatment effectiveness at outcome.

Age at admission for this group of the patients did not relate to outcome. It may be that for borderline adolescents the fact that they are in adolescence carries much more weight than their specific age.

Hospital Factors

Three of the five hospital variables focused on the qualitative differences in each patient's therapeutic experience. It was hypothesized that those patients who had optimal experiences would fare best at outcome. Each of the three variables specific to the treatment captured a different dimension of the therapeutic experience. The Prognosis variable measured the degree to which the patient had achieved the goals of the model (control of acting-out, working-through of the abandonment depression and increased definitive autonomous behavior). The Model Realization variable captured the degree to which the various treatment procedures approximated the ideal of the model for each patient. It included such things as the number of therapist changes and sex composition of the unit. The Patient-Therapist-Supervisor Match variable measured the relative quality of the individual treatment experience. Individual psychotherapy was the crucial feature of the model and the extreme importance of the quality of the therapeutic relationship for prognosis had been established in prior studies (124-127).

The findings supported the hypothesis for all three variables. Patients whose individual and overall therapeutic experiences were optimal looked healthiest at outcome $(r = .74, p = .002; r = .73, p = .002$, respectively).

In addition, those patients who best achieved the goals of the model appeared to have sustained their gains, as reflected in their clinical standing at follow-up $(r = .79, p = .002)$. The strength of these results is enhanced by the fact that the Patient-Therapist-Supervisor Match and Model Realization variables were scaled independently. In addition, no forced distribution was employed for the Prognosis factor.

These results, however, though consistent with prior research, are not strictly comparable since prior follow-up research studies did not define the treatment model or the treatment goals as specifically as this research.

No statistically significant relationship emerged between the duration of the hospital stay and outcome $(r = .11, p < .2)$. It should be noted, however, that it was assumed that only those patients who were hospitalized at least nine months would have a chance to make the gains necessary for sustained success. Our sample, therefore, consisted of only those subjects who were hospitalized over nine months. Levy (73) also found in his sample that a hospital stay of at least six months were necessary to achieve sustained gains. Patients in his sample who were hospitalized for less than six months did poorly at outcome. Both our results and Levy's suggest that a minimal duration of time is essential for a patient to achieve sustained benefit from his inpatient experience.

After the minimal duration of time has been achieved, the remaining additional time needed is idiosyncratic to the specific needs of each patient.

The parental involvement in the borderline adolescent's pathology has been comprehensively described in the literature review. In view of their involvement in the child's continued difficulty, it was hypothesized that patients would fare better at follow-up when their parents gained from their continued counseling. Though 58 percent of the patients felt their parents made gains as a result of their involvement in counseling, no significant relationship emerged between parental counseling gains and patient's outcome standing ($\chi^2 = 2.6$, $p < .9$). It may be that the very fact that parents allowed their adolescent to separate for inpatient treatment may have been sufficient permission to allow him to utilize his therapeutic experience. It should be noted that patients felt their parents gained more from counseling than the parents did. As reported in the clinical findings, in only 46 percent of the families were one or both parents judged to have gained from counseling.

Post-Discharge Variables

A significant correlation did emerge between continuation of treatment and follow-up status ($r = .65$, $p = .002$).* Patients who continued in treatment following discharge fared better at outcome than those who did not continue. The importance of post-discharge treatment has also been well established in prior follow-up research (4, 37, 42). It has also been demonstrated in prior studies that the year following discharge is particularly crucial for formerly hospitalized patients (28). The transition from a highly structured environment to the community, where a self-imposed structure must predominate, typically causes increased anxiety. When outpatient treatment is pursued, the patient is supported during the transition and is provided an opportunity to rework

---

* The Point Biserial Correlation Technique was employed on this because the data did not lend themselves to using Pearson's Product-Moment Correlation Technique.

the underlying issues and internalize and strength the gains made while hospitalized. Without continued treatment, the risk of regression is great and the outcome for most was poor.

The duration of post-discharge treatment for this sample ranged from one month to seven years, with a mean of 2.5 years and a mode of one year $(n = 6)$. While it was not possible to determine the ideal length of post-discharge treatments, several trends did emerge. There was a significant difference in the mean durations of post-discharge treatment between the healthier and disturbed adolescents at outcome. The mean for the healthy adolescents was 31.0 months, while the mean for the most disturbed was 12.0 months. The difference between the means of the two groups was significant $(s(\bar{x}_1 - \bar{x}_2) = 8.82, \; t = 2.17, \; p < .05)$. While there was no statistically significant difference between the middle group and the high and low groups, there was a definite overall trend. As the final index went up, so did the length of post-discharge treatment.

SUMMARY

Our results suggest that the prognosis for borderline adolescents can only be ascertained by viewing the unique clinical picture of each borderline adolescent. The prognostic factors we found, within the spectrum of borderline pathology, to be particularly important were: the degree of early life stress; the level of early ego development; the degree of mastery of early developmental tasks; and the effectiveness of early social relationships (object relations).

Our results also strongly suggest that this specific treatment model, when it can be fully and appropriately applied, exerts a strong influence to help the borderline adolescent overcome his developmental arrest and take his place on the normal pathways to growth. Finally, the findings indicate that continuity of treatment after discharge consolidates and reinforces improvement.

15

Summary and
Discussion

It has been the purpose of this book to report the long-term
results of treatment of the borderline adolescent—a treatment
based upon a developmental theory. We have shown, contrary to
current assumptions, that many of these severely ill adolescents are
actually amenable to the beneficial effects of this therapy. Given
the proper therapeutic support, many can and will overcome their
developmental arrest. More than half of our patients were able to
return to the mainstream of life as functioning, coping individuals.
In other words, therapy had affected the emergence and consolidation of their real and healthy self.

First, a few comments about the usefulness of and limits to the
guiding developmental theory. Theory, as presented here, derives
from a continuously accumulating body of knowledge. It is an

effort to link observed facts and deductions therefrom to provide useful generalizations that enhance their meaning. Theory evolves through a hypothesis formulated from observation, followed by clinical testing, followed by hypothesis revision and still more clinical testing. A good theory must be open-ended and subject to constant revision based on fuller testing and observation. In this way, theory can become a detailed account of what goes on in nature.

The developmental theory has evolved from the treatment of borderline adolescents (and adults) and is a new way of looking at familiar facts of childhood and adolescence. It encourages the construction of new clinical hypotheses that can be put to the clinical test. It is as important to be able to modify or change hypotheses as it is to make them in the first place—for a most-famous example, consider Freud's changing of his seduction hypothesis. This attitude is reflected in the additions to and modifications of the developmental theory described in this book: the broadening of the concept of maternal libidinal unavailability; the further definition of the relationships between the pathologic ego and the rewarding and withdrawing object relations part-units; and the addition of the psychopathology of the self. One must be careful, however, to avoid the trap of circular reasoning by assuming that theory is fact and requires no further validation. Theory is vital to the clinician's task—understanding his patient—but it is equally important to keep in mind its limitations and its malleable state.

Clinical research is without doubt the best method for studying the human personality, because one can recognize and evaluate so many of the dynamic, sometimes fleeting, variables participating at one time in the complex functioning of the patient's personality. However, the phenomena it studies are so complex and the observer who does psychotherapy with the patient so subject to distortions, both conscious and unconscious, that the experience he has with a patient defies the application of a rigorous scientific methodology, which therefore limits the generalization of the findings. Does this mean that because it is not so-called scientifically controlled for the bias of the observer and the variable under study that the findings have no meaning?*

The answer to this question revolves around the differences between the two basic types of research—hypothesis-gathering and hypothesis-testing. Hypothesis-gathering is the first stage of any research where general observations are made about the phenomena under study in order to formulate a hypothesis. This phase of research can be of an indeterminate length and does not require rigorous controls. The second stage of hypothesis-training requires those controls in order to make sure that the research design provides a true test of the theory. The research presented here, like most clinical research, falls under the heading of hypothesis-gathering, and the scientific validity of the findings applies only at that level. It will require many similar studies verifying the same phenomena before the stage is even set for hypothesis-testing research.

Our study sample was small, 31 patients, and contained too high a percentage (73 percent) of patients of middle and upper socioeconomic status. One would have liked a much larger sample, with a more representative socioeconomic status distribution, from which to generalize. The intensive nature of the work mitigates against its ever being done on a large scale. The generalizability of the findings will depend on their replication by other studies. The same problem existed for the 1967 study, but those findings have been regularly replicated and thereby have gained greater generalizability over the last 13 years. In addition, the present study sample was not randomly selected but selected only after careful evaluation of each adolescent's severity of illness and potential for therapy. Therefore, it probably underrepresents those hospitalized borderline adolescents who are not good candidates for therapy.

One of the strengths of the follow-up lies in the fact that a high percentage of the patients were located (89 percent), and a high percentage of interviews were obtained with both adolescent and

---

* I would call your attention to the "uncontrolled" observations reported by Darwin which have had so profound an effect on biological science.

parent (77 percent). These were unusually high percentages for any follow-up study, and it gave a good, solid clinical base to our data. Our data consisted of our own clinical observations through a diagnostic interview rather than reports from schools, letters, phone calls, etc. One of the weaknesses was that only one rather than all three of the interviewers had no prior knowledge of the patient. However, the pilot study demonstrated that the one could serve as a control for the other two. Other weaknesses were the relatively short average length follow-up (3.9 years from hospital discharge) and the average age (20.4).

The fact that most patients had both hospital and later out-patient treatment made it difficult to assess the influence of each of these variables alone on follow-up status. This difficulty was lessened somewhat for hospital therapy by comparing the patient's condition on discharge from the hospital with his severe impairment on admission to the unit.

Many of these methodologic problems sprang from the practical need to finish the study within the time the personnel had available. Suffice it to say that we obtained good clinical data, with some control of interviewer bias because of past knowledge, over a follow-up period long enough in some cases (seven to nine years) to give great confidence in the data and long enough on the average to feel that the patients were, for the most part, past chronologic adolescence.

These disorders began in early childhood and were constantly reinforced throughout childhood and adolescence. All these patients were ill enough to have to be hospitalized after suicide attempts or other desperate pleas for help. Without treatment, many of them would, no doubt, be dead, in hospitals or prisons. From this perspective, the results for many reflect a true triumph over tragedy.

Eighteen out of 20, or 90 percent, of the patients who received inpatient psychotherapy and were discharged as improved have passed the test of time by maintaining that improvement four years later. This represents 58 percent of the total sample and double the percentage reported as improved in the prior follow-up study in 1967, before the developmental theory of the borderline syndrome had been formulated.

The 16 percent of the present study rated as minimally impaired on follow-up had improved not just in symptomatology and functioning but also in ego development and in object relations. They developed until they were close to, if not actually at, the stage of ego autonomy, with full separation of the self representation from the object representation, leading to whole self and object representations, the disappearance of splitting, substantial object constancy with improved capacity to handle separation stress, and with the flowering of individuation—creativity, independence and beginning capacity for intimacy.

Those who were rated mildly impaired at follow-up (42 percent) showed not only dramatic improvement in symptomatology and functioning but also in self-image and capacity for self-assertion. However, they still required pathologic defense mechanisms against separation anxiety and abandonment depression—including a clinging relationship—to maintain a high level of functioning. They, therefore, remained vulnerable to separation stress. Nevertheless, the improved self-assertive capacity markedly lessened the need to sacrifice adaptation to defense.

The improvement with hospital therapy was closely related to the degree to which the patient's clinical course followed the therapeutic model; whether improvement would be maintained four years later could be predicted with a high degree of accuracy at discharge. These findings are compelling evidence that support both the accuracy of the theory and the effectiveness of the therapeutic approach. The method was observational and exploratory rather than hypothesis-testing and, therefore, in the scientific sense, the findings cannot be considered proof—but short of that, their weight and consistency are more than persuasive.

The idiosyncratic clinical course of two patients, who are both now in professional school, is worth attention as a contrast and a caution about prognosis. Their history was remarkable in that they did not improve with hospital therapy and four to five years later would still have been considered severely impaired and perhaps hopeless. In the next two years, both turned around and took hold of themselves, resumed treatment and markedly improved. The reason for this turnabout remains a mystery, except that both patients spontaneously said: "When I was completely down and out, with no one to take care of me, I finally realized I had to take care of me; I finally realized I had to take care of myself."

The salient clinical features of the patients who improved were not returning to live at home again and the continuation of out-patient psychotherapy for many months and sometimes years, thereby supporting their own individuation against the parents' regressive projections and other pressures. The parents were not able to give positive support for separation-individuation. For example, three of the five patients minimally impaired actually had to cut off all contact with their parents for long periods of time to combat the parents' regressive influence.

The patients who were mildly impaired, although they did not achieve full separation with whole self and object representations, nevertheless showed substantial clinical change in adaptive capacity through the gradual transfer of emotional investment from the object representation to the self representation, with gradual improvement of self-image and self-assertive capacity. This finding, by demonstrating the mechanism of change, offers a strong argument for long-term supportive or confrontive psychotherapy of the borderline. In other words, one can expect confrontation psychotherapy to effect slow, gradual improvements in self-image and self-assertion, short of full separation of self-representation from object representation.

The average age on follow-up was 20.4 years, too young to provide more than beginning evidence of the patient's eventual capacity for intimacy. The patients who married seemed to do so as a defense against abandonment depression and not to fulfill mature genital aims for intimacy. The rest of the patients are still experimenting with their capacities for intimacy. Who is not at 21? It would be useful to follow a selected sample through the adult years to trace out the evidence for the capacity for intimacy and, finally and most ultimately important for the assessment of development, to follow this sample into parenthood, to evaluate whether, unlike their parents, these patients, particularly the women, had sufficiently overcome their separation-individuation failure and resultant need for parenting to be able to offer appropriate parenting, particularly during the separation-individuation phases of their own offspring.

The salient clinical features of those who did not improve were more-than-usual overt symptomatology and more environmental separation trauma in childhood, clinical illness having its onset around prepuberty (eight to 10 years), greater difficulty in the hospital psychotherapy with parents' and patients' resistance to separation and more intense countertransference problems with the resident therapist. These difficulties crystallized during the family interviews and later during discharge planning, when the joint resistance would result in continued seemingly insuperable obstacles to appropriate plans. Soon after discharge, the pattern of failure was set when the patient stopped his outpatient psychotherapy and return home to live.

The first post-hospital year was a period of special vulnerability to separation stress, as indicated by the difficulties experienced by those patients whose therapists had to leave them during that time. Some never recovered. To deal with this problem, we tried unsuccessfully to provide a halfway house. This led us to sometimes heroic efforts to find places other than home for the adolescent to live, intensified the adolescent's abandonment depression on discharge, placed a pressure on his capacity to adapt at a time when his new ego structure was most fragile and may well have been the particular or specific straw that broke the camel's back for some of these patients who were moderately impaired.

Although a few of these patients who did not improve received inadequate treatment, a more likely explanation for the majority was the patient's not having the ability to internalize the object in order to achieve separation-individuation. They were able to manage throughout childhood with the support available for their dependency, but the approach of adolescence, with the task of becoming independent, interrupted their defenses, and their inability to internalize the object made it impossible for them to function autonomously; they were thus exposed to an abandonment depression on this loss alone. This sequence was repeated in the hospital, where they were able to manage as long as the hospital reproduced the childhood environment—i.e., gratified their dependency and provided external structure. But when they had to leave, not having internalized the object, they failed to learn new ways to cope; they again had an abandonment depression against which their only defense was to return to the childhood environment of the family—giving up the struggle for individuation and thus sealing their fate. A halfway house could have provided some of them with a longer period in a supportive environment, which would have given a better test of the inability to internalize theory. Perhaps some of them just needed more time.

The relatively poorer results with the parents reflect the severity of their pathology, which limited the therapeutic goal. More mothers improved than fathers, because one of the keys to the mother's intrapsychic system for relieving anxiety was being changed, which compelled her to find other means of adaptation. The tie with the father was less intense, and therefore, he was not compelled in the same way. Let me emphasize that we did not neglect the fathers, and they did attend the sessions regularly. In one case, the father was more attached to his daughter than was the mother; he improved the most and later divorced the mother, who had not improved at all.

Although the decrease and/or the removal of the intensity of the regressive parental projections is no small achievement, nevertheless the goal of the therapy with the parents—their support of the adolescent's individuation—was generally not achieved. This raises questions as to the role the parents should play in the adolescent's treatment. How much therapeutic effort should be employed in the light of such poor prospects? The dilemma springs from the fact that the borderline adolescent is usually a central cog in the family's communication system and removal of that cog creates a disturbance in the rest of the system that must be managed. However, a relatively large amount of therapeutic input achieved a minimal goal for the mothers, less for the fathers, and helped the adolescent indirectly. Should we accept this as a reasonable goal in view of the severity of the parents' psychopathology? Should the parents be advised also to receive psychotherapy on their own, rather than as part of the treatment? Would they be motivated enough to accept it? Should the therapeutic approach with the mother play down confrontation of the destructiveness to her child of her maternal behavior, in favor of emphasizing the need for her to invest her emotion in her own autonomy?

Some perspective is gained by comparing these findings with those of Offer (103, 104), who studied the development of healthy adolescents (age 16 to 24). He divided them into three groups— continuing growth, surgent growth and tumultuous growth—and observed that only the parents of the continuing growth group (25 percent) took pleasure in and were able to give unqualified support to their adolescents' independence. The parents in the other two groups had difficulty letting go, with those in the tumultuous group having the most difficulty. If a minority of parents of healthy adolescents can support emancipation and independence, it may be too much to expect seriously ill parents— even with psychotherapy—to support the earlier, more fateful task of separation-individuation.

There is much confusion in the literature as to whether or not the borderline syndrome is a stable diagnostic entity. The fact that the borderline diagnosis was sustained throughout the follow-up period in 29 of 31 patients is strong evidence that this is indeed a stable entity. The longitudinal history of these patients' psychopathology—from early childhood through the developmental years to adulthood—gave impressive evidence of the stable, enduring quality of their character defenses. Without psychotherapy, they would not have changed.

The inpatient or hospital part of the long course of therapy these patients received was crucial in that it changed a regressive spiral to an adaptive spiral. It changed the balance from defense to adaptation, enabling the patient to participate in later outpatient psychotherapy. These patients then found new capacities to direct their own lives, to perceive realistically and cope with challenges in work and relationships in a constructive, self-motivated manner, and to contain separation stress without sacrificing adaptation. These were new building blocks with which to build a new life whose structure would sustain and support them rather than drag them down. In the minimally impaired most clearly, but also to a lesser extent in the others, the work of the psychotherapy had been internalized and become a part of the patient. He or she had made it his or her own.

PSYCHOTHERAPY

The purpose of the treatment was not insight—to make the unconscious conscious—but rather to promote the reliving of old experiences by the more mature psyche, to discharge and work through the abandonment depression, which resulted from parental failures to support growth, thereby freeing the self representation to separate from the object representation.

Psychotherapy through its requirement that the patient assume responsibility for the initiation, identification and reporting of his feeling states—in other words, he must assume responsibility for the emotional state of the self and its expression, or if not, to examine why not—rekindles the separation-individuation process and immediately brings the patient in the interview up against all the difficulties which have created this defect in the structure of the self in the first place—his need to defend against the abandonment depression that separation-individuation induces. The psychotherapy becomes itself an experiment in individuation. In the therapeutic crucible, when the patient activates his usual defenses, such as avoidance or transference acting-out, these are dealt with by the therapist by confrontation and/or other techniques which refocus and provide a framework for the patient to work through his abandonment depression or reexperience the disappointment, anger and depression that helped to produce the defect in the first place.

As these affects are discharged, other features of the psychotherapy support the patient's further growth: 1. the consistent regular reliability of the therapist; 2. the dyadic character of the relationship, which reinforces the patient's symbiotic projections but also intensifies the patient's availability to introjection once projections have been dealt with; 3. the therapist's activities: a) *listening, understanding*—potent forces which the patient initially sees as a threat, since these experiences of human empathy are often the first the patient has been aware of. They bring with them, by dramatic contrast, the extraordinary pain of the early parental failures in empathy; b) *confrontation*—which does for the patient what he is unable to do for himself because of ego defects and pathologic defense mechanisms—avoidance, denial, projection, projective identification—i.e., perceive reality. The patient identifies with the therapist and then learns to perform this function for himself; c) *interpretation*—which broadens understanding and enhances control; d) *communicative matching*—which provides the responsive, sharing experience with the patient's new individuative thoughts, feelings, actions that compensates for the defect left by mother's withdrawal and fuels and invigorates the patient's individuation.

These therapeutic activities over time establish a harmonious emotional rhythm which meets the patient's emotional therapeutic needs in a manner resembling the optimal mother-child emotional interaction during the crucial symbiotic separation-individuation phases of development. They are not the same—one meets therapeutic needs, the other basic emotional needs for love, support, etc.—but the former resembles the latter in its regularity, consistency, availability of the therapist and in the constructive effect of his actions.

This state of affairs potentiates the patient's working-through of his abandonment depression, as well as his use of the therapist as an object for positive introjections, all of which facilitates individuation and the overcoming of the developmental arrest.

These results go far toward laying to rest, it seems to me, the notion that borderline patients cannot benefit from psychoanalytic psychotherapy. The therapy is arduous, time-consuming, filled with seductive and deceptive obstacles, but it is far from impossible. When it is pursued faithfully, it more than justifies the effort, providing, as it does, a life preserver to rescue and sustain the deprived and abandoned in their struggle and eventually a beacon to guide them to overcome their developmental trauma, reconstruct their psyche and rejoin the mainstreams of life. These objectives—a fulfillment of both the therapist's and patient's deepest wishes—enhance the mutual struggle and endow it with a vitality and nobility that gives the work its enduring satisfaction and significance.

APPENDICES

Appendix I

Systematic
Evaluation Form

I. *Functional Impairment* (Minimal, Mild, Moderate, Severe)

II. *Symptoms* (Intensity, duration, precipitating stress);
(Separation Anxiety, and/or Abandonment Depression)

III. *Psychodynamics* (S-I) (Separation stresses coped with)

IV. *Ego Structure* (Ego defects, pathologic defenses—avoidance,
denial, splitting, projection, acting-out)

V. *Object Relations* (Self and object representations—part or whole; degree of object constancy)

VI. *Developmental Achievements*:

A) Independence—autonomy

B) Intimacy

C) Creativity

Appendix II

Interview Form

Name........................ Birthdate.............Sex......

Address..................... Date of Admission.............

.... Length of Stay.................

Date and Age at Discharge........

Parents:

Father's Name.............. Birthdate or age..................

   Ethnic.................. Religion..........................

Mother's Name............. Birthdate or age..................

   Ethnic.................. Religion..........................

271

Marital Status: Married (with spouse)..... Married (separated)....

                Divorced (remarried)...... Divorced (single)......

                Other (specify)..........

Father: High School.........College (# of years)..........

         College Graduate........Graduate or Professional........

Mother: High School.........College (# of years)..........

         College Graduate........Graduate or Professional........

Siblings (Chronologically):

Name	Birthdate or age	Sex	Grade

Significant Family History:

Father

Mother

PRE-HOSPITAL COURSE

I. *Previous Treatment* (psychiatric)
   Hospitalizations (age, duration, reason, effect, where)
   Psychotherapy (age, duration and frequency, reason, effect,
         with whom)

II. *Early History*
   Birth and Delivery (wanted, health)

   Major Caretaker (mother, other, varied) be specific.

   Developmental Milestones—ages, symptoms, transitional objects,
   walking, training, etc.

   Physical
   Life Stress (moves, losses, illness of parents, death) and age of
   child at time

   Birth of Siblings—age, reaction, sex of baby

   School History (level of success, changes and why, social, type
   of school)

   Other

PATIENT STATUS AT ADMISSION

Age and Attitude toward Hospital

Precipitant to Hospitalization

Chief Complaint (parents and child)

Events Leading to Hospitalization

Symptoms (acting-out—drugs, sexual activity, legal, assaultive,
depression, suicidal, withdrawal, somatic, complaints,
anorexia; other—truancy, underachievement)

School Assessment (name, type, grade level; attendance, behavior,
achievement, length of attendance)

Social Adjustment (quality, quantity, sex, type of involvement with peers, siblings, parents and other significant figures)

Sublimatory Activities (hobbies, sports, skills, strengths)

Psychological Test Results

IQ Full Scale   Verbal   Performance

Projectives Striking Themes

Impression

Other

HOSPITAL STAY ITSELF

Therapists

Name	Sex	Length of Time	Supervisor
a.			
b.			
c.			

Point at which sessions switched from daily to three times a week......
(implies movement into depression and working through stage)

Significant Life Events which occurred while in hospital

Familial moves, illnesses

Hospital suicidal gestures, illness, losses, sign out letters, run aways and positive—poetry

Individual Treatment Summary

Discharge (Plan or Unplanned)

Disposition Plans—treatment where to, with whom

Final Diagnosis

Prognosis

Appendix III

Operational
Definitions

The following operational definitions provided the rater and judges with the relevant dimensions to be considered in the rating of patients. Since the aim of the study was to establish the relative within-group standing of patients, rather than an individualized health rating, it was not deemed necessary to establish absolute criteria when defining each variable. Thus, for example, while actual academic grades were considered in the rating of patient's academic functioning, no predetermined grade accomplishment was necessary to obtain a specific score. Rather, each specific score reflected the quality of the patient's academic functioning in relation to other patients.

In all cases, the rater had to consider age differences among patients when making final ratings.

Outcome Variables

1. *Independence and Autonomy*: The degree to which patients had achieved emotional and/or physical separation from their parents and/

or substitutes, were able to manage, plan and take responsibility for their own lives. For the high school student, the above necessitated consideration of their management of school, involvement in social activities and their increased focus on their lives away from parents. For the college or post-college student, actual physical and financial independence and career focus became more crucial.

2. *Ego Functioning—Self-Regulatory Functioning*: Patient's relative ability: to tolerate anxiety; to continue pursuing sublimatory activities; to employ effective and adaptive defenses and maintain reality perception when faced with stress (response to loss of girlfriend, school changes, illness, graduation, discharge).

3. *Ego Functioning—Defensive Structure*: The predominate level and effectiveness of patient's defensive armamentarium. Defenses were viewed on a continuum moving from the most primitive—denial, avoidance, acting-out, projection and splitting—to the more sophisticated—rationalization, displacement, suppression, repression, intellectualization and sublimation.

The Ego Mean was calculated by averaging the scores on numbers 2 and 3.

4. *Object Relations—Parental*: The degree to which patients could realistically assess and accept the strengths and weaknesses of their parents and the predominant level of parental-patient interaction (ranging from reciprocal, passive-aggressive, overtly hostile to dependent).

5. *Object Relations—Peer/Sexual*: A qualitative assessment of sexual functioning, bearing in mind different ages and developmental expectations among patients. This included reviewing whether patients performed sexually or were symptomatic (avoided sexual encounters completely, frigidity, impotence or promiscuity), and the predominant function sexual activity served, i.e., did the sexual activity reflect mature, gratifying and reciprocal interpersonal interaction, was sexual activity avoided completely because of fears of loss of autonomy or was sexual activity *primarily* defensive (acting-out) to avoid abandonment depression, a way of satiating oral dependent wishes for fusion (i.e., recapturing the rewarding object).

6. *Object Relations—Peer/Nonsexual*: The degree and quality of patient interaction and relationships with peers as measured by the number of friends, sex, appropriateness and basis of the involvements (reciprocal, shared interest, to act out or dependency), tenacity and

duration of these relationships and degree of gratification reported.

The *Object Relations Mean* was calculated by averaging the obtained scores on numbers 4, 5 and 6.

7. *Symptomatology—Recognition*: The degree to which patients expressed awareness (i.e., symptoms not denied and understanding of underlying conflictual precipitants of symptoms), degree of ego-alienness to symptoms and degree to which patients have taken adaptive appropriate steps to cope with symptoms (self-analysis, discussion of in ongoing treatment, return to treatment, versus denial or resignation).

8. *Symptomatology—Type and Severity*: The incidence, chronicity and severity of symptomatology manifested since discharge. Symptoms were viewed on the following lesser to greater continuum of severity: circumscribed transient anxiety; reactive and short-lived depression; circumscribed inhibitions like stifled creativity and sexual problems; pervasive and functionally inhibiting anxiety and/or depression; substance abuse (alcohol and/or drugs) ; and suicidal behavior and/or gestures. Chronicity referred to the relative period of time patients suffered since discharge from these symptoms.

9. *Symptomatology—Source of Conflict*: Degree to which patient's symptoms seemed reflective of continual difficulty in separation-individuation or were more reflective of higher-level developmental conflicts (oedipal or genital). These ratings were made on the basis of patients' self-reports of their life circumstances (precipitants) prior to the onset of their symptoms, self-reports of the thoughts and feelings that predominated during their symptomatic phase and the actual steps taken to cope with the symptoms and/or conflicts. It was anticipated that patients might experience a transient recurrence of separation anxieties during critical periods but that when the conflicts had been for the most part worked through they would be transient and coped with adaptively.

10. *Symptomatology—Social and Psychic Cost to Functioning*: The degree to which symptomatology inhibited, interfered with or blocked adaptive functioning. Patients who were able to continue to function in spite of symptomatology were given the highest ratings. When, however, symptoms like heroin addiction or suicidal behavior made functioning impossible, lower ratings were assigned.

The *Final Symptomatology Score* was achieved by averaging the scores on variables 7, 8, 9, and 10.

The *Final Follow-Up Index* was calculated by summing the score on variable 1, the ego mean, the object relations mean, and the final symptomatology score.

PROGNOSTIC VARIABLES

Qualitative Variables

Pre-admission

1. *Pre-admission—Life Stress* was defined as any event which typically disrupts children's development and over which they have no control from birth to the onset of the illness. It, therefore, measures the incidence, nature, age of onset and effects (where discernible): physical illness in patient or caretaking figures; death and/or losses of significant figures; serious mental illness in parents; birth of siblings (carried less weight); and family moves. Where these events did not predominate, patients were considered to have had benign early-life experiences and received a higher score on this variable. A five-point scale was used on this variable with a 7-3 point spread.

2. *Pre-admission—Early Academic Functioning* prior to the onset of the illness leading to hospitalization: The degree of congruence between the relative capability and actual performance and the degree of gratification experienced by patients during their early school years. The results of the psychological testing done at admission were used to substantiate that all patients were capable of at least average intellectual potential. The history of actual performance was assessed from the parental and patient reports of their grades, attendance records, behavioral reports, incidence of grade holdovers and necessity for tutoring. For some patients, school reports were also included in the charts. The degree of gratification was inferred from the actual reports of patients and parental views. For example, one boy maintained average grades throughout his early grades but clearly hated school and resisted going by feigning illness.

3. *Pre-admission—Early Social Functioning*: The relative quality and degree of success patients had in peer relationships outside the family prior to the onset of the illness leading to hospitalization; the number, age, appropriateness and duration of early childhood friendships outside the immediate family. In addition, the basis for the in-

volvements was reviewed (mutual interest as in sports, hobbies, scouting or dependency) and the degree of satisfaction derived from these involvements.

Admission

4. *Admission—Ego Self-Regulatory Functioning*: Patient's relative ability: to tolerate anxiety; to continue pursuing sublimatory activities (art, dance, music, writing, etc.); to employ effective and adaptive defenses (repression, intellectualization, sublimation rather than denial, withdrawal, somatization, acting-out); and to maintain reality perception as measures by their responses to stress (including school changes, losses, illness, menarche, etc.) from the onset of illness and/or puberty to actual admission.

5. *Admission—Independence and Autonomy*: The degree of physical and/or emotional separation patients had achieved from parents and/or parental substitutes at the time of admission. Self-reports, parental reports and admitting-resident evaluations were used to determine the actual amount of time patients spent on their own, the capacity of patients to realistically assess their parents and the predominant level of patient-parent interaction (reciprocal, passive-aggressive, overtly hostile, or infantile dependency).

6. *Admission—Object Relations*: The degree and quality of patient interaction with peers as measured by the actual number of friends, sex and age appropriateness, basis for involvement (reciprocal, shared interest, acting-out, dependent), tenacity and duration of relationships and level of satisfaction as reported by patients and parents at the point of admission.

7. *Admission—Symptomatology—Chronicity*. The actual duration of time between the onset of the symptomatology leading to hospitalization and actual admission. Patients who were symptomatic for the longest period of time received the lowest scores.

8. *Admission—Symptomatology—Recognition*: Patients' awareness of their symptomatology (as measured by the degree of congruence between self-reports and the parental and resident reports of behavior), how ego-alien symptomatology was at admission ("there's nothing wrong with drugs, they make me feel good," versus "I hate wanting to die all the time") and the degree of motivation for help ("the hospital is better than jail," versus "I want to be in better control of my life").

A six-point rather than seven-point scale was employed on this variable.

9. *Admission—Symptomatology—Social and Psychic Cost to Functioning*: The severity of symptomatology as measured by how seriously it interfered with age-appropriate functioning (somatic complaints versus poor school attendance and performance versus serious suicidal gestures). Patients who were using heroin or who made serious suicidal attempts were given the lowest ratings.

The *Symptomatology Mean* is an index of symptomatology at admission. The index reflects the mean of numbers 7, 8 and 9.

10. *Final Admission Index* provided a final admission index which reflected patients' overall health impairment at admission. It was calculated by summing the scores on variables 2, 3, 4, and 6, and the symptomatology index.

Hospital

11. *Hospital—Model Realization*: The degree to which various treatment procedures approximated the ideal of the model for each patient. It was assumed that though the model was theoretically sound, patients' experiences would qualitatively vary because of the presence or absence of reality factors which could not be controlled. These reality factors included: primary therapist changes; number of temporary breaks in treatment with the primary therapist (vacations, ill health); incidence of intervening life stress (parental interference, patient or parental ill health, passage of 1971 law which subsequently involved the legal system in patients' continued treatment, losses of family, patient or staff members, family financial problems, parental separations) ; patient composition of the unit (sexual, proportion of newly-admitted, acting-out patients, number of signouts against medical advice); and the stability of the unit (during its early organization, many procedures were worked out as problems arose, and when the unit was slated to close, staff and patient morale was low).

12. *Hospital—Patient-Therapist-Supervisor Match*: The quality of each patient's individual treatment experience. The senior author, who was familiar with all patients' treatment, provided the original ratings which were then judged by Dr. William Lulow, who was equally familiar with all patients' treatment courses. The ratings necessitated review of the individual characteristics of the patient, therapist and supervisor and an assessment of the quality of the patient-therapist and therapist-supervisor rapport. It was, therefore, possible that a highly

skilled therapist who had countertransference difficulties may have had less therapeutic impact than a less-skilled therapist who was able to therapeutically relate to both the patient and supervisor.

13. *Hospital—Prognosis at Discharge* (a natural distribution employed): The degree to which patients achieved the goals of the model, the degree of readiness at discharge to proceed with age-appropriate developmental tasks. This included an assessment of: the degree to which self-destructive acting-out behavior was controlled and replaced by direct and verbal confrontation of feelings and stress; the degree to which the abandonment depression had been worked through (i.e., mood lifted, less emphasis in individual sessions on feelings of abandonment, rage, disappointment at parents) and replaced by an increased focus on self-actualization and the establishment of autonomy; and the degree to which patients' behavior at discharge reflected more autonomous, responsible and independent functioning (as seen in patients' taking an active role in discharge planning). A five-point scale was adopted ranging from excellent to poor. The resultant distribution was as follows: 3 excellent, 5 good, 12 fair to good, 7 fair, 4 poor.

Objective Variables

Pre-admission

14. *Age of Admission*: Patient age at entry reported in months.

Hospital

15. *Duration of Hospital Stay*: The number of weeks each patient remained in the program.

Post-discharge

16. *Continuation of Post-Discharge Treatment*: Whether patients did or did not continue in treatment following discharge.

17. *Duration of Post-Discharge Treatment*: The actual number of months patients continued in treatment following discharge.

Subjective Variable

Post-discharge

18. *Patient Perception of the Effectiveness of Parents' Concomitant*

Counseling: Patients' perceptions of the effect counseling had had on their parents were organized and rated on a three-point scale. When patients felt their parents were more tolerant of their individuation and related appropriately to them, parents were rated as improved. The other two ratings were no change or worse. The latter reflected those parents who were threatened by their child's improvement and either functionally deteriorated themselves or stepped up their inappropriate involvement in their child's life.

Bibliography

1. ABELIN, E. The role of the father in the separation-individuation process. In Settlage, C. F. and McDevitt, J. B. (Eds.), *Separation-Individuation—Essays in Honor of Margaret S. Mahler.* New York: Int. Univ. Press, 1971, pp. 229-252.
2. ANNESLEY, P. T. Psychiatric illness in adolescence: Presentation and prognosis. *Journal of Mental Science,* 107 (268):268-278, 1961.
3. BARDONA, D. T., MacKEITH, S. A., and CAMERON, K. Symposium on the inpatient treatment of psychotic adolescents. *British Journal of Medical Psychology,* 23:107-118, 1950.
4. BEAVERS, W. and BLUMBERG, S. A follow-up study of adolescents treated in an inpatient facility. *Diseases of the Nervous System,* 29, 1968, 606-612.
5. BENEDEK, T. Adaptation of reality in early infancy. *Psa. Quart.,* 7:200-215, 1938.
6. BENEDEK, T. The psychosomatic implications of the primary unit: Mother-child. *Amer. J. Orthopsychiat.,* 19:642-654, 1949.
7. BENEDEK, T. Psychobiological aspects of mothering. *Amer. J. Orthopsychiat.,* 26:272-278, 1956.
8. BENEDEK, T. Parenthood as a developmental phase. *J. Amer. Psa. Ass.,* 7:389-417, 1959.
9. BERGIN, A. Some implications of psychotherapy for therapeutic practice. *International Journal of Psychiatry,* 3, 1967, 136-150.

285

10. BOWLBY, J. Separation anxiety. *Int. J. Psa.,* 41:89-113, 1960.
11. BOWLBY, J. Grief and mourning in infancy and early childhood. *Psa. Study Child,* 15:9-52, 1966.
12. BOWLBY, J. *Attachment and Loss, Vol. I, Attachment.* New York: Basic Books, 1969.
13. BOWLBY, J. The nature of the child's tie to his mother. *Int. J. Psa.,* 39:350-371, 1958.
14. BOWLBY, J. Process of mourning. *Int. J. Psa.,* 42:317-340, 1961.
15. BOWLBY, J. *Attachment and Loss, Vol. II, Separation.* New York: Basic Books, 1973.
16. CARTER, B. The prognostic factors of adolescent psychosis. *Journal of Mental Science,* 88:31-81, 1947.
17. ERICKSON, R. Outcome studies in mental hospitals: A review. *Psychological Bulletin,* 82:4, 519-540, 1973.
18. EYSENCK, H. *The Effects of Psychotherapy.* New York: International Science Press, 1966.
19. FAIRBAIRN, W. R. D. A revised psychopathology of the psychoses and psychoneuroses. In: *Psychoanalytic Studies of the Personality (An Object-Relations Theory of the Personality).* London: Tavistosk, 1952; New York; Basic Books, 1954.
20. FRAIBERG, S. Libidinal object constancy and mental representation. *Psa. Study Child,* 24:9-47, 1969.
21. FREUD, S. Fetishism (1927). In: Strachey, J. (Ed.), *Collected Papers, Vol. V.* London: Hogarth Press, 1950, pp. 198-204.
22. FREUD, S. Splitting of the ego in the defensive process (1938). In: Strachey, J. (Ed.), *Collected Papers, Vol. V.* London: Hogarth Press, 1950, pp. 372-375.
23. FREUD, S. On narcissism: An introduction (1914). In: *Riviere,* J. (Ed.), *Collected Papers, Vol. IV.* London: Hogarth Press, 30-59, 1948.
24. FROSCH, J. Severe regressive states during analysis. *J. Amer. Psa. Assn.,* 15:491-507, 1967.
25. FROSCH, J. The psychotic character: Clinical psychiatric consideration. *J. Psych. Quart.,* 38:81-96, 1964.
26. FROSCH, J. Psychoanalytic considerations of the psychotic character. *J. Amer. Psa. Assn.,* 15-606-625, 1967.
27. FROSCH, J. Severe regressive states during analysis summary. *J. Amer. Psa. Assn.,* 15:607-625, 1967.
28. GARBER, B. and POLSKY, R. Follow-up of hospitalized adolescents: A preliminary report. *Archives of General Psychiatry,* 22:179-187, February, 1970.
29. GARBER, B. *Follow-Up of Hospitalized Adolescents.* New York: Brunner/Mazel, 1972.
30. GIOVACCHINI, P. L. The submerged ego. *J. Amer. Child Psych.* 3:430-442, 1964.
31. GIOVACCHINI, P. L. Maternal introjection and ego defect. *J. Amer. Acad. Child Psych.,* 4:279-292, 1965.
32. GIOVACCHINI, P. S. Transference incorporation and synthesis. *Int. J. Psa.,* 46:287-296, 1965.
33. GIOVACCHINI, P. S. Frustration and externalization. *Psa. Quart.,* 36:571-583, 1967.
34. GIOVACCHINI, P. S. The frozen introject. *Int. J. Psa.,* 48:61-67., 1967.
35. GIOVACCHINI, P. S. et al. On regression: A workshop. In: Lindon, J. A. (Ed.), *The Psychoanalytic Forum,* 2:4, Winter, 1967.

36. GIOVACCHINI, P. L. Effects of adaptive and disruptive aspects of early object relationships and later parental functioning. In: Anthony, E. and Benedek, T. (Eds.), *Parenthood.* Boston: Little, Brown, Inc., 1970.

37. GOSSETT, J., LEWIS, S., LEWIS, J., and PHILLIPS, V. Follow-up of adolescents treated in a psychiatric hospital: A review of studies. *American Journal of Orthopsychiatry*, 42:4, 602-610, July, 1973.

38. GRINKER, R., WERBLE, B., and DRYE, R. *The Borderline Syndrome: A Behavioral Study of Ego Functions.* New York: Basic Books, Inc., 1968.

39. GUNTRIP, H. *Personality Structure and Human Interaction.* London: Hogarth Press; New York: Int. Univ. Press, 1964.

40. GUNTRIP, H. *Schizoid Phenomena, Object Relations and the Self.* New York: Int. Univ. Press, 1968.

41. HAMILTON, D., McKINLEY, R., MOORHEAD, H., and WALL, J. Results of mental hospital treatment of troubled youth. *American Journal of Psychiatry*, 117:811-819, 1961.

42. HARTMANN, E., GLASSER, B., SOLOMON, M., and LEVENSON, D. *Adolescents in a Mental Hospital.* New York: Grune & Stratton, 1968.

43. HERRERA, E., LIFSON, B., HARTMANN, E., and SOLOMON, M. A ten year follow-up of fifty-five hospitalized adolescents. *American Journal of Psychiatry*, 131:7, 769-774, July, 1974.

43a. HOLLINGSHEAD, A. and REDLICH, F. *Social Class and Mental Illness.* New York: John Wiley & Sons, 1958.

44. JACOBSON, E. Denial and repression. *J. Amer. Psa. Assn.*, 5:61-92, 1957.

45. JACOBSON, E. *The Self and the Object World.* New York: Int. Univ. Press, 1964.

46. KERNBERG, O. The psychotherapy research project of the Menninger Foundation: Summary and conclusions. *Bulletin of the Menninger Clinic*, 36:181-195, 1975.

47. KERNBERG, O. Borderline personality organization. *J. Amer. Psa. Assn.*, 15:641-685, 1967.

48. KERNBERG, O. A psychoanalytic classification of character pathology. *J. Amer. Psa. Assn.*, 18:800-822, 1970.

49. KERNBERG, O. The treatment of patients with borderline personality organization. *Int. J. Psa.*, 49:600-619, 1968.

50. KERNBERG, O. Notes on countertransference. *J. Amer. Psa. Assn.*, 13:38-56, 1965.

51. KERNBERG, O. Prognostic considerations regarding borderline personality organization. Presented at the 57th Annual Meeting of the American Psychoanalytic Assn., San Francisco, Calif., 1970.

52. KERNBERG, O. Factors in the psychoanalytic treatment of narcissistic personalities. *J. Amer. Psa. Assn.*, 18:51-85, 1970.

53. KERNBERG, O. New developments in psychoanalytic object relations theory. Presented at the 58th Annual Meeting of the American Psychoanalytic Assn., Washington, D.C., 1971.

54. KERNBERG, O. Early ego integration and object relations. *Ann. N. Y. Acad. Sci.*, 193:233-247, 1972.

55. KERNBERG, O. Structural derivatives of object relationships. *Int. J. Psa.*, 47:236-253, 1966.

56. KERNBERG, O. Further considerations to the treatment of narcissistic personalities. *Int. J. Psa.*, 55:215-240, 1974.

57. KERNBERG, O. *Borderline Conditions and Pathological Narcissism.* New York: Science House, 163-177, 1975.
58. KERNBERG, O. *Object Relations Theory and Clinical Psychoanalysis.* New York: Aronson, 1976.
59. KING, L. and PITTMAN, G. A six year follow-up study of sixty-five adolescent patients: Natural history of affective disorders. *Archives of General Psychiatry,* 20:230-236, March, 1970.
60. KING, L. and PITTMAN, G. A six year follow-up study of sixty-five adolescent patients: Predictive value of presenting clinical picture. *British Journal of Psychiatry,* 115:1437-1441, 1969.
61. KIVOWITZ, J., FORGOTSON, J., GOLDSTEIN, F., and GOTTLIEB, F. A follow-up study of hospitalized adolescents. *Comprehensive Psychiatry,* 15:35-42, January-February, 1974.
62. KLEIN, M. *The Psychoanalysis of Children.* London: Hogarth Press, 1932.
63. KLEIN, M. Contribution to the psychogenesis of manic depressive states. In: *Contributions to Psychoanalysis 1921-1945.* London: Hogarth Press, 1948.
64. KLEIN, M. Mourning and its relation to manic depressive states. In: *Contribution to Psychoanalysis 1921-1945.* London: Hogarth Press, 1948.
65. KLEIN, M. Notes on some schizoid mechanisms. In: Riviere, Jr. (Ed.), *Developments in Psychoanalysis.* London: Hogarth Press, 1946.
66. KOHUT, H. Autonomy and integration. *J. Amer. Psa. Assn.,* 13:851-856, 1965.
67. KOHUT, H. Forms and transformations of narcissism. *J. Amer. Psa. Assn.,* 14:243-272, 1966.
68. KOHUT, H. Psychoanalytic treatment of narcissitic personality disorder: Outline of a systematic approach. *Psa. Study Child,* 23:86-113, 1968.
69. KOHUT, H. Panel on narcissistic resistance. (N. P. Segal, Reporter), *J. Amer. Psa. Assn.,* 17:941-954, 1969.
70. KOHUT, H. *The Analysis of the Self: A Systematic Approach to the Psychoanalytic Treatment of Narcissistic Personality Disorders.* New York: Int. Univ. Press, 1971.
71. KOHUT, H. *Restoration of the Self.* New York: Int. Univ. Press, 1978.
72. LEVENSTEIN, S., POLLACK, M., and KLEIN, D. Follow-up of formerly hospitalized psychiatric patients: Procedural considerations in data collection. *Journal of Hillside Hospital,* 16:152-164, 1965.
73. LEVY, E. Long-term follow-up of former inpatients at the children's hospital of the Menninger Clinic. *American Journal of Psychiatry,* 125:12, 1633-1639, June, 1969.
74. LEWIS, S. and others. Follow-up study of adolescents treated in a psychiatric hospital: Operational solutions to some methodological problems of clinical research. *American Journal of Orthopsychiatry,* 45 (5):813-823, Oct., 1975.
75. MAHLER, M. S. *On Human Symbiosis and the Vicissitudes of Individuation.* New York: Int. Univ. Press, 1968.
76. MAHLER, M. S. Thoughts about development and individuation. *Psa. Study Child,* 18:307-324, 1963.
77. MAHLER, M. S. Autism and symbiosis—Two extreme disturbances of identity. *Int. J. Psa.,* 39:77-83, 1958.
78. MAHLER, M. S. On the significance of the normal separation-individuation phase. In: Schur, M. (Ed.), *Drives, Affects and Behavior, Vol. 2.* New York: Int. Univ. Press, 161-169, 1965.
79. MAHLER, M. S. and FURER, M. Certain aspects of the separation-individuation phase. *Psa. Quart.,* 32:1-14, 1963.

80. MAHLER, M. S. and LAPERRIERE, R. Mother-child interactions during separation-individuation. *Psa. Quart.*, 34:483-489, 1965.

81. MAHLER, M. S. and McDEVITT, JR. Observations on adaptation and defense in statu nascendi. *Psa. Quart.*, 37:1-21, 1968.

82. MAHLER, M. S., PINE, F., and BERGMAN, A. The mother's reaction to her toddler's drive for individuation. In: Anthony, E. and Benedek, T. (Eds.), *Parenthood*. Boston: Little, Brown, 1970.

83. MASTERSON, J. F. Prognosis in adolescent disorders. *Journal of Nervous and Mental Diseases*, 124:3, 219-232, Sept., 1956.

84. MASTERSON, J. F. *Treatment of the Borderline Adolescent: A Development Approach*. New York: John Wiley & Sons, Inc., 1972.

85. MASTERSON, J. F. Intensive psychotherapy of the adolescent with the borderline syndrome. In G. Caplan (Ed.), *American Handbook of Psychiatry*. New York: Basic Books, 1974.

86. MASTERSON, J. F. The splitting defense mechanism of the borderline adolescent: Developmental and clinical aspects. In: Mack, J. (Ed.), *Borderline States*. New York: Grune & Stratton, 1975.

87. MASTERSON, J. F. and RINSLEY, D. B. The borderline syndrome: The role of the mother in the genesis and psychic structure of the borderline personality. *Int. J. Psa.*, 56:163-178, 1975.

88. MASTERSON, J. F. Prognosis in adolescent disorders. *American Journal of Psychiatry*, 114:1097-1103, 1957-58.

89. MASTERSON, J. F. *Psychiatric Dilemma of Adolescence*. Boston: Little, Brown and Company, 1965.

90. MASTERSON, J. F. Treatment of the adolescent with borderline syndrome: A problem in separation-individuation. *Bulletin of the Menninger Clinic*, 35: 5-18, 1971.

91. MASTERSON, J. F. *Psychotherapy of the Borderline Adult*. New York: Brunner/ Mazel, 1976.

92. MASTERSON, J. F. Therapeutic alliance and transference. *American Journal of Psychiatry*, 135:4, 437-441, 1978.

93. MASTERSON, J. F. Transference acting out and working through. In: Masterson, J. F. (Ed.), *New Perspectives on Psychotherapy of the Borderline Adult*. New York: Brunner/Mazel, 1978.

94. MASTERSON, J. F. Primary anorexia nervosa in the borderline adolescent. In: P. Hartocollis (Ed.), *An Object Relations View in Borderline Personality Disorders, The Concept, The Syndrome, The Patient*. New York: Int. Univ. Press, 1977.

95. MASTERSON, J. F. Prognosis in adolescent disorders. *American Journal of Psychiatry*, 114:1097, 1958.

96. MASTERSON, J. F. Borderline and narcissistic disorders: An integrated developmental approach. Presented to American Psychiatric Association, Chicago, 1979.

97. McDEVITT, J. B. Separation-individuation and object constancy. *J. Amer. Psa. Assn.*, 23:713-742, 1975.

98. OFFER, D. and OFFER, J. Four issues in the developmental psychology of adolescents. In: Howells, J. (Ed.), *Modern Perspectives in Adolescent Psychiatry*. New York: Brunner/Mazel, 1971.

99. OFFER, D. and OFFER, J. Growing-up: A follow-up study of normal adolescents. *Seminars in Psychiatry*, I:1, 46-56, Feb., 1969.

100. OFFER, D. and OFFER, J. *Normal Adolescents: From Teenager to Young Manhood.* New York: Basic Books, Inc., 1975.
101. OFFER, D., OFFER, J., and MARCUS, D. A longitudinal study of normal adolescent boys. *American Journal of Psychiatry,* 126:7, 41-48, Jan., 1970.
102. OFFER, D., MAROHN, R., and OSTROV, E. *The Psychological World of the Juvenile Delinquent.* New York: Basic Books, Inc., 1979.
103. OFFER, D. *The Psychological World of the Teenager.* New York: Basic Books, Inc., 1969.
104. OFFER, D. and OFFER, J. *From Teenager to Young Manhood.* New York: Basic Books, Inc., 1975.
105. PIAGET, J. *The Construction of Reality in the Child.* New York: Basic Books, 1954.
106. PIAGET, J. *Play, Dream and Imitation in Childhood.* New York: Norton, 1951.
107. PIAGET, J. *The Psychology of Intelligence.* London: Routledge and Kegan, Paul, 1950.
108. POLLACK, M., LEVENSTEIN, S., and KLEIN, D. A Three-year post hospital follow-up of adolescent and adult schizophrenics. *American Journal of Orthopsychiatry,* 38:94-109, 1968.
109. RINSLEY, D. Psychiatric hospital treatment of adolescents. *Archives of General Psychiatry,* 8:78-86, Oct., 1962.
110. RINSLEY, D. Theory of practice of intensive residential treatment of adolescents. *Psychiatric Quarterly,* 42:611-638, 1968.
111. RINSLEY, D. B. Economic aspects of the object relations. *Int. J. Psa.,* 41:389-395, 1965.
112. RINSLEY, D. B. The adolescent inpatient: Patterns of depersonification. *Psych. Quart.,* 45:1-20, 1971.
113. RINSLEY, D. B. An object relations view of borderline personality. Presented at International Meeting on Borderline Disorders. The Menninger Foundation and the National Institute of Mental Health, Topeka, Kansas, March 19-21, 1976.
114. SINNETT, R., STIMPERT, W., and STRAIGHT, B. A five-year follow-up study of psychiatric patients. *American Journal of Orthopsychiatry,* 35:572, 280, 1965.
115. SLAVIN, M. and SLAVIN, J. Two patterns of adaptation in late adolescent borderline personalities. *Psychiatry,* 39:41-50, Feb., 1976.
116. SPITZ, R. A. Anaclitic depression. *Psa. Study Child,* 2:313-341, 1946.
117. SPITZ, R. A. *The First Year of Life (A Psychoanalytic Study of Normal and Deviant Development of Object Relations).* New York: Int. Univ. Press, 1965.
118. SPITZ, R. A. The smiling response: A contribution to the ontogenesis of social relations. *Genet. Psychol. Mong.,* Vol. 34. Provincetown, Mass.: Journal Press, 1957.
119. SPITZ, R. A. *No and Yes.* New York: Int. Univ. Press, 1957.
120. SPITZ, R. A. The evolution of dialogue. In: Schur, M. (Ed.), *Drives, Affects, Behavior,* Second Edition. New York: Int. Univ. Press, 170-190, 1965.
121. SPITZ, R. A. Relevancy of direct infant observations. *Psa. Study Child,* 5:66-75, 1950.
122. SPITZ, R. A. Hospitalism: An inquiry into the genesis of psychiatirc conditions of early childhood. *Psa. Study Child,* 1:53-74, 1945.
123. SPITZ, R. A. Hospitalism: A follow-up report. *Psa. Study Child,* 2:313-342, 1946.

124. The Psychotherapy Research Project of the Menninger Foundation: Preliminary Report. *Bulletin of the Menninger Clinic,* 20:5, 221-279, Sept. 1956.
125. The Psychotherapy Research Project of the Menninger Foundation: Second Report. *Bulletin of the Menninger Clinic,* 22:4, 115-166, July, 1958.
126. The Psychotherapy Research Project of the Menninger Foundation: Third Report. *Bulletin of the Menninger Clinic,* 24:4, 157-216, July, 1960.
127. The Psychotherapy Research Project of the Menninger Foundation: Final Report. *Bulletin of the Menninger Clinic,* 36, 1975.
128. VAILLANT, G. Theoretical hierarchy of adaptive ego mechanisms. *Archives of General Psychiatry,* 24:107-115, Feb., 1971.
129. WARREN, W. A study of psychiatric inpatients and the outcome six or more years later: II. The follow-up study. *Journal of Child Psychology,* 6:12, 141-160, 1965.
130. WALLERSTEIN, R. The problem of assessment of change in psychotherapy. *International Journal of Psychoanalysis,* 44:31-41, 1963.
131. WEIL, J. The basic core. *Psa. Study Child,* 25:442-460, 1970.
131a. WEISS, R. and GLASSER, B. Social adjustment of adolescents released from a mental hospital. *Mental Hygiene,* 40:378-385, July, 1965.
132. WINNICOTT, D. W. The capacity to be alone. In: *The Maturational Processes and the Facilitating Environment.* New York: Int. Univ. Press, 29-36, 1965.
133. WINNICOTT, D. W. The theory of the parent-infant relationship. In: *The Maturational Processes and the Facilitating Environment.* New York: Int. Univ. Press, 37-55, 1965.
134. WINNICOTT, D. W. Ego integration in child development. In: *The Maurational Processes and the Facilitating Environment.* New York: Int. Univ. Press, 56-63, 1965.
135. WINNICOTT, D. W. The development of the capacity for concern. In: *The Maturational Processes and the Facilitating Environment.* New York: Int. Univ. Press, 73-82, 1965.
136. WINNICOTT, D. W. From dependence towards independence in the development of the individual. In: *The Maturational Processes and the Facilitating Environment.* New York: Int. Univ. Press, 83-92, 1965.
137. WINNICOTT, D. W. Ego distortions in terms of true and false self. In: *The Maturational Processes and the Facilitating Environment.* New York: Int. Univ. Press, 140-152, 1965.
138. ZETZEL, E. R. A developmental model and the theory of therapy (1965). In: *The Capacity for Emotional Growth.* New York: Int. Univ. Press, 182-196, 1970.
139. ZETZEL, E. R. On the incapacity to bear depression (1965). In: *The Capacity for Emotional Growth.* New York: Int. Univ. Press, 82-114, 1970.
140. ZETZEL, E. R. The depressive position (1953). In: *The Capacity for Emotional Growth.* New York: Int. Univ. Press, 63-81, 1970.
141. ZETZEL, E. R. Depressive illness (1960). In: *The Capacity for Emotional Growth.* New York: Int. Univ. Press, 53-62, 1970.
142. ZETZEL, E. R. Anxiety and the capacity to bear it (1949). In: *The Capacity for Emotional Growth.* New York: Int. Univ. Press, 33-52, 1970.

Index

293

absence of, 171, 183, 193
and admission index variable, 89
anxiety about, 130, 133, 163
capacity for, 189, 212, 235, 236
data on, 83
establishment of, 282
failure in, 136
as goal, 9
and independence, 246, 276-77
measurement of, 86, 87
needs for, 58
parental view of in child, 166
as prognostic variable, 88
unfolding of, 9
Avoidance, 20, 37, 38, 43, 50, 51, 102, 103,
    108, 141, 152, 159, 163, 172, 212, 213,
    224, 265, 269, 277

Barbiturates, 188
Beavers, W., 244, 285n.
Behavior Disorders of Adolescence, 238
Benedek, T., 6, 285n.
Beskind, 242
Blumberg, S., 244, 285n.
Body image, differentiation of, 11
Borderline syndrome, 80-81, 238, 242, 248.
    See also Development theory on
    borderline syndrome
cognitive functioning in, 249-50
developmental theory on, 5-28, 256
as diagnostic entity, viii, xvi
as label, xvi
prognosis on, viii
self in, 29-39
treatment of, developmental approach
    to, xviii-xix
Bowlby, J., xix, 6, 286n.

Carter, B., 240, 244, 286n.
Character disorder, 241
Clinging, 20, 24, 37, 50, 103, 133, 166, 224
Clinical diagnosis/model of treatment, 43-
    60
psychodynamic approach to, 43-50
    diagnosis, 44
    and family communication, 48-50
    fixation, 46-47
    and patient distress, 46
    present illness, 44-45
therapeutic model on, 50-60
    approaches, 55-60
    inpatient service, 50-51

limits/restrictions, 54-55
    milieu design, 51-53
Clinical evaluation and therapeutic
    change, 211-15
Cocaine, 136, 193
Cognitive functioning in borderlines, 249-
    50
Communication:
    in families, 44, 48-50
    matching for, 265
Cornell University Medical College, 50
Cortisone, 199
Costello, 62, 78, 85, 86, 88, 89, 90, 91
Countertransference, 118, 122, 126, 200,
    210, 261
Creativity, 99, 101, 116, 183, 270
    absence of, 159, 193
    capacity for, 189, 212
    data on, 83
    evidence of, 142
    failure of, 136

Defense mechanisms, 101
    projective identification, 21, 50, 163, 265
Denial, 19, 20, 21, 25, 37, 38, 43, 44, 50, 51,
    102, 103, 112, 119, 134, 141, 152, 153,
    159, 163, 164, 165, 172, 212, 213, 224,
    225, 265, 269, 277
Dependency, 51, 192, 195
    acting-out of, 103, 119, 124, 166
    gratification of, 262
    and parents, 108
    prolonged, 47
    regressive, 47
    on therapist, 143
Depersonification, 104
Depression, 18, 28, 37, 58, 105, 110, 111,
    123, 129, 138, 159, 160, 167, 187,
    233, 278
    abandonment, viii, 16, 19-21, 26, 36, 38,
        44-48, 50, 51, 56, 102, 103, 112, 113,
        124, 128, 129, 130, 134, 147, 151, 153,
        155, 166, 175, 177, 179, 181, 193, 198,
        202, 211, 213-14, 224, 229, 231, 251,
        259, 261, 262, 264
    and acting-out, 179
    and activity, 172
    anaclitic, 17
    denial of, 225
    drug treatment of, 120
    of ego, 24-25